ERICH ZEISL
Wiens verlorener Sohn in der Fremde

ERIC ZEISL
Vienna's Lost Son in Foreign Lands

Michael Haas
E. Randol Schoenberg
Karin Wagner
Tina Walzer

Herausgegeben von | *Edited by* Gerold Gruber

Ausstellung des | *Exhibition at the* Exilarte Zentrum der mdw
– Universität für Musik und darstellende Kunst Wien

Böhlau

Gerold Gruber (Hg.)

Exilarte Zentrum der mdw – Universität für Musik und darstellende Kunst Wien

Erich Zeisl. Wiens verlorener Sohn in der Fremde
Eric Zeisl. Vienna's Lost Son in Foreign Lands

Bibliografische Information der Deutschen Nationalbibliothek :
Die Deutsche Nationalbibliothek verzeichnet diese Publikation
in der Deutschen Nationalbibliografie ; detaillierte bibliografische
Daten sind im Internet über http://dnb.d-nb.de abrufbar.

© 2025 Böhlau, Zeltgasse 1, A-1080 Wien, ein Imprint der Brill-Gruppe
(Koninklijke Brill NV, Leiden, Niederlande; Brill USA Inc., Boston MA, USA; Brill Asia Pte Ltd, Singapore;
Brill Deutschland GmbH, Paderborn, Deutschland ; Brill Österreich GmbH, Wien, Österreich)
Koninklijke Brill NV umfasst die Imprints Brill, Brill Nijhoff, Brill Hotei, Brill Schöningh,
Brill Fink, Brill mentis, Vandenhoeck & Ruprecht, Böhlau und V&R unipress.
Alle Rechte vorbehalten. Das Werk und seine Teile sind urheberrechtlich geschützt.
Jede Verwertung in anderen als den gesetzlich zugelassenen Fällen bedarf der vorherigen schriftlichen Einwilligung des Verlages.

Konzeption: Karin Wagner
Gestaltung, Layout und Satz: Iby-Jolande Varga
Übersetzungen: Michael Haas, Karin Wagner
Lektorat: Birgit Trinker, Michael Strand
Umschlagfotos: Erich Zeisl im Exil in Los Angeles, ca. 1955 (U1, A-Weaz),
Erich Zeisl mit seiner Tochter Barbara an der Küste in Santa Monica, Dezember 1947 (U4, A-Weaz)
Druck und Bindung: Finidr, Český Těšín
Printed in the EU

Vandenhoeck & Ruprecht Verlage | www.vandenhoeck-ruprecht-verlage.com
ISBN 978-3-205-22192-0

INHALT | CONTENTS

Gerold Gruber – Michael Haas
    Vorwort   6
    Preface   8

Karin Wagner
    Erich Zeisl (1905–1959). Wiens verlorener Sohn in der Fremde   10
    Eric Zeisl (1905–1959). Vienna's Lost Son in Foreign Lands   34

Tina Walzer
    Das Café Tegetthoff der Familie Zeisl in der Heinestraße 42   56
    Café Tegetthoff of the Zeisl Family at 42 Heinestrasse   66

Michael Haas
    A Tale of Two Viennese Jewish Composers. Eric Zeisl and Walter Bricht   76
    Eine Geschichte zweier jüdischer Komponisten aus Wien. Erich Zeisl und Walter Bricht   86

E. Randol Schoenberg
    The Convergence of Schoenberg and Zeisl   98
    Die Konvergenz zwischen Schönberg und Zeisl   120

Michael Haas
    Rabbi Sonderling and His Commissions   138
    Rabbi Sonderling und seine Aufträge   146

Karin Wagner
    „A sort of Hebrew Tanglewood" Erich Zeisl im Brandeis Music Camp   156
    "A sort of Hebrew Tanglewood" Eric Zeisl at the Brandeis Music Camp   168

    Bildnachweise   180

Gerold Gruber – Michael Haas

VORWORT

Seit der Etablierung des Forschungszentrums Exilarte im Jahr 2016 wurden bereits an die 40 Nachlässe europäischer Komponist:innen und Künstler:innen, die vor der nationalsozialistischen Diktatur fliehen mussten, in dessen Archiv aufgenommen. Dabei wurde zunehmend deutlich, dass das Exilerlebnis unter Komponist:innen ein eigenständiges, bislang weitgehend unerforschtes Kapitel der Kulturgeschichte des 20. Jahrhunderts darstellt. Das Wechselspiel zwischen Exil und Kreativität äußerte sich in einer Vielzahl unterschiedlicher Konstellationen – geprägt vom jeweiligen Zufluchtsort, dem Alter und Geschlecht der Komponist:innen sowie ihrer individuellen Anpassungsfähigkeit. In all diesen Variationen entstand eine Synthese, die alte und neue Heimat ebenso verband wie alte und neue Identitäten.

Jüdische Komponist:innen aus Österreich empfanden sich mehrheitlich als Teil einer spezifischen deutschen Tradition – einer Identität, die weit über die bloße Staatsbürgerschaft hinausging. Trotz der österreichischen Staatsbürgerschaft sahen sie sich als Repräsentant:innen deutscher und österreichischer Komponierpraxis, die bis zu Johann Sebastian Bach und Johann Joseph Fux zurückreichte. Ihre Werke betrachteten sie als organische Fortsetzungen dieser Tradition – selbst radikale Neuerer wie Arnold Schönberg, die die Grundlagen der westlichen Musik in Frage stellten, verstanden ihre Kompositionen nicht als Bruch, sondern als Weiterentwicklung des übergeordneten Gefüges deutscher und österreichischer Musik.

Mit Hitlers „Anschluss" Österreichs im März 1938 und der damit zusammenhängenden Auslöschung des Staates und Einverleibung in das „Deutsche Reich" verloren diese Komponist:innen ihre österreichische Staatszugehörigkeit. Doch als Jüdinnen und Juden durften sie auch keine Deutschen mehr sein – die nationalsozialistische Ideologie erklärte Judentum und Deutschtum für unvereinbar. Ihrer Identität als Österreicher:innen und Deutsche beraubt, wandten sie sich oft ihrer jüdischen Herkunft zu. Vielfach hatte die jahrzehntelange Assimilation jedoch den Bezug zu den jüdischen Wurzeln entfremdet.

Die unermüdliche Forschung von Dr. Karin Wagner zum Komponisten Eric(h) Zeisl hat eine musikalische Synthese zwischen seiner Wiener Vergangenheit und seiner postmigratischen Identität als Jude offengelegt. Zeisl war dankbar, dass er als Komponist weiterarbeiten konnte – doch keine Dankbarkeit konnte darüber hinwegtäuschen, dass sein Exilland ihm immer fremd bleiben würde. Die amerikanische Staatsbürgerschaft machte ihn nicht automatisch zu einem amerikanischen Komponisten, doch zugleich konnte er sich nicht länger als österreichischen Komponisten betrachten. Dennoch blieben in ihm der Amerikaner und der Jude ebenso lebendig wie der Wiener und der Österreicher. Daraus entstand ein einzigartiges musikalisches Idiom – eine Musik, die kein in den USA oder Österreich geborener Komponist seiner Generation ohne Zeisls prägende Erfahrung von Vertreibung und Selbstneuerfindung hätte schreiben können.

Im Jahr 2024 wurde das Exilarte Zentrum der mdw von der Familie Zeisl-Schönberg ausgewählt, den gesamten Nachlass von Eric(h) Zeisl zu beherbergen – eine Entscheidung, für die das Zentrum und die Leitung der mdw äußerst dankbar sind. Eine erste Bestandsaufnahme der mehr als 5.000 Korrespondenzen wurde bereits durchgeführt, während der musikalische Nachlass, der bis vor Kurzem an der UCLA aufbewahrt wurde, derzeit wissenschaftlich aufgearbeitet wird.

Ein so anspruchsvolles Projekt wie die vorliegende Ausstellung kann nur mit der Unterstützung vieler umgesetzt werden – dafür möchten wir uns herzlich bedanken:

Rektorin Ulrike Sych hat uns seit der Gründung des Exilarte Zentrum stets zur Seite gestanden. Der Nationalfonds und der Zukunftsfonds der Republik Österreich haben die Ausstellung und den Katalog mit großzügigen Subventionen unterstützt. Karin Wagner brachte als Kuratorin ihr Fachwissen und ihre Begeisterung ein, während Katharina Reischl, Leiterin des Exilarte Archivs, die Bestandsaufnahme des Zeisl-Nachlasses in Angriff nahm und die Materialien bereitstellte. Architekt Checo Sterneck hat – wie immer mit großem Interesse und Feingefühl – die Gestaltung übernommen. Die grafische Umsetzung wurde von Thomas Reinagl für die Ausstellung und von Iby-Jolande Varga für den Katalog mit gewohntem ästhetischem Gespür realisiert. Schließlich sorgten Birgit Trinker und Michael Strand mit akribischer Sorgfalt für das Lektorat.

Unser aufrichtiger Dank gilt allen, die zum Gelingen dieses Projekts beigetragen haben.

Gerold Gruber – Michael Haas

PREFACE

Since the establishment of the Exilarte Research Center in 2016, nearly 40 estates of European composers and artists who were forced to flee from the National Socialist dictatorship have been added to its archive. Over time, it has become increasingly evident that the experience of exile among composers represents an independent and largely unexplored chapter of 20th-century cultural history. The interplay between exile and creativity manifested itself in a wide variety of different constellations—shaped by the particular place of refuge, the age and gender of the composers, as well as their individual adaptability. In all of these variations, a synthesis emerged that linked old and new homelands just as much as it connected old and new identities.

Jewish composers from Austria largely perceived themselves as part of a specific German tradition—an identity that extended far beyond mere citizenship. Despite being Austrian nationals, they saw themselves as representatives of German and Austrian compositional practice, which reached back to Johann Sebastian Bach and Johann Joseph Fux. They viewed their works as organic continuations of this tradition—even radical innovators such as Arnold Schoenberg, who fundamentally questioned the foundations of Western music, did not see their compositions as a rupture but rather as a further development of the overarching edifice of German and Austrian music.

With Hitler's annexation of Austria in March 1938, these composers were no longer Austrian, since Austria was now integrated into the "German Reich", but as Jews, they were no longer allowed to be German, since the Nazis felt that being Jewish was incompatible with being German. Deprived of their identities as Austrians and Germans, they often turned to their identities as Jews, yet assimilation meant that few had a concept as to how this might manifest itself.

The tireless research of Dr Karin Wagner into the composer Eric(h) Zeisl has revealed a musical synthesis between his Viennese past and his post-migrant identity as a Jew. Zeisl was grateful that he could continue his work as a composer—yet no amount of gratitude could obscure the fact that his country of exile would always remain foreign to him. American citizenship did not automatically make him an American composer, yet at the same time, he could no longer consider himself an Austrian composer. Nevertheless, the American and the Jew remained as present within him as the Viennese and the Austrian. From this emerged a unique musical idiom—music that no composer born in the United States or Austria of his generation could have written without Zeisl's formative experience of displacement and self-reinvention.

In 2024, the Exilarte Center at the mdw was chosen by the Zeisl-Schoenberg family to house the entire estate of Eric(h)

Zeisl—a decision for which the center and the leadership of mdw are deeply grateful. An initial inventory of more than 5,000 letters has already been carried out, while the musical estate, which until recently was housed at UCLA, is currently undergoing academic analysis.

A project as ambitious as this exhibition can only be realized with the support of many people—for this, we express our heartfelt gratitude: President of the mdw, Ulrike Sych has supported us since the founding of the Exilarte Center. The National Fund and the Future Fund of the Republic of Austria have generously subsidized the exhibition and the catalogue. Karin Wagner, as curator, contributed her expertise and enthusiasm, while Katharina Reischl, head of the Exilarte Archive, undertook the inventory of the Zeisl estate and provided the materials. Architect Checo Sterneck—as always, with great interest and sensitivity—took charge of the exhibition design. The graphic implementation was carried out by Thomas Reinagl for the exhibition and by Iby-Jolande Varga for the catalogue, both with their signature aesthetic sensibility. Finally, Birgit Trinker and Michael Strand ensured meticulous proofreading with great care.

Our sincere thanks go to everyone who contributed to the success of this project.

„Das grosse Universal Quartett". Handbemaltes Quartett-Kartenspiel von Hans Kohn, Wien 1932. Das Café Zeisl ist als eines der „lustigsten Vergnügungslokale" Wiens verewigt.
Archiv des Exilarte Zentrum der mdw, Wien (A-Weaz)

Karin Wagner

ERICH ZEISL (1905–1959)
Wiens verlorener Sohn in der Fremde

Café Tegetthoff

> Am staerksten hab ich Dich „innerlich erlebt" als ich vor mehr als einem Jahr nach fuenfzehnjaehriger Abwesenheit in Wien war und in den Naechten allein um Praterstern, Heinestrasse und ehemaliges Cafe Zeisl herumgeschlichen bin ... Beschreiben laesst sich das schwer, am wenigsten in ein paar Zeilen.[1]

Das schrieb der in Wien geborene Dichter und Psychoanalytiker Alfred Farau (1904–1972) am 11. Juli 1955 aus New York an seinen Freund Erich Zeisl in Los Angeles; Farau war gerade erst von Wien nach New York zurückgekehrt. Unter dem Namen Fred Hernfeld hatte er in den 1930er-Jahren den interdisziplinären Wiener Kulturzirkel „Junge Kunst" geleitet, dem auch Erich Zeisl angehörte. Im November 1938 wurde Farau verhaftet und nach Dachau deportiert, nach der Freilassung gelang ihm die Flucht in die Vereinigten Staaten. Nach dem Krieg kam er in die Stadt seiner Jugend zurück, um an der Universität Wien in Psychologie zu promovieren. Vor seiner Flucht hatte er in Wien als Schüler Alfred Adlers eine psychotherapeutische Praxis betrieben und in den frühen 1930er-Jahren an der Volkshochschule und dem Schubert-Konservatorium unterrichtet. Alfred Faraus Heimat blieb nach dem Krieg New York, von dort berichtete er 1955 über Wien im Wiederaufbau und seinen Versuch, das Café Tegetthoff zu finden, in dem Erich Zeisl aufgewachsen war.

Auch Ernst Toch (1887–1964), Zeisls Freund im kalifornischen Exil, durchstreifte bei einem Aufenthalt in Österreich nach Kriegsende die Gegend um den Praterstern und suchte auf Zeisls Bitte hin das Café Tegetthoff. Am 5. Mai 1950 schrieb er nach Los Angeles:

> Das Zirkus Renz Gebäude neben dem Gymnasium (ausgerechnet dieses) ist total zerbombt. Ausser diesem fand ich nur noch den Tempel in der Tempelgasse, natürlich, und diesen nicht durch Bomben, bis auf wenige Reste der Aussenmauern dem Erdboden gleich gemacht. Aber ein Café Tegethoff [sic] gibt es nicht mehr. Café Praterstern, Schreyvogel, Dogenhof, alles da – aber kein Tegetthoff! Ich fragte viele Leute, und niemand konnte mir Auskunft geben, natürlich auch nicht das Telephonbuch. Alle wussten, dass es es [sic] <u>einmal</u> irgendwo dort war! Und ich hätte mich doch so gern hineingesetzt, vielleicht einer Chanteuse auf den Schoß, und Ihnen eine Ansichtskarte von dort geschickt, die Zeislsche Jugend in Stellvertretung <u>durchlebend</u>![2]

Rückblick

Erich Zeisl wurde 1905 geboren, er war ein Kind der Leopoldstadt, seine Eltern betrieben am Praterstern das bis zur „Arisierung" im Jahr 1938 im Familienbesitz stehende Café Tegetthoff. Die Zeisls waren eine assimilierte jüdische Familie des kleinbürgerlichen Mittelstandes, mit Egon (geb. 1901), Walter (geb. 1902) und Wilhelm (geb. 1907) hatte Erich drei Brüder. Wohl spielte Musik im Hause Zeisl eine Rolle – der Vater Siegmund war aktives Mitglied im Wiener Kaufmännischen Gesangverein und die Brüder Egon und Wilhelm übten sich als Sänger –, doch musste der bereits im Knabenalter komponierende Erich sich die Möglichkeit zum Studium an der damaligen Akademie für Musik und darstellende Kunst gegen den Willen der Eltern erkämpfen. Er bestand die Aufnahmeprüfung bravourös, wenngleich er danach keinen vollständigen Studiengang in Theorie, Komposition oder Klavier durchlief: Die pianistische Ausbildung musste er wegen Problemen mit den Händen beenden, und die „Harmonielehre" Richard Stöhrs (1874–1967) besuchte er nur im Studienjahr 1920/21. Stöhr unterrichtete den auffallend begabten Zeisl aber privat.

Richard Stöhrs Lehrbücher in Formenlehre, Harmonielehre und Kontrapunkt waren „viel verbreitet und für gewisse Prüfungen obligatorisch"[3], so der Wiener Musikkritiker Paul Stefan (1879–1943). Der Musiksprache des späten 19. Jahrhunderts verpflichtet, zählte Stöhr zu jenen Wiener „Neuromantikern", die der Avantgarde um Arnold Schönberg (1874–1951) fernstanden. Zeisl setzte diese Tradition des Rückbezugs auf die Romantik fort. Stöhr, der zuvor schon Lehrer von Erich Leinsdorf (1912–1993), Marcel Rubin (1905–1995), Paul Reif (1910–1978) oder Josef Dichler (1912–1993) gewesen war, schrieb im Mai 1938 vielsagend über Zeisl: „In meiner mehr als 35jährigen Tätigkeit als Lehrer war er ohne Übertreibung gesprochen der begabteste Schüler, den ich je hatte und auf den die denkbar größten Hoffnungen zu setzen waren."[4] Mit der in romantischem Gestus gehaltenen *Klaviertrio-Suite*, op. 8 (ca. 1920–1924), schuf Zeisl ein repräsentatives und stiltypisches Jugendwerk, die „temperamentvolle, begabte Arbeit eines Sechzehnjährigen"[5], wie in der *Arbeiter-Zeitung* anlässlich der Uraufführung im Wiener Konzerthaus im April 1928 zu lesen war. Das mit der Kammermusik Franz Schuberts oder Gustav Mahlers in Verbindung stehende Stück vermittelt Wiener Tradition, es wurde auch als „das Ergebnis gesunder und kräftiger musikalischer Impulse" mit einer Satztechnik von „stattlichem Entwicklungsstand"[6] gehört.

Lieder

Vornehmlich Lieder bestimmten die Zusammenarbeit zwischen Zeisl und Stöhr. Zeisl verstand es, die Singstimme und den Klavierpart in fein nuancierter Textausdeutung zueinander in Beziehung zu setzen und spätromantische Idiomatik um moderat moderne Stilelemente zu erweitern. Es war auch die Welt des Kunstliedes, die Zeisl für kurze Zeit zum „Traditionshüter" Joseph Marx (1882–1964) führte, ehe mit Hugo Kauder (1888–1972) eine innovative und der Moderne zuge-

Erich Zeisl, ein junger österreichischer Komponist, ca. 1930
Archiv des Exilarte Zentrum der mdw, Wien (A-Weaz)

wandte Lehrerpersönlichkeit in sein Leben trat. Im Austausch mit Kauder entstand als wichtiges Instrumentalwerk das *Erste Streichquartett* (ca. 1930–1933), das Zeisl dem im Wiener Konzertbetrieb etablierten Galimir Quartett „in Bewunderung & Freundschaft" zueignete. Auch über Felix Galimir (1910–1999), den Primgeiger des Quartetts, lässt sich eine Brücke zum Zirkel „Junge Kunst" schlagen: Bei einer Veranstaltung des Zirkels interpretierte Galimir mit seinem Ensemble Zeisls *Erstes Streichquartett*.

In die Zeit der Entstehung dieses Streichquartetts fiel das besondere Jahr 1931, in dem Zeisl ausschließlich Kunstlieder komponierte und sich ein „Liederjahr" im besten Sinne schuf. Sein Liedschaffen besticht durch den großen Reichtum an Melodien, breit ist die Palette an fein ausgeloteten Gefühlszuständen, die in gleißender Helligkeit aufblitzen oder in düsterstes Dunkel kippen, die seufzen, klagen, toben und schreien. Stimmungsbilder, Momentaufnahmen und groteske Miniaturen sind ebenso Teil dieser Liederwelt. Ein tonaler Bezug bleibt stets gewahrt, dissonante Akkordgebilde unterstreichen die Textaussage, Rückungen in entfernte Tonarten bringen Färbung.

Unter dem Einfluss von Hugo Kauder verknappte Zeisl seine Tonsprache, manifest wird dies etwa an den Nietzsche-Vertonungen *Das trunkene Lied* (1931) oder *Die Sonne sinkt* (1931). Der Klavierpart ist hier im Vergleich zur früheren Klangfülle reduziert und bildet den nun harmonisch auffallend interessanten Rahmen, Motivbildung scheint nicht mehr von vordergründiger Bedeutung. *Das trunkene Lied* zeigt durchaus Anklänge an Gustav Mahler – nicht zuletzt durch den Lehrer Kauder stand Zeisl in seiner Tradition. Besonders die Lieder nach Nietzsche verdeutlichen diesen Bezug: Sowohl in Nietzsches Texten als auch in Mahlers Musik spielt der „Lichtgedanke" eine tragende Rolle. Gemäß Nietzsches Vorlage liegt auch Zeisls *Trunkenem Lied* die Entwicklung „durch Dunkel zum Licht" zugrunde, musikalisch dargestellt durch die Bewegung von einer anfänglichen Moll-Klangsphäre in die Dur-Variante.

An zwei Punkten greift Zeisl minimal in den Text ein – das beginnende „Oh Mensch" wird wiederholt, ebenso das tragende „Weh spricht: Vergeh!". Genau hier und in den jeweils folgenden Takten hebt die ansonsten konsequent syllabisch gehaltene Singstimme zu charakteristischen signalartigen Triolenmelismen an, die als hommageartiges Herbeizitieren von Mahlers Art der Gestaltung in dessen *Zweiter* und *Dritter Symphonie* gedeutet werden können. Zeisls Lehrer Kauder verehrte Mahler tief, auch vertonte er viele Texte von Friedrich Nietzsche. In seinen Nietzsche-Liedern wandelt auch Zeisl auf diesen Pfaden.

Bemerkenswert innerhalb der Vielzahl vertonter Texte (Zeisl schrieb unter anderem nach Dehmel, Eichendorff, Goethe, Lenau, Morgenstern, Bierbaum, Ringelnatz oder Busch) ist die Auseinandersetzung mit Alfons Petzold (1882–1923). Der „Arbeiterdichter" Petzold rückte vermutlich durch die österreichische Literatin Hilde Spiel (1911–1990) in Zeisls Blickfeld. Als enge Freundin von Zeisls späterer Frau Gertrud Susanne Jellinek (1906–1987) stand Hilde Spiel dem Komponisten ebenfalls nahe; Freundschaftsbande, die auch im Exil hielten, bis zu Zeisls Tod. Hilde Spiel war engagierte Sozialdemokratin und zutiefst erschüttert von den Ereignissen, die zum Bürgerkrieg 1934 führten. Der Gedanke liegt nahe, dass sie den sonst nie „politisch" schreibenden Zeisl für Petzold sensibilisierte: 1932 entstanden die vier Lieder *Der tote Arbeiter*, *Ein buckliger Waisenknabe singt*, *Die Arbeiter* und *Wanderlied* nach Alfons Petzold. Fanfarenmotive und

Ein verschollenes Portrait Erich Zeisls von Lisel Salzer, abgebildet in der Zeitschrift *Radio Wien*, 1932/12.
Von diesem Gemälde, das 1938 in Wien blieb und bis heute verschwunden ist, fertigte Salzer im Exil ein Remake an.
Archiv des Exilarte Zentrum der mdw, Wien (A-Weaz)

Triolen stützen den harschen Trauermarsch im *Toten Arbeiter*, wenn der Leib nach größter Qual im „leuchtenden Sonnenstrahl" aufsteigt. Der Gedanke der Befreiung im Tod leitet auch das Lamento des Waisenknaben: Markante harmonische Wendungen kennzeichnen dort die „Heimat im Grabe" als einzige Perspektive. Solch typische Muster der „Proletarierdichtung" verwendete Zeisl ausschließlich hier.

Hilde Spiel

> In einem neuen Zirkel von Freunden, in den ich geraten war, spielte ich in improvisierten Theateraufführungen mit, hörte bei kleinen Hauskonzerten den Komponisten Erich Zeisl ganze Symphonien von Bruckner und Mahler auf dem Klavier simulieren [...] oder versuchte mich im Chor seiner eben entstehenden Messe; ich wurde von der Künstlerin Lisel Salzer gemalt und sah das nach dem Anschluß verschollene Bild im Hagenbund ausgestellt [...].[7]

So blickte Hilde Spiel zurück auf die gemeinsame Zeit mit der Malerin Lisel Salzer (1906–2005), dem Komponisten Erich Zeisl und der Juristin Gertrud Susanne Jellinek. Lisel und Gertrud kannten einander seit Kindheitstagen. Die beginnenden 1930er-Jahre führten dieses Quartett von künstlerischen Begabungen zusammen: Man traf sich zum Gedankenaustausch und verbrachte die Sommermonate am Wolfgangsee, wo Salzer der „Zinkenbacher Malerkolonie" angehörte. Unverkennbar hielt Hilde Spiel den musikbesessenen Zeisl in ihrem Romanerstling *Kati auf der Brücke* (1933, ausgezeichnet mit dem Julius-Reich-Preis der Stadt Wien) in der Figur des Musikers fest: „Dann spielte er wieder. [...] kleine lyrische Lieder, vertonten Morgenstern und Ringelnatz, endlich sein erstes Streichquartett, so blühend lebendig, daß man die Geige zu hören vermeinte und die Bratsche."[8] Malerei, Musik und Literatur nährten und bedingten einander in diesem Kreis, der durch Hilde Spiels Flucht nach London im Jahr 1936 auseinandergerissen wurde. Ein aufschlussreiches Konvolut von Exildokumenten aber blieb in Form der Korrespondenz zwischen den Zeisls und Hilde Spiel erhalten; Schriftstücke, die Erich Zeisls Leben nachzeichnen. Lisel Salzer flüchtete 1939 in die Vereinigten Staaten und lebte bis 2005 als letzte Vertreterin der „Zinkenbacher Malerkolonie" in Seattle, Washington.

„Eine der stärksten Persönlichkeiten"

Als gerade noch nicht 30-jähriger Komponist konnte Zeisl im Jahr 1934 auf eine Reihe von Aufführungen sowohl im Wiener Konzerthaus als auch im Musikverein zurückblicken. Nach seinen Anfängen in den 1920er-Jahren hatte er sich nun im Rahmen der moderaten Wiener Moderne etabliert. Menschen wie Karl Weigl (1881–1949), Egon Kornauth (1891–1959), Kurt Pahlen (1907–2003), Franz Mittler (1893–1970), Ernst Kanitz (1894–1978), Friedrich Bloch

Die junge Malerin Lisel Salzer vor einem ihrer Kunstwerke, Wien 1932
Archiv des Exilarte Zentrum der mdw, Wien (A-Weaz)

(1899–1945), Rudolf Réti (1885–1957), Victor Urbancic (1903–1958) oder Othmar Wetchy (1892–1951) bildeten sein Umfeld. 1934 nahm Paul Amadeus Pisk (1893–1990) in einer verheißungsvollen Rezension auf Zeisls bis dahin vorliegendes Œuvre Bezug:

> Eine der stärksten Persönlichkeiten der noch nicht dreißigjährigen Wiener Komponisten ist Erich Zeisel [sic]. [...] Außer diesem Quartett hat der heute erst achtundzwanzig Jahre alte Komponist eine Violinsonate, ein Klaviertrio und mehrere Chöre geschrieben, darunter Jazzchöre [...] und Volksliedbearbeitungen. Eine ganze Messe für Chor, Orgel und Streicher liegt in seiner Lade, ein Ballett ‚Pierrot in der Flasche' und neuerdings ein ‚Requiem', das der Fertigstellung entgegensieht. Einige dieser Werke sind schon zur Aufführung gekommen, da jeder Musiker, der sie hört, von dem eigenwüchsigen Temperament Zeisels [sic] gefangen ist. [...] Zeisels [sic] Musik ist wohl immer leicht verständlich, doch nie banal. Der noch sehr junge Komponist verdient es, daß man nachdrücklich auf ihn hinweist und sein Schaffen der Öffentlichkeit näher bringt.[9]

Zeisls Werk umfasste zu jener Zeit Kunstlieder, Kammermusik- und Chorwerke, die frühe Oper *Die Sünde* (1927/28), das mit „Jazzyness" kokettierende Ballett *Pierrot in der Flasche* (1929), die *Kleine Messe* (1932) und das im Entstehen begriffene *Requiem Concertante* (1933/34). Mit dem sinnlich tanzenden *Pierrot in der Flasche* nach Gustav Meyrinks Erzählung *Der Mann auf der Flasche* bewegte Zeisl sich in der Welt der Groteske; mit dem ein Jahr zuvor entstandenen Liederzyklus *Mondbilder* (nach Christian Morgenstern) hatte er sie bereits durchwandert. Aktualität und Experimentierfreude vermitteln zwei spätere Chorwerke: Das ins Populäre reichende *Afrika singt* (1930/31) nach Texten der 1929 veröffentlichten Anthologie *Afrika singt. Eine Auslese neuer afro-amerikanischer Lyrik* knüpft als erstes Werk dieser Gattung an den jazzinspirierten *Pierrot* an, während die suggestive *Spruchkantate* (1935) nach Sprüchen von Silesius, Salomon und Goethe neue Effekte in der Chormusik auslotet. In den nachfolgenden symphonischen Werken wie der *Passacaglia* (1933/34) und der *Kleinen Symphonie* (1935/36) nach Bildern von Roswitha Bitterlich (1920–2015) nützt Zeisl die Vorzüge des romantischen Orchesterapparats und erscheint traditioneller. Dirigenten wie Karl Oskar Alwin (1891–1945), Kurt Herbert Adler (1905–1988) und Rudolf Nilius (1883–1962) nahmen sich Zeisl'scher Orchesterwerke an.

Eine Erscheinung anderen Zuschnitts in Zeisls Wiener Leben war der in Brünn geborene Hugo F. Königsgarten (später Koenigsgarten, 1904–1975), der 1933 vor dem Nationalsozialismus aus Deutschland nach Österreich floh und 1938 abermals flüchtete, diesmal nach England. Königsgarten war am literarischen Kabarett „Der liebe Augustin" Akteur der Wiener Kleinkunstszene, mit Zeisl verband ihn die gemeinsame Arbeit an *Leonce und Lena* nach Georg Büchner (1813–1837): Königsgarten verfasste das Libretto, Zeisl komponierte die Musik. Nach einer Idee von Königsgarten war das Stück als Singspiel mit gesprochenen Dialogen und Musik konzipiert. Heiterkeit und Übermut durchziehen den Text, als Lustspiel lebt das Stück von Anmut und Leichtigkeit. In krassem Gegensatz zu den Umständen der Entstehungszeit vermittelt *Leonce und Lena* eine Unbeschwertheit, die nur in der fiktiven Welt der Büchner'schen Königreiche „Popo" und „Pipi" möglich ist. Zeisls Musik dazu schwelgt im Märchenkolorit. Eine Aufführung des Lustspiels war für April/Mai 1938 unter Kurt Herbert Adlers Dirigat im Schlosstheater Schönbrunn geplant, der „Anschluss" im März 1938 zerstörte diese Perspektive.

Der „Telefonbuchzeisl"

Im Frühjahr 1938 war Zeisl in geistige Lähmung und tiefe Depression verfallen. *Leonce und Lena* blieb in Österreich sein letztes Werk größeren Zuschnitts, die danach nur zögerlich zu Papier gebrachten Werke – die Klavier- beziehungsweise Orchesterstücke *November* (entstanden zwischen November 1937 und Mai 1938), das Lied *Komm süsser Tod* (Jänner 1938) und die A-cappella-Chöre *In tiefem Schlummer* (Februar 1938) und *Am Abend* (Februar 1938) – haben alles Lichte verloren und klingen dunkel und resignativ. An die 100 Kunstlieder komponierte Zeisl bis in das Jahr 1938, mit *Komm süsser Tod* hinterließ er seinen Abgesang an die Welt des deutschen Kunstlieds. In dieser Abschiedsgeste verwendete er eine aus deutsch-österreichischer Liedtradition herrührende Sprachlichkeit. *Komm süsser Tod* suggeriert „Todeseinverständnis" und Sehnsucht nach Ruhe, das Lied ist durch seine dem Text entsprechende Dur-Moll-Polarität charakterisiert. Zeisl setzte, wie oft auch Franz Schubert oder Hugo Wolf, ausschließlich halbe Noten und Viertelnoten und inszenierte bewusst ein gleichförmiges Fortschreiten. Als typisch „schubertisch" mutet der Kunstgriff der Bekräftigung der Singstimme durch den nachfolgend imitierenden Klavierpart an. Zeisl wusste, welche kulturelle Welt er verlassen würde, und er wusste, in welchen Chiffren dieser Verlust zum Ausdruck gebracht werden konnte.

Im Mai 1938 berichtete Zeisl der Freundin Hilde Spiel nach London: „Ich schreibe momentan gar nichts. Bin nicht in Stimmung. Nur manchmal habe ich das Gefühl, dass noch Grosses in mir steckt. Es kommt aber leider nichts heraus. – Vielleicht werde ich nicht mehr komponieren können. Es wäre entsetzlich und mein Leben verwirkt."[10] Um dem Naziterror in Wien zu entfliehen, wichen die Zeisls nach dem „Anschluss" über die Ostertage 1938 nach Baden bei Wien aus. Dort wollten sie auch die Sommermonate verbringen. Ein Schreiben der Stadtgemeinde Baden vom 29. Juni 1938 mit dem Befehl, „das Gebiet der Stadt- und Kurgemeinde Baden b. Wien binnen 48 Stunden nach Empfang dieser Aufforderung zu verlassen"[11], machte die Hoffnung auf Sicherheit zunichte.

In der Not durchforstete Gertrud das New Yorker Telefonbuch nach Namensgleichen, die eventuell ein Affidavit für die Vereinigten Staaten vermitteln konnten. Solch ein „Telefonbuchzeisl" fand sich dann tatsächlich in Morris Zeisel. Der den Wiener Zeisls bis dahin unbekannte Namensvetter stellte das dringend erforderliche Dokument zur Verfügung und ermöglichte so den Zeisls die Ausreise aus Österreich und die Einreise nach Frankreich. Dieses „Affidavit of Support"[12] wurde am 20. September 1938 von einem amerikanischen Notariat freigegeben: Der in Österreich geborene Morris Zeisel war damals 44 Jahre alt, hielt sich seit 1913 in den Vereinigten Staaten auf, war seit 1921 amerikanischer Staatsbürger und wohnte in 1555 West 11th Street, Brooklyn, New York. Als „Verwandtschaftsverhältnis" zu Erich und Gertrud gab der zweifache Vater „Cousin" an. Neben der Wohnadresse war in Morris Zeisels Brief die Firmenadresse Manbrook, Plumbing and Heating Co., Inc., 541 10th Avenue, New York, angeführt. Der „Telefonbuchzeisl" war ein „Master Plumber" aus New York – und Lebensretter.

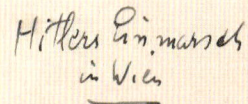

Ankündigung zur Erstaufführung von Zeisls *Scherzo und Fuge für Streichorchester* am 10. März 1938 in Wien. Zeisl vermerkte: „Hitlers Einmarsch in Wien"
Archiv des Exilarte Zentrum der mdw, Wien (A-Weaz)

Schreiben der Stadtgemeinde Baden an Erich Zeisl mit dem Befehl, die Stadt innerhalb 48 Stunden zu verlassen, 29. Juni 1938
Archiv des Exilarte Zentrum der mdw, Wien (A-Weaz)

Seite 21: Das letzte Foto vor der Flucht aus Wien: Zeisls Schwiegermutter Ilona Jellinek, Zeisls Frau Gertrud, die Freundin Hilde Hirschenhauser und Erich Zeisl, November 1938
Archiv des Exilarte Zentrum der mdw, Wien (A-Weaz)

Hiob

Am 10. November 1938 verließen Erich, Gertrud und Wilhelm Zeisl mit Gertruds Mutter Ilona Jellinek Wien. Vergleichsweise spät nach Paris gelangt, fanden sie in der französischen Metropole relativ schwierige Bedingungen vor. Dennoch – und vor allem mit Blick zurück auf die verheerende Situation in Wien – eröffnete die Ankunft in Paris denkbar gute Perspektiven. Überwältigend war das Gefühl neu gewonnener Freiheit und groß die Dankbarkeit für die gelungene Flucht. Das von einer schlechten Wirtschaftslage, einer hohen Arbeitslosenrate und einer immensen Zahl von Geflüchteten gezeichnete Frankreich zeigte ohnehin früh genug seinen für die Asylsuchenden beschämenden Bürokratismus. Die Zeisls mussten nervenzermürbende Behördengänge erledigen, um den weiteren Verbleib in Paris zu sichern.

Von eminenter Bedeutung war daher das Zusammentreffen mit Darius Milhaud (1882–1974), der den Zeisls mit einem Schreiben des französischen Innenministers Albert Sarraut im März 1939 (das er erwirkt hatte) einen längeren Aufenthalt in Paris ermöglichte. Milhauds Zutun öffnete ihnen auch die Türen zum Pariser Kulturleben, das mit einer Gedenkveranstaltung für den österreichischen Autor Joseph Roth (1894–1939) ein besonders gewichtiges Ereignis verzeichnete: Roth war am 27. Mai in Paris verstorben, sein Roman *Hiob* wurde am 3. Juli im Théâtre Pigalle in einer Bühnenfassung aufgeführt. Ein deutschsprachiges Emigrantenensemble mit Mitgliedern des Reinhardt-Ensembles (etwa Hugo Haas, Josef Meinrad oder Leon Askin) spielte die Geschichte um die Leiden Hiobs. Den Auftrag für die Bühnenmusik erhielt Zeisl, der das *Organ Prelude*, *Menuhim's Song* für Violine und Klavier und den *Cossack Dance* für Klavier lieferte. Trotz widrigster Umstände und eklatanter organisatorischer Mängel wurde die *Hiob*-Aufführung ein großer Erfolg; das Projekt bestach nicht zuletzt aufgrund der Aktualität des Stoffs.

Während Arnold Schönbergs Aufenthalt in Paris von seinem Nachdenken über Stellung und Zukunft des Judentums und seinem Wiedereintritt in die jüdische Glaubensgemeinschaft (als letzte Konsequenz eines erneuerten und gestärkten jüdischen Bewusstseins) bestimmt war, besann Erich Zeisl sich im Exil erstmals auf seine jüdischen Wurzeln. Dies hatte starken Nachhall in seinem weiteren Komponieren. Nicht „wieder zum Juden geworden", sondern, pointiert formuliert, „erstmals zum Juden geworden" – und das durch Hitler –, stellte Zeisl sich dem NS-Rassenwahn entgegen. Nie hatte er in Österreich nach jüdischen Sujets gearbeitet, nie war seine Tonsprache von „jüdischer" Idiomatik gefärbt gewesen; erst mit *Hiob* veranschaulichte er seine jüdische Herkunft im Werk. Die Auseinandersetzung mit dem Stoff bedeutete eine Konfrontation mit dem eigenen Schicksal. Roths Roman, Sinnbild des Leids und der Verfolgung der europäischen Jüdinnen und Juden, war 1930 erschienen, wenige Jahre vor der Zerstörung alles Jüdischen durch den Nationalsozialismus.

Zeisl intonierte nun eine quasijüdische Sprache und führte in Stücken wie *Menuhim's Song* Themen ein, die in späteren Werken zu Schlüsselthemen wurden. Auffälligstes Merkmal in *Menuhim's Song* ist die oftmals betonte übermäßige Sekund, die maßgeblich für die „jüdisch-traditionelle" Intonation verantwortlich ist. Rezitierende Sequenzen und eine freie Fortspinnung des Anfangsmotivs geben dem Stück Gebetscharakter, der zusätzlich durch gehäufte seufzerartige Vorhalte unterstrichen wird. Das Motiv wird dabei stilbildend improvisatorisch weitergeführt.

Als die Musikwissenschaftlerin Anneliese Landau (1903–1991) den Komponisten 1951 fragte, ab welchem Zeitpunkt „Jüdisches" in seinem Werk Relevanz hatte, gab er zur Antwort: „I believe it was in Paris when I was commissioned to set music to Joseph Roth's book on 'Job'. The story of the persecuted Jew who escaped from Poland to America suggested in itself an outspoken Jewish music."[13]

Über die Pariser *Hiob*-Aufführung hatte Paul Stefan geschrieben: „Der hochbegabte Wiener Komponist überzeugte auch sein Theater-Publikum. Man empfing einen starken Eindruck namentlich von der einleitenden Orgelmusik, die einen Prolog im Himmel vorstellt, ernst, mächtig, weit ausgreifend."[14]

Der Schönberg-Schüler Paul Stefan, auf den Zeisl in Paris traf, war ihm wohlbekannt. Sie bewegten sich beide in einem Exilzirkel, dem auch der Richard-Stöhr-Schüler Marcel Rubin (1905–1995) angehörte; dieser war in Wien tätig gewesen. In Paris kamen die Zeisls außerdem mit Franz Werfel (1890–1945) und Alma Mahler-Werfel (1879–1964) in freundschaftlichen Kontakt; man traf sich regelmäßig, auch später im kalifornischen Exil. Anfangs wohnten die Zeisls wie viele Geflüchtete im Hotel Perey, Cité du Retiro, Paris 8, ab Juni 1939 konnten sie außerhalb von Paris ein Haus mieten. Der neue Wohnort mit der passenden Adresse „39, route de l'Asile, Le Vésinet" wurde zum Ort der Begegnung; Zeisl teilte das Haus mit dem österreichischen Exilschriftsteller Hans Kafka (1902–1974). Ab der Pariser Zeit verband Kafka und Zeisl eine künstlerische Zusammenarbeit: Kafka verfasste das Libretto zur späteren Oper *Hiob*.

Nach seiner Tätigkeit als Literatur-, Film- und Theaterkritiker in Berlin, einem Aufenthalt in Chicago, erneuter Tätigkeit in Wien (ab 1934) und Arbeit für den Film in London (1936) war Kafka 1937 nach Paris gelangt. Nach Kriegsausbruch wurde er in Frankreich für fünf Monate interniert; seine Frau, die Schauspielerin Trude Burr, konnte Visa für die Vereinigten Staaten erwirken. Nach seiner Entlassung brachen sie im Jahr 1940 dorthin auf. Die Zeisls erreichten die Vereinigten Staaten im September 1939, ein zweites Affidavit von einem Arnold Zeissl aus Milwaukee hatte die Ausreise aus Paris ermöglicht; dieser war tatsächlich ein entfernter Verwandter.

Misere Hollywood

Als Passagiere der „Volendam" landeten die Zeisls in New York, und im Oktober gingen von dort die ersten Zeilen an Hilde Spiel in London: „Wir sind nach endlosen Strapazen hier angekommen und fühlen uns sehr glücklich. Du machst Dir gar keine Vorstellung von der gigantischen Grösse New Yorks. Die Stadt mutet einen fast wie eine Marsstadt an. Wie auf einem Planeten. Wie das alles in den Himmel ragt! Unglaublich! Könnt ihr nicht herkommen? Ich glaube es ist der richtige Platz für uns alle!"[15]

Zeisls erste Berührung mit dem amerikanischen Kulturleben verlief erstaunlich positiv, am 28. November 1939 war im *Morning Telegraph* unter der Headline „Zeisl's Music in U.S. Debut" zu lesen: „The American premiere of a modern symphony by Erich Zeisl, brilliant young Austrian composer, will be given on the 'Radio City Music Hall on the Air' next Sunday [...]."[16] Offenbar traf die *Little Symphony* (*Kleine Symphonie*, 1935/36) den amerikanischen Publikumsgeschmack punktgenau. Der in Budapest geborene Dirigent Ernö Rapée

(1891–1945) war 1939 einer der Künstler des großen New Yorker Filmtheaters Radio City Music Hall. Kurzerhand inkludierte er Zeisls Orchestersätze nach Bildern von Roswitha Bitterlich in das Programm seiner landesweiten Radiostunde, für die er mit dem Music Hall Symphony Orchestra klassisches Repertoire aufbereitete. Über die Stationen WJZ und NBC Blue Network lief am 3. Dezember 1939 die erste US-Radioaufführung Zeisl'scher Musik.

Nach dem anfänglichen Aufenthalt in einem Hotel fand sich für die Zeisls über den Winter 1939/40 ein unmöbliertes „one-room apartment" an der Adresse 315 West 91st Street. Der Lebensstandard war mehr als bescheiden, der finanzielle Rückhalt fehlte; und dennoch erlebten Erich und Gertrud New York als Neustart: Im Mai 1940 wurde die Tochter Barbara geboren. Der Umzug in ein gemietetes Haus auf Long Island kam der kleinen Familie entgegen. Mittlerweile zu „Eric" amerikanisiert, knüpfte Zeisl beruflich wichtige Kontakte; die weitere Zusammenarbeit mit dem Radio unter Dirigenten wie Howard Barlow (1892–1972) oder Wilfrid Pelletier (1896–1982) machte seinen Namen auch in den Vereinigten Staaten klingend.

Dennoch hoffte Zeisl, dass New York das Sprungbrett für ein Leben in Hollywood sein werde. Konkretisiert wurden diese Visionen durch Hans Kafka, der ab Mai 1940 in Hollywood lebte. Mit den Strukturen des Filmgeschäfts bestens vertraut, sah er als Mitglied des MGM-Personals eine „terrific Chance"[17], auch den Freund Zeisl in die Company zu holen. Kafka war als „personal Zeisl representative"[18] der Hauptakteur in Zeisls Transfer vom Osten in den Westen, mit Geschick und Hartnäckigkeit arrangierte er Zeisls Start bei MGM. Kafkas Korrespondenz aus Hollywood an die Zeisls in New York von Juli/August 1941 spricht Bände: Um die Vita des künftigen Filmkomponisten für Hollywood passend zu machen, setzte Kafka Zeisls Alter herab, „da eine Tendenz gegen zu ‚alte' Leute"[19] bestand, bagatellisierte seine vertragliche Bindung an Associated Music Publishers in New York und beschrieb ihn als „zwei Jahre im Land" befindlich und mit „first papers"[20] ausgestattet. Kafka bestand darauf, dass Zeisl Englisch „like hell"[21] lernen müsse, gab Anweisungen zum Erwerb aller „erdenkbaren technischen Ausdrücke", stellte „500 Dollar Musiker", die „gefeuert" werden, in Aussicht, und sprach von einziehenden „75 Dollar Musikern"[22].

Hanns Eisler (1898–1962) versuchte ebenso, durch seine Kontakte zum Filmbetrieb Zeisl „plus Familie nach Hollywood zu verpflanzen"[23]. Und auch später noch unterstützte er den zum Freund gewordenen Zeisl mit einem Empfehlungsschreiben an Herbert Kline (1909–1999), den Regisseur des Semidokumentarfilms *The Forgotten Village*, für den er, Eisler, die Musik komponierte. „He is a very gifted fellow" – so Eisler an Kline im Juli 1942 – „and I think he would be splendid for your new picture. Listen to his music!"[24]

Erich Zeisl, seine Frau Gertrud und die Tochter Barbara starteten ihr Leben in Los Angeles dennoch in Ungewissheit. Der Vertragsabschluss mit MGM kam zu schlechteren Konditionen zustande als ursprünglich vereinbart, und auch das erst nach der Drohung Zeisls, Hollywood umgehend wieder zu verlassen. Die Bindung an MGM begann schließlich mit der unterbezahlten Arbeit an den damals populären *Fitzpatrick Traveltalks*, landschaftsbeschreibenden Kurzfilmen, die nach illustrativer Musik verlangten. In der Folge war er an vielen Spielfilmen beteiligt – einen „credit", eine namentliche Nennung im Vor- oder Abspann, erhielt er jedoch nie. Dass mehrere Komponisten für eine Produktion schrieben und nur die „großen Namen" mit einem „credit" gewürdigt wurden, war

Erich und Gertrud Zeisl mit Tochter Barbara
im neuen Zuhause in New York City, 1940
Archiv des Exilarte Zentrum der mdw, Wien
(A-Weaz)

Hanns und Lou (Louise) Eisler am Strand in Los Angeles, 1943
Arnold Schönberg Center Privatstiftung, Wien (A-Was)

gängige Praxis in Hollywood. Zeisl arbeitete in dieser Manier mit Kollegen wie Franz Waxman, Walter Jurmann, Bronisław Kaper, Mario Castelnuovo-Tedesco, Herbert Stothart, Daniele Amfitheatrof oder Nathaniel Shilkret.

Die anfängliche Hollywood-Euphorie ging in Desillusionierung und Frustration über; nach nur 18 Monaten löste MGM den Vertrag. Anschließend war Zeisl freischaffend tätig, arrangierte und orchestrierte für Komponistenkollegen und arbeitete auch für Universal International. Zwar gewann er über den Film bedeutende Freunde wie Alexandre Tansman (1897–1986) und Mario Castelnuovo-Tedesco (1895–1968), doch litt er massiv darunter, in Hollywood auf das „Produzieren" von Musik reduziert zu sein, die fernab seiner künstlerischen Ansprüche stand. Die in die „Traumfabrik" gesetzten Erwartungen blieben gänzlich unerfüllt, vielmehr driftete er in eine veritable Schaffenskrise. Entrinnen konnte er der Hollywood-Misere allein durch die Komposition des *Requiem Ebraico* (1944/45).

Ein Requiem für das jüdische Volk

„It is so refreshing to find a composer in Hollywood who can still divorce himself from the false glitter of film music and devote his spare time to writing music to a religious text."[25] So lautete eine Reaktion auf die Uraufführung der Orgelfassung des *Requiem Ebraico* beim „Hollywood Inter-Faith Forum" am 8. April 1945 in Los Angeles. Das *Requiem Ebraico* ist keine lateinische Totenmesse nach der katholischen Liturgie; der dem Werk zugrunde liegende Psalm 92 enthält keine textliche Anlehnung an einen Totengesang. Mit der Nachricht von der Ermordung seines Vaters Siegmund und seiner Stiefmutter Malvine, die 1942 von Theresienstadt in das Vernichtungslager Treblinka deportiert worden waren, änderte sich die Bedeutung des Kompositionsauftrags, den Zeisl vom Reformrabbiner Jacob Sonderling (1878–1964) für den Synagogendienst erhalten hatte. Das Wissen um die Verbrechen des Holocaust drang nun auch nach Übersee, Zeisl widmete den Psalm als Requiem für das jüdische Volk seinem ermordeten „Vater und den unzähligen Opfern der jüdischen Tragödie in Europa"[26]. Das *Requiem Ebraico* gilt heute als eine der frühesten musikalischen Bezugnahmen auf den Holocaust.

Stilistisch setzte Zeisl den Weg fort, den er in Paris mit der Komposition zu *Hiob* beschritten hatte; im Intonieren quasi-jüdischer Idiomatik begründete er seinen „synagogalen Stil". Diese Sprache formte in unterschiedlicher Ausprägung weitere Kompositionen wie die *Songs for the Daughter of Jephtha* (1948), das Chorwerk *From the Book of Psalms* (1952), die auf biblische Themen gestützten Ballette *Naboth's Vineyard* (1953) und *Jacob and Rachel* (1954) oder Instrumentalwerke ohne programmatischen Bezug zum Judentum wie die *Sonata Barocca* (1948/49) für Klavier, die *Brandeis Sonata* (1949/50) für Violine und Klavier, die *Viola Sonata* (1950) und das *Second String Quartet* (1953). Die letztgenannten Kammermusikwerke lassen die „neue" Stilistik in unterschiedlicher Intensität hören – deutlich offenkundig ist sie in den Stücken mit biblischem Kontext.

Die Beschäftigung mit jüdischer Kunstmusik eröffnete im Exil neue Bezugs- und Betätigungsfelder: Von 1948 bis 1950 unterrichtete Zeisl in den Sommermonaten mit den Kollegen Max Helfman (1901–1963) und Julius Chajes (1910–1985; ehemals ein Mitstreiter im Wiener Zirkel „Junge Kunst") als „composer in residence" am Brandeis Camp Institute in Santa Susana im nordwestlich von Los Angeles gelegenen Simi Valley. Hier brachte ein Kurs- und Freizeitangebot jüdischen Jugendlichen sowohl tradierte als auch zeitgenössische jüdische Kunst- und Volksmusik näher. Im Camp stellte Zeisl im Sommer 1950 seine *Brandeis Sonata* für Violine und Klavier fertig. Israel Baker (1919–2011) und Yaltah Menuhin (1921–2001) führten das Stück im September 1950 in Santa Monica auf – eine „Voraufführung" fand im Brandeis Camp statt. Zeisls Verbundenheit mit den die jüdische Kunstmusik fördernden Organisationsstrukturen und Musiziergemeinschaften wirkte sinn- und stilstiftend.

Julius Chajes, der nach seiner Flucht aus Österreich und vor seiner Ankunft in den Vereinigten Staaten in Palästina lebte, war der jüdischen Kunstmusik bedeutend mehr und auch differenzierter verbunden als Zeisl. Als Leiter der Klavierabteilung der Musikakademie in Tel Aviv war er mit dem praktischen Musikleben in Palästina auf Tuchfühlung und entwickelte großes Interesse an den Quellen jüdischer Musik der Antike und an der Folklore der Region. Chajes orientierte sich an der so bezeichneten Eastern Mediterranean School, an arabischer Folklore oder an anderen das Land durchflutenden Musikstilen – das färbte viele seiner künftigen Kompositionen charakteristisch ein. Die Kantate *The Promised Land*, die Oper *Out of the Desert*, die ursprünglich für Kammerensemble gedachte und zum Orchesterwerk revidierte *Hebrew Suite* oder die Psalmvertonung *Old Jerusalem* vermitteln einen Eindruck von Chajes' Adaption tradierter jüdischer Musik und von seinem optimistischen und lebensfrohen Zugriff auf die Folklore, der auch im Geiste der zionistischen Bewegung stand. Dass Chajes in den Vereinigten Staaten Leiter des Jewish Community Center in Detroit wurde, wo er ein Orchester gründete, und später auch als Musikdirektor am Detroiter Temple Beth-El wirkte, bezeugt, wie intensiv er von seiner jüdischen Identität durchdrungen war.

Die musikalischen Biografien und Äußerungen von Jüdinnen und Juden unter dem NS-Rassenwahn stellten sich verschieden dar; sosehr Zeisl im Exil eine neue Sprache definierte, so sehr blieb er doch den Kompositionstechniken und -verfahren treu, die er aus der Heimat kannte. Das unterschied ihn von Julius Chajes. Interessant in diesem Kontext erscheint die „Synthese" der deutschen Hoch- und Spätromantik und eines kämpferisch zionistischen Textes von Karl Wolfskehl (1869–1948), die Richard Fuchs (1887–1947; geboren in Karlsruhe, Exil und Tod in Neuseeland) im Oratorium *Vom jüdischen Schicksal* (1936) vollzog. Das Werk gewann den Preis des „Reichsverbandes Jüdischer Kulturbünde" und wurde aufgrund eines Verbots durch die „Reichskulturkammer" nicht mehr aufgeführt. Fuchs verharrte in dem Stück in der Sprache der deutschen Romantik und näherte sich dem Text von Wolfskehl in keiner Weise über „jüdische" Anklänge an.

Familienausflug in Kalifornien.
Erich und Gertrud Zeisl, Ilona
Jellinek und Barbara Zeisl,
Juli 1955
Archiv des Exilarte Zentrum der
mdw, Wien (A-Weaz)

Küsschen von Korngold

Galt das Brandeis Camp den Exilierten als besonderer Kommunikationsort, so waren allgemein gesehen die Stätten der inspirativen Auseinandersetzung in Los Angeles dünn gesät. Plätze wie der den Vertriebenen wichtige Diskussionsort Farmers Market waren die Ausnahme. Um dieses Manko auszugleichen, wurden die Privathäuser in Hollywood, Brentwood, Beverly Hills oder den Küstenvororten Pacific Palisades und Santa Monica zu beliebten Treffpunkten. So auch das Haus der Zeisls in 8578 West Knoll Drive, Hollywood 46, wohin etwa Alma Mahler-Werfel schrieb: „Dear dear friends Tausend tausend Dank für das entzückende Geschenk – ich komme bald und dann wollen wir uns gründlich sehen! Alles Liebe Alma Maria!"[27]

Die Zeisls sorgten für eine kleine österreichische Insel: Immer wieder gaben Erich und Gertrud Abend- und Nachmittagsgesellschaften, zu denen sich Erich Wolfgang und Luzi Korngold gerne einfanden. Mit den Zeisls befreundet waren etwa Alma Mahler-Werfel, Alexandre Tansman, Darius Milhaud, Ernst Toch oder Lion Feuchtwanger. Mit Hanns Eisler und Igor Strawinsky stand Zeisl in guter Verbindung. Das Haus am West Knoll Drive lud zu einem Mix, der durch Wiener Mehlspeisen eine besonders authentische Note erhielt – und dennoch auch Illusion blieb. Die Urlaubspost innerhalb dieser Runde lässt Vertrautheit erahnen: So schrieb Toch an seine „Zeiserln" oder an das „Gezeisl" und sprach von den „Korngöldern", Zeisl an seine „lieben Korngolds", Korngold wiederum an die „Liebe[n], gute[n] Zeisls". Es waren dann und wann auch schnell aufgesetzte Nachrichten, die Korngold den Zeisls übermittelte: eine Postkarte aus Burbank etwa, wo Warner Brothers Studios betrieb (ganz in der Nähe von Korngolds Haus in Toluca Lake), oder flott geschriebene Zeilen, die Korngold im Vorbeifahren und mit „Küsschen" den Zeisls an ihrem Urlaubsort Desert Hot Springs hinterließ.

Korngold schrieb auch „hinauf" nach Lake Arrowhead, in die San-Bernardino-Berge, die klimatisch wie landschaftlich an Europa erinnern und den naturverliebten Zeisls in den späten 1950er-Jahren ein Ferienparadies waren. Am 27. Juli 1955 fragte Korngold von Burbank aus in Lake Arrowhead nach – scherzend im Namen der „ganzen Korngoldfamilie" –, ob Zeisl sein Klavier umgestellt habe:

> Liebe, gute Zeisls –
> Nur eine Zeile des Danks für die höchst angenehmen Stunden am vergangenen Sonntag wie für das prächtige und opulente Zimmer und alle guten Wünsche für den weiteren Sommerverlauf nebst guter Komponierlaune!
> Habt Ihr das Klavier umgestellt? Bestimmt nicht!! –
> Wir kommen sicherlich noch einmal hinauf zu Euch. Bis dahin:
> lasst es Euch gut gehen und seid herzlich gegrüsst und umarmt!
> Die ganze Korngoldfamilie.[28]

Und keck war die Notiz aus Desert Hot Springs vom 30. Dezember 1955:

> Lieber alter Zeisl!
>
> Wir kommen über San Diego u. Palm Springs eigens, um Euch für ein paar Küsschen zu besuchen!
> Nachdem wir über eine halbe Stunde angenehm die „Siesta" gemacht haben – niemand konnte uns eine definitive Adresse bekannt geben – habe ich sie endlich in der „Fiesta" (5. Street) ausfindig gemacht, um gerade 2 Minuten nach Eurer Abfahrt einzutreffen!!! Das nenne ich Pech! Auf baldigst in L.A. Prosit Neujahr!
> Herzlich: Dein EWK.[29]

„Diese Wiener ‚Schleimhäute'. Pfui Teufel!"

Mit dem scherzenden „Prosit Neujahr" verabschiedete Erich Wolfgang Korngold das Jahr 1955; ein Jahr, in dem Zeisl gemeinsam mit der Exilcommunity in Los Angeles seinen 50. Geburtstag gefeiert hatte. Zu Ehren ihres Freundes verfasste Hilde Spiel einen Text für die Zeitung *Neues Österreich*: „Heute feiert der Wiener Musiker Erich Zeisl, fern der Heimat, seinen fünfzigsten Geburtstag [...]."[30] So die ersten Zeilen. Ein „Komitee der Freunde Erich Zeisls" mit Personen wie Igor Strawinsky, Darius Milhaud, Arnold Schönbergs Witwe Gertrud, Erich Wolfgang Korngold und Alma Mahler-Werfel organisierte aus diesem Anlass einen Konzertabend in Los Angeles, um „Wiens verlorene[n] Sohn in der Fremde"[31] zu ehren. In einem kurzen Abriss blickt Hilde Spiel zurück auf Zeisls Wiener Jahre, um dann pointiert festzustellen: „Diesen Urwiener, diesen Vollmusiker in kalifornische Erde zu verpflanzen, mochte ein Ding der Unmöglichkeit sein. Immerhin, was gelingen mußte, gelang schließlich auch."[32] Im letzten Absatz verbindet die Autorin die zwei so verschiedenen Welten in einem Bild: „Als wir ihn in seinem weißen Blockhaus am West Knoll Drive besuchten, führte er uns voll Stolz in den Garten, um uns seine tropischen Sträucher und Gewächse zu zeigen. Im Biedermeiersalon mit der gestreiften Tapete stand ein Wiener Flügel. Im Garten blühte der Avokado-Birnbaum. So hat ein Österreicher, der er bis zum letzten Atemzug bleiben wird, in einem Ausgleich zweier Zivilisationen seine neue Lebensgrundlage gefunden."[33]

Nach dem Kriegsende war Wien für die Zeisls wieder näher gerückt; vor allem als Hilde Spiel 1946 als Korrespondentin in britischer Uniform erstmals wieder nach Österreich gereist war, um für den *New Statesman* über die sozialen und politischen Umstände in ihrer ehemaligen Heimat zu berichten. Den Zustand der Zerrissenheit fühlte sie intensiv am „topographisch genau bestimmbaren Ursprung"[34] ihrer „Einheit mit Wien" – dem Pfarrplatz in Heiligenstadt. Ihre Eindrücke sendete sie an die Zeisls, die in Kalifornien im Zustand permanenter „homesickness" lebten. Aufgewühlt und pendelnd zwischen heftiger Sehnsucht nach Wien und Trauer, Wut und Schock über die dort verübten Verbrechen antwortete Erich Zeisl im Mai 1946: „Nach Wien würde ich lange Zeit nicht

Hilde Spiel, Korrespondentin für den britischen *New Statesman*, im Grinzinger Bad, Juli 1946
Archiv des Exilarte Zentrum der mdw, Wien (A-Weaz)

gehen. Beide Eltern verloren! Diese Wiener ‚Schleimhäute'. Pfui Teufel!"[35] Und: „Ich kann mir überhaupt nicht vorstellen, wie man dies aushalten kann. Ich glaube ich würde vor seelischer Erschütterung tot umfallen."[36]

Im Februar 1959, nach einer Vorlesung am Los Angeles City College – wo er seit 1949 unterrichtet hatte und wo 1952 im Opera Workshop unter der Leitung von Hugo Strelitzer (1896–1981) die Uraufführung von *Leonce und Lena* „nachgeholt" worden war –, starb Erich Zeisl im Alter von nur 53 Jahren durch einen Herzinfarkt. Völlig unerwartet war er „tot umgefallen". Ein Schock für alle Freund:innen sowie Wegbegleiter:innen, ein Schock, der Gertrud und Barbara Zeisl natürlich besonders tief und schmerzhaft traf. Seine Heimatstadt Wien hatte Erich Zeisl nicht wiedergesehen.

1. Alfred Farau an Erich Zeisl, 11. 7. 1955, zit. n. Karin Wagner (Hg.), ... es grüsst Dich Erichisrael. Briefe von und an Eric Zeisl, Hilde Spiel, Richard Stöhr, Ernst Toch, Hans Kafka u. a., Wien 2008, S. 332.
2. Ernst Toch an Erich und Gertrud Zeisl, 5. 5. 1950, zit. n. ebd., S. 255.
3. Paul Stefan, *Neue Musik und Wien*, Leipzig/Wien/Zürich 1921, S. 28.
4. Richard Stöhr, Empfehlungsschreiben, 22. 5. 1938, Erich-Zeisl-Nachlass, Exilarte Zentrum, Wien.
5. *Arbeiter-Zeitung*, 7. 5. 1928.
6. Zeitungsausschnitt ohne Angaben, Erich-Zeisl-Nachlass, Exilarte Zentrum, Wien.
7. Hilde Spiel, *Die hellen und die finsteren Zeiten. Erinnerungen 1911–1946*, München 1965, S. 93.
8. Hilde Spiel, *Kati auf der Brücke*, Berlin/Wien/Leipzig 1933, S. 164.
9. Paul A. Pisk, „Erich Zeisel [sic]", in: *Radio Wien*, 26. 1. 1934, S. 2–3.
10. Erich Zeisl an Hilde Spiel, 3. 5. 1938, zit. n. Wagner 2008, wie Anm. 1, S. 28.
11. Schreiben der Stadtgemeinde Baden b. Wien, 29. 6. 1938, Erich-Zeisl-Nachlass, Exilarte Zentrum, Wien.
12. Morris Zeisel, Affidavit of Support, 20. 9. 1938, Erich-Zeisl-Nachlass, Exilarte Zentrum, Wien.
13. Zit. n. Malcolm S. Cole, Barbara Barclay, *Armseelchen. The Life and Music of Eric Zeisl*, Westport, Conn./London 1984, S. 40.
14. P. Stf. [Paul Stefan], Zeitungsausschnitt ohne Angaben, Erich-Zeisl-Nachlass, Exilarte Zentrum, Wien.
15. Erich Zeisl an Hilde Spiel, 12. 10. 1939, zit. n. Wagner 2008, wie Anm. 1, S. 65.
16. *The Morning Telegraph*, 28. 11. 1939, Erich-Zeisl-Nachlass, Exilarte Zentrum, Wien.
17. Hans Kafka an Erich und Gertrud Zeisl, undatiert, zit. n. Wagner 2008, wie Anm. 1, S. 122–124, hier S. 123.
18. Hans Kafka an Erich und Gertrud Zeisl, undatiert, zit. n. ebd., S. 126–127, hier S. 127.
19. Hans Kafka an Erich und Gertrud Zeisl, undatiert, zit. n. ebd., S. 122–124, hier S. 122.
20. Ebd.
21. Ebd.
22. Hans Kafka an Erich und Gertrud Zeisl, undatiert, zit. n. Wagner 2008, wie Anm. 1, S. 126.
23. Hanns Eisler an Erich Zeisl, undatiert, zit. n. ebd., S. 113.
24. Hanns Eisler an Herbert Kline, 2. 7. 1942, Erich-Zeisl-Nachlass, Exilarte Zentrum, Wien.
25. *The Tidings*, 13. 4. 1945, Erich-Zeisl-Nachlass, Exilarte Zentrum, Wien.
26. Vorwort zu Erich Zeisls *Requiem Ebraico*, Transcontinental Music Corporation 1946, TCL Nr. 266.
27. Alma Mahler-Werfel an Erich und Gertrud Zeisl, undatiert, Erich-Zeisl-Nachlass, Exilarte Zentrum, Wien.
28. Erich Wolfgang Korngold an Erich Zeisl, 27. 7. 1955, zit. n. Wagner 2008, wie Anm. 1, S. 339.
29. Erich Wolfgang Korngold an Erich Zeisl, 30. 12. 1955, zit. n. ebd., S. 340.
30. Hilde Spiel, „Erich Zeisl, fünfzig Jahre", in: *Neues Österreich*, 22. 5. 1955, S. 8.
31. Ebd.
32. Ebd.
33. Ebd.
34. Spiel 1965, wie Anm. 7, S. 226.
35. Erich Zeisl an Hilde Spiel, 17. 5. 1946, zit. n. Wagner 2008, wie Anm. 1, S. 205.
36. Ebd.

Karin Wagner

ERIC ZEISL (1905–1959)
Vienna's Lost Son in Foreign Lands

Café Tegetthoff

> I had the strongest "inner experience" of you when I was in Vienna more than a year ago after a fifteen-year absence, wandering alone at night around the area around Praterstern, Heinestrasse, and what used to be Café Zeisl ... It's hard to describe, least of all in a few lines.[1]

Thus wrote Vienna-born poet and psychoanalyst Alfred Farau (1904–1972) on July 11, 1955, to his friend Eric Zeisl in Los Angeles. Farau had just returned to New York from revisiting the city of his youth. Known in the 1930s as Fred Hernfeld, Farau had led Vienna's interdisciplinary "Young Art" cultural circle, which Zeisl had also belonged to. Arrested in November 1938 and deported to Dachau, Farau eventually escaped to the United States. Postwar studies at the city's university brought him back to Vienna, where he, a student of Alfred Adler, had once worked as a psychotherapist in private practice and taught at Vienna's Volkshochschule (Adult education college) and the Schubert Conservatory in the early 1930s. After the war, however, New York had become his home. From there, he reported back in 1955 on the reconstruction of Vienna, including the fate of Café Tegetthoff, the café where Eric Zeisl had spent his youth.

Another friend, Ernst Toch (1887–1964), also exiled in California, roamed the Praterstern area at Zeisl's request, searching for Café Tegetthoff. On May 5, 1950, Toch wrote to Los Angeles:

> The Circus Renz building next to the high school (of all places) is completely bombed out. Apart from that, I only found the Temple on Tempelgasse, of course, razed to the ground, but not by bombs, except for a few remnants of the outer walls. But there is no longer a Café Tegetthoff [sic]. Café Praterstern, Schreyvogel, Dogenhof, all still there—but no Tegetthoff! I asked around, yet no one had any information, and of course, it wasn't in the phone book. Everyone knew it it [sic] had <u>once</u> been around there somewhere. I would have loved to sit there, maybe on the lap of a chanteuse, and send you a picture postcard, vicariously enjoying the life of a youthful Zeisl![2]

Retrospective

Eric Zeisl, born in 1905, was a native of Vienna's Leopoldstadt district. His family ran Café Tegetthoff on the Praterstern plaza until it was "aryanized" in 1938. The Zeisls were a lower-middle-class, music-loving Jewish family. Eric had three brothers—Egon (b. 1901), Walter (b. 1902), and Wilhelm (b. 1907). Their father, Siegmund, sang in the Vienna Commercialists' Choral Society, while Egon and Wilhelm showed early promise as singers. But it was Eric, composing from a young age, who fought for the chance to study at Vienna's Academy of Music and Performing Arts, despite his parents' reluctance. He passed the entrance exam with distinction but did not complete courses in theory, composition, or piano. Hand problems cut short his piano studies, and he chose not to continue the harmony courses under Richard Stöhr (1874–1967) he started in the 1920/21 semesters. Instead, Stöhr, recognizing Zeisl's exceptional talent, tutored him privately.

According to Viennese music critic Paul Stefan (1879–1943), Stöhr's textbooks on theory, harmony, and counterpoint were "widely used and compulsory for certain exams."[3] A proponent of late-nineteenth-century Romanticism, Stöhr was part of Vienna's "Neo-Romantics," who distanced themselves from the avant-garde circle around Arnold Schoenberg (1874–1951). Zeisl, too, embraced the legacy of Romanticism. Stöhr, who had taught prominent musicians such as Erich Leinsdorf (1912–1993), Marcel Rubin (1905–1995), Paul Reif (1910–1978), and Josef Dichler (1912–1993), exuberantly described Zeisl in 1938 by saying that "without exaggeration, in the more than thirty-five years I have taught, he was my most talented student, in whom I have placed the highest hopes."[4] Written in the spirit of Romanticism, Zeisl's *Piano Trio Suite*, op. 8 (ca. 1920–1924), which premiered in Vienna's Konzerthaus on April 1928, was praised by the Socialist *Arbeiter-Zeitung* as the "spirited, talented work of a sixteen-year-old,"[5] a precociously youthful work that demonstrated his talent, echoing Schubert's and Mahler's chamber music and capturing the Viennese tradition. Another review characterized the work as the result of "sound and vigorous musical impulses" with a compositional technique at a "considerable level of development."[6]

Lieder

Eric Zeisl's collaboration with his teacher Richard Stöhr focused largely on lieder, or art songs. Zeisl knew to balance voice and piano in delicately nuanced interpretations of the lyrics, infusing the late Romantic style with touches of modernism. Art song even briefly brought him to traditionalist Joseph Marx (1882–1964) before a more innovative and modernist-minded teacher came into his life in the person of Hugo Kauder (1888–1972). Zeisl's *First String Quartet* (ca. 1930–1933), a key instrumental work from this period, was dedicated "in admiration and friendship" to the acclaimed Galimir Quartet. Its first violinist Felix Galimir (1910–1999) also was a connection to Vienna's "Young Art" circle, where Galimir and his ensemble performed Zeisl's quartet.

A milestone during this time was 1931, Zeisl's "year of lieder," when he focused exclusively on art song. His lieder are known for their melodic richness and emotional depth, flashes of glaring brightness, plunges into the blackest darkness, sighs and lamentation, raging and screaming. The world of Zeisl's songs is made up of atmospheric sketches, momentary moods, and sometimes grotesque miniatures, always grounded in tonality but laced with dissonant chords that emphasize the lyrics, with modulations and key changes adding dramatic color and intensity.

Under Kauder's influence, Zeisl refined his musical idiom, as becomes evident in his 1931 Nietzsche settings, *Das trunkene Lied* (*The Drunken Song*, 1931) and *Die Sonne sinkt* (*The Setting Sun*, 1931). Compared to his earlier sonority, these works present a pared-down piano accompaniment that highlights harmony, giving less prominence to motivic development. *Das trunkene Lied* includes clear references to Mahler, emphasizing the influence Kauder had in anchoring Zeisl in Mahler's tradition. The Nietzsche settings explore the theme of "light" as a journey from darkness to illumination—a concept reflected in Zeisl's musical shift from minor to major, echoing Nietzsche's idea of moving "through darkness to light."

Zeisl even modified Nietzsche's text, if minimally, repeating the opening "Oh Mensch" and the crucial "Weh spricht: Vergeh!"—moments where the normally syllabic vocal line lifts into Mahler-inspired triplet melismas that can be heard as a reverence to Mahler's compositional style in his *Second* and *Third Symphonies*. Kauder, who was a devoted admirer of Mahler and also set several Nietzsche texts to music, passed this affinity on to Zeisl, who continued in this vein with his own Nietzsche settings.

Zeisl set music to a variety of texts, including poems by Dehmel, Eichendorff, Goethe, Lenau, Morgenstern, Bierbaum, Ringelnatz and Busch. Among these, his work with the poetry of Alfons Petzold (1882–1923) stands out. The "working-class poet" Petzold may have come to Zeisl's attention through Austrian writer Hilde Spiel (1911–1990), a friend of Zeisl's future wife, Gertrud Susanne Jellinek (1906–1987), and a close companion of the composer until his death. A lifelong dedicated social democrat, Spiel was deeply affected by the events that led to Austria's civil war in 1934, and most likely introduced Zeisl to Petzold's work. In 1932, Zeisl composed four songs based on Petzold's poems: *Der tote Arbeiter, Ein buckliger Waisenknabe singt, Die Arbeiter,* and *Wanderlied*. In *Der tote Arbeiter*, fanfare motifs and triplets accentuate the harsh funeral march, where the worker's body rises as a "shining ray of sunlight." The orphan's lament similarly envisions the grave as place of liberation, a "home," offering a grim sense of peace. Zeisl reserved such themes of "proletarian poetry" for Petzold's works alone.

Eric Zeisl and Gertrud Jellinek on a visit to the country, early 1930s
Archiv des Exilarte Zentrum der mdw, Wien (A-Weaz)

Eric Zeisl and Gertrud Jellinek, early 1930s
Archiv des Exilarte Zentrum der mdw, Wien (A-Weaz)

Verein für Internationale Kulturarbeit

veranstaltet am 3. März 1932
8 Uhr abends im Spiegelsaale
des Primatialpalais einen

LITERARISCH - MUSIKALISCHEN ABEND

der „Jungen Kunst-Jugendvereinigung
der Radiowelt, Wien" mit folgendem
Programm:

1. Einleitende Worte: FRED HERNFELD.
2. JULIUS CHAJES: „Melodie für Cello" Konzertmeister THEO SALZMANN (Cello) am Flügel der Komponist
3. LISL HIRSCHFELD: „Meinem unbekannten Soldaten..." Es liest die Autorin
4. LIZZI POLTEN (Ravag): bringt die Autoren: GERTRUDE SCHAFRAN
   HILDE GOMBRICH
   ALFRED WERNER
5. ERICH ZEISL: Ernste Lieder. WILLY ZEISL (Gesang) am Flügel der Komponist
6. ALEXANDER WEISS: Aus dem Cyklus: „Marionetten des Lebens..." Es liest der Autor
7. JULIUS CHAJES: Trio d-Moll in drei Sätzen: Konzertmeister FERDINAND ADLER (Ravag) (Violine)
   Konzertmeister THEO SALZMANN (Ravag) (Cello)
   Der Komponist (Klavier)

PAUSE

8. MAX EUGEN KÜHNEL: „Krause Gedichte" Es liest der Autor
9. ANNY MARGULIES: bringt die Autoren: FANJA LEWKOWA
   HANS WITTMANN
   ERNST FANTL
   FRED HERNFELD
10. WALTER HANS BÖSE: bringt lyrische Dichtungen in Prosa von JULIUS SIEGFRIED SEIDENSTEIN
11. FRED HERNFELD: Prolog aus „Das optimistische Manifest"
12. ERICH ZEISL: Heitere Lieder. WILLY ZEISL (Gesang) am Flügel der Komponist
13. ALEXANDER WEISS: Aus dem Cyklus: „Ironie und ähnliches Ungeziefer..." Es liest der Autor
14. JULIUS CHAJES: Capriccio für Violine. Konzertmeister FERDINAND ADLER (Violine)
    am Flügel der Komponist

Kartenvorverkauf: Buchhandlung Steiner, Venturgasse 22, „Grenzbote",
Franziskanerplatz 4, Slovenské knihkupectvo, Rosengasse 12

Program of "The Young Art Youth Federation of Vienna's Radio World", 1932. Many members of this group went into exile with Zeisl remaining mostly in touch with Julius Chajes and Fred Hernfeld (Alfred Farau).
Archiv des Exilarte Zentrum der mdw, Wien (A-Weaz)

Hilde Spiel, c. 1930
Archiv des Exilarte Zentrum der mdw, Wien (A-Weaz)

Hilde Spiel

> In the new circle of friends in which I found myself, I participated in improvised theater performances, listened to the composer Eric Zeisl simulate entire symphonies by Bruckner and Mahler on the piano at intimate house concerts [...], or joined the choir for his Mass that was still being written. I was painted by the artist Lisel Salzer and saw the painting—which disappeared after the Anschluss—exhibited at the Hagenbund [...].[7]

Hilde Spiel reflected on her time with painter Lisel Salzer (1906–2005), composer Eric Zeisl, and lawyer Gertrud Susanne Jellinek. Lisel and Gertrud had known each other since childhood. In the early 1930s, this quartet of Viennese artistic talents came together, meeting to exchange ideas and spending summers at Wolfgangsee, where Lisel worked within the Zinkenbach Painters' Colony. In her debut novel, *Kati auf der Brücke* (Kati on the bridge), published in 1933 and awarded the Julius Reich Prize by the City of Vienna, Spiel unmistakably portrayed the music-obsessed Zeisl: "Then he played again [...] little lyrical songs, Morgenstern and Ringelnatz set to music, finally his first string quartet, so vibrantly alive that one thought one could hear the violin and the viola."[8] In this circle, painting, music, and literature nourished and influenced one another, until it was torn apart by Spiel's flight to London in 1936. Yet, a revealing collection of exile documents was preserved through the correspondence between the Zeisls and Hilde Spiel, tracing Eric Zeisl's life. Lisel Salzer fled to the United States in 1939 and lived in Seattle, Washington, until 2005, as the last representative of the Zinkenbach Painters' Colony.

Wedding photograph of Eric and Gertrud Zeisl. The ceremony took place on December 29, 1935.
Archiv des Exilarte Zentrum der mdw, Wien (A-Weaz)

Zeisl and friends swimming: Eric's brother Egon Zeisl, Hilde Spiel, Gertrud Zeisl, a married couple who were friends with the Zeisls and Eric Zeisl, c. 1935
Archiv des Exilarte Zentrum der mdw, Wien (A-Weaz)

"One of the Strongest Personalities"

By 1934, not yet thirty years old, Eric Zeisl had established himself in Vienna's musical scene, with performances at both the Vienna Konzerthaus and the Musikverein. In contrast to his early work in the 1920s, Zeisl had secured a place within Vienna's trend towards moderate modernism. Figures like Karl Weigl (1881–1949), Egon Kornauth (1891–1959), Kurt Pahlen (1907–2003), Franz Mittler (1893–1970), Ernst Kanitz (1894–1978), Friedrich Bloch (1899–1945), Rudolf Réti (1885–1957), Victor Urbancic (1903–1958), or Othmar Wetchy (1892–1951), among others, shaped this circle he moved in. Music critic Paul Amadeus Pisk (1893–1990) wrote an enthusiastic review in 1934:

> Erich Zeisel [sic] is one of the strongest personalities among Viennese composers not yet thirty years old. Besides this quartet, the composer—only twenty-eight years old—has written a violin sonata, a piano trio, and several choral works, including jazz choruses [...] and folk song arrangements. In his drawer lies an entire mass for choir, organ, and strings, a ballet titled "Pierrot in der Flasche," and recently a "Requiem" that is nearing completion. Some of these works have already been performed, as every musician who hears them is captivated by Zeisel's [sic] unique temperament. [...] Zeisel's [sic] music is always readily understandable, yet never banal. This still very young composer deserves to be prominently highlighted and his work introduced more widely to the public.[9]

Zeisl's work at this time spanned art songs, chamber music, choral pieces, and larger works. His early opera *Die Sünde* (1927/28), his jazz-inflected ballet *Pierrot in der Flasche* (1929), the *Kleine Messe* (1932), and the in-progress *Requiem Concertante* (1933/34) showcase his versatility. With *Pierrot in der Flasche*, inspired by Gustav Meyrink's story *The Man on the Bottle*, Zeisl explored the grotesque, building on themes he had first tackled in his song cycle *Mondbilder* (after Christian Morgenstern). Later choral works like *Afrika singt* (1930/31) and *Spruchkantate* (1935) draw from diverse sources, experimenting with choral textures and harmonies. *Afrika singt* (Africa sings), which was based on a 1929 anthology of African-American poetry of that title, is the first work in this genre to pick up from the jazz-inspired *Pierrot*, while *Spruchkantate* (1935), based on saws from Silesius, Solomon, and Goethe, explores new effects in choral music. In symphonic pieces such as *Passacaglia* (1933/34) and *Kleine Symphonie* (1935/36), the latter inspired by the paintings of Roswitha Bitterlich (1920–2015), Zeisl embraced the Romantic orchestral palette, taking a more traditional approach and winning the support of conductors like Karl Oskar Alwin (1891–1945), Kurt Herbert Adler (1905–1988), and Rudolf Nilius (1883–1962).

Zeisl's collaboration with Hugo F. Königsgarten (later Koenigsgarten, 1904–1975), a native of Brno in Moravia, added a new dimension to his work. Königsgarten fled Nazi Germany in 1933, first to Austria and then in 1938 to England. In Vienna, he worked as a writer for the literary cabaret "Der liebe Augustin." He was connected with Zeisl in that he wrote the libretto for *Leonce und Lena* as a singspiel (musical comedy) with spoken dialogue and music, based on Georg Büchner's (1813–1837) romantic play. The comedic piece breathes graceful light-heartedness, a sense of carefree merriness that was in stark contrast to the sinister circumstances of its time of creation and seemed possible only in Büchner's fictional kingdoms of "Popo" and "Pipi." Zeisl's music echoes this insouciance with fairy-tale colors. A premiere at Schönbrunn Palace Theater was scheduled in April/May 1938 under Kurt Herbert Adler, but the Nazi annexation of Austria ("Anschluss") in March 1938 shattered these plans.

The "Phone Book Zeisl"

By spring 1938, Eric Zeisl had fallen into a stupor of deep depression. *Leonce und Lena* marked his last major work in Austria, while the pieces that followed—such as *November* (a piano and orchestral work, written between November 1937 and May 1938), the lied *Komm süsser Tod* (January 1938), and the two a cappella choruses *In tiefem Schlummer* and *Am Abend* (both February 1938)—were resonant with dark, resigned tones. Up to this point, Zeisl had composed around one hundred art songs, and with *Komm süsser Tod*, he bid his farewell to the genre, using a language long rooted in the Austro-German song tradition that speaks of a haunting acceptance of death and a yearning for peace given expression in the major-minor polarity of the music. Like Franz Schubert and Hugo Wolf, Zeisl used only half and quarter notes, crafting a deliberately uniform progression. A typical "Schubertian" device is the reaffirmation of the vocal line by a subsequent imitative piano part. Zeisl knew precisely the cultural world he was leaving behind and also knew the symbolic codes to express this loss.

In May 1938, Zeisl wrote to his friend Hilde in London: "I'm not writing anything at the moment. I'm not in the mood. Sometimes I feel there's still something great in me. But nothing comes out.—Perhaps I won't be able to compose anymore. It would be terrible, and my life would be forfeited."[10] After the Nazi annexation, and during the Easter holidays, the Zeisls relocated to the small town of Baden near Vienna, hoping for safety throughout the summer months. However, a letter from the Nazi-controlled municipality of June 29, 1938, ordering them to "leave the area of the Town and Spa Resort of Baden near Vienna within 48 hours upon receipt of this notification,"[11] shattered any thought of safety.

Desperate, Gertrud searched the New York phone directory, hoping to find someone with a similar last name who might help them secure an affidavit. Against the odds, they found one "phone book Zeisl" named Morris Zeisel in Brooklyn, New York. Though a stranger, he provided the crucial affidavit that enabled the Zeisls to leave Austria for France. Issued by an American notary and dated September 20, 1938, this "Affidavit of Support"[12] listed Morris Zeisel's details: a forty-four-year-old "master plumber," originally from Austria and father of two, living at 1555 West 11th Street, Brooklyn. He had declared himself a "cousin" to Eric and Gertrud. Morris's business address, Manbrook Plumbing and Heating Co. on 541 10th Avenue, completed the paperwork. This unexpected connection—a namesake in a New York phone book—ultimately saved their lives.

Hiob

On November 10, 1938, Eric Zeisl, his wife Gertrud, his brother Wilhelm, and Gertrud's mother left Vienna, ultimately arriving in Paris. Despite the harsh conditions facing refugees in France—marked by economic hardship, high unemployment, and bureaucratic challenges—Paris offered a gratefully appreciated sense of newfound freedom after their escape from Nazi Austria. Still, the Zeisls had to keep running nerve-racking bureaucratic errands to secure their residence permit.

Meeting composer Darius Milhaud (1882–1974) in March 1939 proved pivotal. Milhaud secured a letter from the French Interior Minister, Albert Sarraut, allowing the Zeisls to stay longer in France. And Milhaud opened the doors to Paris's cultural scene. When Austrian author Joseph Roth (1894–1939) died in Paris on May 27, a stage adaptation of his novel Hiob based on the biblical figure of Job (in German Hiob) was performed at the Théâtre Pigalle on July 3, featuring an exiled German-speaking cast from Max Reinhardt's ensemble, including Hugo Haas, Josef Meinrad and Leon Askin. Zeisl was commissioned to compose the music, producing pieces like Organ Prelude, Menuhim's Song for violin and piano, and Cossack Dance for piano. Despite adverse conditions and major organizational challenges, the performance of Job was a success, resonating deeply in light of the political climate.

While Arnold Schoenberg's time in Paris prompted a reconsideration of Judaism at large and an eventual reconnection with his Jewish identity, Zeisl's exile brought him to artistically explore his Jewish roots for the first time, which strongly reverberated in his work. The Job project reconnected him with a heritage he had never previously expressed in music, and it became his first work to reflect his Jewish origins. Roth's novel, a powerful epitome of Jewish suffering and persecution, had been published in 1930, anticipating the atrocities that were soon to unfold in the wake of the Nazi attempt to annihilate once and for all anything Jewish.

Zeisl now switched to a quasi-Jewish musical language, introducing in pieces like Menuhim's Song themes that would influence later works, marked most conspicuously by his frequent use of the augmented second interval that echoed traditional Jewish intonation. The piece's prayer-like quality, emphasized by frequent sigh-like suspensions, came through recitative sequences and improvisationally developed motifs, evoking a meditative, almost liturgical atmosphere.

When musicologist Anneliese Landau (1903–1991) asked Zeisl in 1951 when "Jewishness" began to appear in his work, he replied crediting Job: "I believe it was in Paris when I was commissioned to set music to Joseph Roth's book on 'Job.' The story of the persecuted Jew who escaped from Poland to America suggested in itself an outspoken Jewish music."[13]

Music critic Paul Stefan wrote about the Paris performance of Job: "The highly talented Viennese composer also convinced his theater audience. One received a strong impression, particularly from the introductory organ music, which presents a prologue in heaven, earnest, powerful, far-reaching."[14]

Paris also reunited Zeisl with Paul Stefan, a Schoenberg pupil and fellow Austrian émigré, as well as the Stöhr pupil Marcel Rubin (1905–1995). Also in Paris, the Zeisls became friends with Franz Werfel (1890–1945) and Alma Mahler-Werfel (1879–1964), with whom they would later reconnect in California. Upon their arrival in Paris, the Zeisl family, like many other émigrés, set up residence at the Hôtel Perey, Cité du Retiro, Paris 8. In June 1939, they were able to rent a house just outside Paris at the telltale address "39, route de l'Asile" in Le Vésinet, which they shared with Austrian writer Hans Kafka (1902–1974), who would later write the libretto for Zeisl's opera adaptation of *Job*.

Following a job as a book, film, and theater critic in Berlin, a stay in Chicago, renewed activity as a writer in Vienna from 1934, and some work in film 1936 in London, Kafka came to Paris in 1937. After the outbreak of the war, he was interned in France for five months, until his wife, actress Trude Burr, managed to obtain visas to the United States. When Kafka was released, they both left Europe in 1940. The Zeisls reached the United States in September 1939, due to a second affidavit from one Arnold Zeissl of Milwaukee, which had enabled them to leave Paris; this time, he was, in fact, a distant relative.

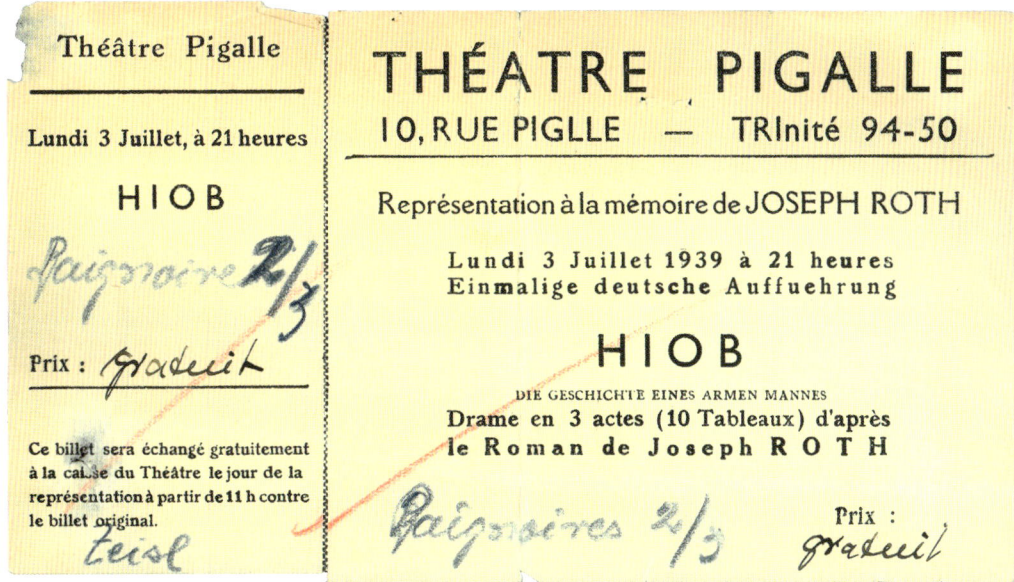

The theater production that changed Zeisl's music. Ticket for the play based on Joseph Roth's novel *Job*, July 3, 1939 at the Théâtre Pigalle, Paris
Archiv des Exilarte Zentrum der mdw, Wien (A-Weaz)

Hollywood Misery

Arriving on the "Volendam," Eric Zeisl and his family landed in New York, sending their first message to Hilde Spiel in London that October 1939: "We've arrived after endless hardships and feel very happy. You have no idea of the huge size of New York. It feels almost like a city on Mars—like another planet. The way everything rises up into the sky! Unbelievable! Can't you come here? I think it's the right place for all of us!"[15]

Zeisl's initial exposure to American culture was surprisingly promising. On November 28, 1939, *The Morning Telegraph* headlined, "Zeisl's Music in U.S. Debut." The article then read: "The American premiere of a modern symphony by Erich Zeisl, brilliant young Austrian composer, will be given on the 'Radio City Music Hall on the Air' next Sunday [...]."[16] His *Little Symphony* (1935/36) seemed to resonate with American audiences. In 1939, Budapest born conductor Ernö Rapée (1891–1945) was one of the conductors working at New York's Radio City Music Hall, then the world's largest movie theater. He was quick to include Zeisl's orchestral movements based on paintings by Roswitha Bitterlich in the program of his nationwide radio hour, in which he performed a classical music repertoire with the Music Hall Symphony Orchestra. The stations WJZ and NBC Blue Network thus broadcast the first U.S. performance of Zeisl's music on December 3, 1939.

Making a modest start in New York, the Zeisls left their life in a hotel for a small unfurnished one-room apartment on the Upper West Side on 315 West 91st Street. While finances were tight, their future felt hopeful. Their daughter Barbara was born in May 1940. The move to a rented house on Long Island suited the young family better. Americanizing his first name to Eric, Zeisl began to make contacts in New York's musical circles, with his works aired on the radio under conductors like Howard Barlow (1892–1972) and Wilfried Pelletier (1896–1982).

Yet, Zeisl soon looked westward, aiming for a life in Hollywood. This vision was put into practice by Hans Kafka, who by May 1940 had managed to establish himself in Hollywood working for MGM. With his inside knowledge of the film business, he was determined to bring his friend into MGM's fold, which he explained was a "terrific chance" for Zeisl.[17] Kafka worked tirelessly as a "personal Zeisl representative,"[18] using his skills and persistence to pave Zeisl's way into the business. Kafka's correspondence from Hollywood in July/August 1941 to the Zeisls, who were still waiting in New York, speaks volumes. To tailor the résumé of the future film composer for Hollywood, Kafka lowered Zeisl's age, noting there was "a tendency against people who were too 'old,'"[19] downplayed his New York contract with Associated Music Publishers, and described him as having been "two years in the country" and holding "first papers."[20] Kafka insisted that Zeisl would have to learn English "like hell,"[21] instructed him on how to make himself familiar with "all conceivable technical terms," and made remarks about "500 dollar musicians" being "fired," while "75 dollar musicians" were coming in.[22]

Hanns Eisler (1898–1962) also tried to use his contacts in the film industry to "transplant Zeisl plus family to Hollywood."[23] And even later, he supported Zeisl, who had become a friend, with a letter of recommendation to Herbert Kline (1909–1999), the director of the semidocumentary film

The Forgotten Village, for which Eisler composed the music. "He is a very gifted fellow," Eisler wrote to Kline in July 1942, "and I think he would be splendid for your new picture. Listen to his music!"[24]

Yet, when the Zeisls, Eric, his wife Gertrud, and their daughter Barbara, finally reached Los Angeles, they started a precarious new life. The longed-for MGM contract had worse terms than originally agreed upon and was signed only after Zeisl threatened to leave Hollywood again right away. His MGM engagement began with underpaid projects for the popular *Fitzpatrick Traveltalks*, scenic shorts that demanded illustrative incidental music. Although he subsequently worked on many feature films, he never received a "credit" in the opening or end titles, as was standard practice in Hollywood, where multiple composers might contribute to a score but only "big names" earned a mention. Zeisl worked alongside colleagues such as Franz Waxman, Walter Jurmann, Bronisław Kaper, Mario Castelnuovo-Tedesco, Herbert Stothart, Daniele Amfitheatrof or Nathaniel Shilkret.

Zeisl's initial euphoria for Hollywood soon gave way to disillusionment and frustration; after only eighteen months, MGM terminated his contract. From then on, Zeisl worked freelance, arranging and orchestrating for fellow composers and also collaborating with Universal International. Although his work in film brought significant friends like Alexandre Tansman (1897–1986) and Mario Castelnuovo-Tedesco (1895–1968), Zeisl suffered greatly from being reduced in Hollywood to merely "manufacturing" music, which was way below his own artistic standards. The expectations he had placed in the "dream factory" remained completely unfulfilled, and Zeisl drifted into a veritable creative crisis. He was only able to overcome the Hollywood misery by composing the *Requiem Ebraico* (1944/45).

A Requiem for the Jewish People

"It is so refreshing to find a composer in Hollywood who can still divorce himself from the false glitter of film music and devote his spare time to writing music to a religious text."[25] This was one reaction to the premiere of the organ version of *Requiem Ebraico* at the "Hollywood Inter-Faith Forum" concert on April 8, 1945, in Los Angeles. *Requiem Ebraico* is not a Latin requiem mass of the Catholic liturgy, and Psalm 92, on which the work is based, contains no textual reference to a funeral hymn. With the news of the murder of his father Siegmund and stepmother Malvine, who were deported from Theresienstadt to the Treblinka extermination camp in 1942, the significance of the composition commission Zeisl had received from Reform Rabbi Jacob Sonderling (1878–1964) for use in the synagogue changed. Knowledge of the atrocities of the Holocaust was now reaching overseas, and Zeisl dedicated the psalm as a requiem for the Jewish people to his murdered "father and the countless victims of the Jewish tragedy in Europe."[26] *Requiem Ebraico* is today regarded as one of the earliest musical references to the Holocaust.

Stylistically, Zeisl continued on the path he had begun in Paris with the composition for *Job*; intoning a "quasi-Jewish" idiom, he established his "synagogal style." This language shaped other compositions to varying degrees, such as the *Songs for the Daughter of Jephtha* (1948), the choral work

In Los Angeles exile, 1940s
Archiv des Exilarte Zentrum der mdw, Wien (A-Weaz)

Front and back of Zeisl's ID card, no. 11702, 1942
Archiv des Exilarte Zentrum der mdw, Wien (A-Weaz)

Barbara, Gertrud and Eric Zeisl, c. 1956
Archiv des Exilarte Zentrum der mdw, Wien (A-Weaz)

From the Book of Psalms (1952), the biblically themed ballets *Naboth's Vineyard* (1953) and *Jacob and Rachel* (1954) as well as instrumental works without programmatic references to Judaism, such as the *Sonata Barocca* (1948/49) for piano, the *Brandeis Sonata* (1949/50) for violin and piano, the *Viola Sonata* (1950), and the *Second String Quartet* (1953). The latter chamber music works reveal the "new" stylistic approach in varying degrees of intensity—most clearly evident in the pieces with a biblical context.

The engagement with Jewish art music opened up new spheres of reference and activity in exile. From 1948 to 1950, Zeisl taught as composer in residence during the summer months with colleagues Max Helfman (1901–1963) and Julius Chajes (1910–1985, formerly one of his companions in Vienna's "Young Art" circle), at the Brandeis Camp Institute in Santa Susana in the Simi Valley, northwest of Los Angeles. Here, a course and leisure program introduced young Jewish people to both traditional and contemporary Jewish art and folk music. At the camp in summer 1950, Zeisl completed his *Brandeis Sonata* for violin and piano. Israel Baker (1919–2011) and Yaltah Menuhin (1921–2001) performed the piece in Santa Monica in September 1950, following a "preview" performance at Brandeis Camp. Zeisl's close ties to the organizations and musical communities that promoted Jewish art music were meaningful and stylistically defining for him.

Julius Chajes, who lived in Palestine after fleeing Austria and before arriving in the United States, was significantly more deeply and diversely connected to Jewish art music than Zeisl. As head of the piano department at the music academy in Tel Aviv, he was in close contact with practical musical life in Palestine and developed a great interest in the sources of ancient Jewish music as well as in the folklore of the region. Chajes drew inspiration from the so-called Eastern Mediterranean School, Arabic folklore, and other musical styles that were pervasive in the country, which lent many of his future compositions their distinct character. The cantata *The Promised Land*, the opera *Out of the Desert*, the *Hebrew Suite* (originally intended for chamber ensemble and later rearranged into an orchestral work), and the psalm setting *Old Jerusalem* all reflect Chajes' adaptation of traditional Hebrew music and an optimistic, joyful take on folklore that was in line with the spirit of the contemporary Zionist movement. Chajes' later role in the United States as director of the Jewish Community Center in Detroit, where he founded an orchestra, and his work as music director at Temple Beth-El testified to his profound connection with his Jewish identity.

Jewish musical biographies and expressions in the face of the racial fanaticism of the Nazis varied widely; even while defining a new compositional language in exile, Zeisl always remained faithful to the compositional techniques and procedures he knew from his old home country. This set him apart from Julius Chajes. Particularly interesting in this context is the "synthesis" achieved by Richard Fuchs (1887–1947; born in Karlsruhe, died in exile in New Zealand) in combining the tonality of German High and Late Romanticism with a militant Zionist text by Karl Wolfskehl (1869–1948) in his oratorio *Vom jüdischen Schicksal* (1936). The work won the prize of the "Reich Federation of Jewish Cultural Leagues" but was no longer performed due to a ban by the "Reich Chamber of Culture". In this piece, Fuchs adhered strictly to the language of German Romanticism, approaching Wolfskehl's text without any "Jewish" modulations.

Kisses from Korngold

The Brandeis Camp was considered a special communication hub by exiles, but generally speaking, places for inspirational exchange in Los Angeles were few and far between. Spots like the Farmers Market, an important place for discussion among the displaced, were an exception. To make up for this shortage, private homes in Hollywood, Brentwood, Beverly Hills, or the coastal suburbs of Pacific Palisades and Santa Monica became much-frequented gathering and meeting places. This included the Zeisl home at 8578 West Knoll Drive, Hollywood 46, where Alma Mahler, for example, once wrote: "Dear dear friends A thousand thousand thanks for the delightful gift. I am coming soon and then we can see each other thoroughly! All my love Alma Maria!"[27]

The Zeisls made their home a small Austrian isle, with Eric and Gertrud hosting afternoon and evening parties for émigré friends like Erich Wolfgang and Luzi Korngold. The Zeisls also were friends with Alma Mahler-Werfel, Alexandre Tansman, Darius Milhaud, Ernst Toch and Lion Feuchtwanger. Eric Zeisl again was on good terms with Hanns Eisler and Igor Stravinsky. The atmosphere—authenticated by Viennese pastries—of their house on West Knoll Drive was that of a social mix, which nevertheless remained something of an illusion. Playful holiday messages kept the community connected: Toch affectionately addressed the Zeisls using the uniquely Viennese diminutive of "Zeiserln" or "Gezeisl," and coined the playful plural form of "Korngölder." Zeisl spoke of the "dear Korngolds," and Korngold of the "dear, good Zeisls." Every now and then, Korngold, always whimsical, sent spontaneous notes, like a postcard from Burbank, where Warner Brothers had studio branches close to his Toluca Lake home. He also dropped quick lines that he left at the Zeisls' vacation spot at Desert Hot Springs, while driving past and tossing them "kisses."

Lake Arrowhead in the San Bernardino Mountains, which reminded them of Europe, became a favorite retreat for the nature-loving Zeisls in the 1950s. On July 27, 1955, Korngold sent greetings from Burbank to Lake Arrowhead, playfully inquiring if Zeisl had moved his piano and signing off on behalf of "the whole Korngold family."

> Dear, good Zeisls—
> Just a line of thank you for the most enjoyable hours this last Sunday, as well as for the magnificent and opulent room, and all good wishes for the rest of the summer, along with a positive mood for composing!
> Have you moved the piano? Most likely not!!—
> We will surely come up to see you again. Until then:
> Take care and be warmly greeted and hugged!
> The whole Korngold family.[28]

And the cheeky note from Desert Hot Springs dated December 30, 1955:

> Dear old Zeisl!
>
> We're coming via San Diego a. Palm Springs especially to visit you for a few kisses!
>
> After pleasantly taking a "siesta" for over half an hour—no one could give us a definite address—I finally found it at "Fiesta" (5th Street), only to arrive just 2 minutes after you left!!! Now that's what I call bad luck! See you soon in L.A. Happy New Year!
> Warmly: Your EWK.[29]

"Those Viennese 'Slimy Snakes.' Yuck, Nauseating!"

With the playful "Happy New Year," Erich Wolfgang Korngold bid farewell to the year 1955—the year in which Zeisl celebrated his fiftieth birthday together with the Los Angeles exile community. In honor of her friend, Hilde Spiel wrote an article for *Neues Österreich*: "Today, the Viennese musician Erich Zeisl celebrates his fiftieth birthday, far from his home country [...]."[30] These were the opening lines. A "Committee of Friends of Eric Zeisl," including people like Igor Stravinsky, Darius Milhaud, Arnold Schoenberg's widow Gertrud, Erich Wolfgang Korngold, and Alma Mahler-Werfel, organized a concert evening in Los Angeles in tribute to "Vienna's lost son in foreign lands."[31] In a brief overview, Spiel recapitulates Zeisl's Viennese years, pointedly noting: "Transplanting this quintessential Viennese, this consummate musician, into Californian soil may have been an impossibility. Still, what had to be done finally was done."[32] In the final paragraph, she brings those two very different worlds together in a single image: "When we visited him in his white log house on West Knoll Drive, he proudly took us to the garden to show us his tropical shrubs and plants. In the Biedermeier-style living room with striped wallpaper stood a Viennese grand piano. Outside, the avocado tree was in bloom. Thus, an Austrian, who would remain so until his last breath, found his new livelihood in a balance of two civilizations."[33]

After the end of the war, Vienna began to move into sharper focus for the Zeisls, especially when Hilde Spiel traveled back to Austria for the first time in 1946 as a correspondent in British uniform to report for the *New Statesman* on the social and political conditions in her former home country. She intensely felt the sense of disruption at the "precisely determinable topographic origin" of her "unity with Vienna"[34]—the Pfarrplatz in Heiligenstadt. She sent her impressions to the Zeisls, who were living in California in a constant state of "homesickness." Agitated and torn between an intense longing for Vienna and grief, anger, and shock over the crimes committed there, Eric replied in May 1946: "I wouldn't go to Vienna for a long time to come. Both parents murdered! Those Viennese 'slimy snakes.' Yuck, nauseating!"[35] And: "I can't even imagine how one could endure that. I think I would drop dead from emotional shock."[36]

Photo of Hilde Spiel taken during a lecture
Archiv des Exilarte Zentrum der mdw, Wien (A-Weaz)

In February 1959, following a lecture at Los Angeles City College—where Zeisl had been teaching since 1949 and where, in 1952, the belated world premiere of *Leonce und Lena* was staged in the opera workshop under the direction of Hugo Strelitzer (1896–1981)—Eric Zeisl died from a heart attack at the age of only fifty-three. He had "dropped dead" completely unexpectedly. It was a shock for all his friends and companions—and a shock that struck Gertrud and Barbara Zeisl especially deeply and painfully. Eric Zeisl died without seeing his hometown of Vienna again.

Autograph of Zeisl's last German lied, composed in January 1938: *Komm süsser Tod*
Archiv des Exilarte Zentrum der mdw, Wien (A-Weaz)

1 Alfred Farau to Eric Zeisl, July 11, 1955, quoted in Karin Wagner (ed.), ... es grüsst Dich Erichisrael: Briefe von und an Eric Zeisl, Hilde Spiel, Richard Stöhr, Ernst Toch, Hans Kafka u. a. (Vienna, 2008), p. 332.

2 Ernst Toch to Eric and Gertrud Zeisl, May 5, 1950, quoted in ibid., p. 255.

3 Paul Stefan, *Neue Musik und Wien* (Leipzig, 1921), p. 28.

4 Stöhr's recommendation of Eric Zeisl, May 22, 1938, Eric Zeisl Estate, Exilarte Center, Vienna.

5 *Arbeiter-Zeitung*, May 7, 1929.

6 Newspaper clipping without any details, Eric Zeisl Estate, Exilarte Center, Vienna.

7 Hilde Spiel, *Die hellen und die finsteren Zeiten: Erinnerungen 1911–1946* (Munich, 1965), p. 93.

8 Hilde Spiel, *Kati auf der Brücke* (Berlin, 1933), p. 164.

9 Paul Amadeus Pisk, „Erich Zeisel [sic]", *Radio Wien*, Jan. 31, 1934.

10 Eric Zeisl to Hilde Spiel, May 3, 1938, quoted in Wagner, *... es grüsst Dich Erichisrael*, p. 28.

11 Correspondence from Baden Municipality, June 29, 1938, Eric Zeisl Estate, Exilarte Center, Vienna.

12 Morris Zeisel, Affidavit of Support, Sept. 20, 1938, Eric Zeisl Estate, Exilarte Center, Vienna.

13 Quoted in Malcolm Cole and Barbara Barclay, *Armseelchen: The Life and Music of Eric Zeisl* (Westport, CT, 1984), p. 40.

14 P. Stf. [Paul Stefan], Newspaper clipping without any details, Eric Zeisl Estate, Exilarte Center, Vienna.

15 Eric Zeisl to Hilde Spiel, Oct. 12, 1939, quoted in Wagner, *... es grüsst Dich Erichisrael*, p. 65.

16 *The Morning Telegraph*, Nov. 28, 1939, Eric Zeisl Estate, Exilarte Center, Vienna.

17 Hans Kafka to Eric and Gertrud Zeisl, undated, quoted in Wagner, *... es grüsst Dich Erichisrael*, pp. 122–124 at 122.

18 Hans Kafka to Eric and Gertrud Zeisl, undated, quoted in ibid., pp. 126–127 at 127.

19 Hans Kafka to Eric and Gertrud Zeisl, undated, quoted in ibid., pp. 122–124 at 122.

20 Ibid.

21 Ibid.

22 Hans Kafka to Eric and Gertrud Zeisl, undated, quoted in Wagner, *... es grüsst Dich Erichisrael*, p. 126.

23 Hanns Eisler to Eric Zeisl, undated, quoted in ibid., p. 113.

24 Hanns Eisler to Herbert Kline, July 2, 1942, Eric Zeisl Estate, Exilarte Center, Vienna.

25 *The Tidings*, Apr. 13, 1945, Eric Zeisl Estate, Exilarte Center, Vienna.

26 Dedication in Eric Zeisl's *Requiem Ebraico*, Transcontinental Music Corporation 1946, TCL no. 266.

27 Alma Mahler-Werfel to Eric and Gertrud Zeisl, undated, Eric Zeisl Estate, Exilarte Center, Vienna.

28 Erich Wolfgang Korngold to Eric Zeisl, July 27, 1955, quoted in Wagner, *...es grüsst Dich Erichisrael*, p. 339.

29 Erich Wolfgang Korngold to Eric Zeisl, Dec. 30, 1955, quoted in ibid., p. 340.

30 Hilde Spiel, "Erich Zeisl, fünfzig Jahre," *Neues Österreich*, May 22, 1955, p. 8.

31 Ibid.

32 Ibid.

33 Ibid.

34 Spiel, *Die hellen und die finsteren Zeiten*, p. 226.

35 Eric Zeisl to Hilde Spiel, May 17, 1946, quoted in Wagner, *... es grüsst Dich Erichisrael*, p. 205.

36 Ibid.

Hochzeitsfoto von Erich Zeisls Eltern
Siegmund Zeisl und Kamilla Feitler
Archiv des Exilarte Zentrum der mdw,
Wien (A-Weaz)

Tina Walzer

DAS CAFÉ TEGETTHOFF DER FAMILIE ZEISL IN DER HEINESTRASSE 42
Gewaltsamer Umbruch im jüdischen Nordbahnviertel 1938

Das Café Tegetthoff war ein alteingesessener Familienbetrieb in der Heinestraße 42, an der Ecke zum Praterstern. Siegmund Zeisl hatte das gut eingeführte Lokal am 11. März 1897 von seinem Vater Emanuel Zeisl übernommen und führte es ein Vierteljahrhundert, bis 1921. In den folgenden Jahren verpachtete er es bis 1937. Einer seiner Pächter wohnte auch im Haus, so wie die Zeisls selbst. Das Café beschäftigte zum Zeitpunkt von Zeisls Enteignung im März 1938 drei nichtjüdische Angestellte. In 23 Logen waren Marmortischchen aufgestellt, zur Unterhaltung der Gäste gab es einen Billardtisch und ein großes Schachspiel. Lichtreklame und Kühlgerät wurden von der Brauerei Nussdorf zur Verfügung gestellt. Vier große Fenster gaben den Blick auf den Praterstern und die Heinestraße frei. Kurz nach einer umfassenden Renovierung im Frühjahr 1938 wurde der Betrieb durch das NS-Regime enteignet und aufgelöst. Das Schicksal der Familie Zeisl spiegelt die Entwicklung eines ganzen Stadtgebiets.

Heinestraße 42

Nach der nationalsozialistischen Machtübernahme im März 1938 wurde das Kaffeehaus „arisiert"[1], das heißt, Zeisl wurde seine Konzession entzogen, sein Betrieb behördlich geschlossen und das Inventar eingezogen. Zu dem Zeitpunkt waren seine Söhne 37 (Egon), 36 (Walter), 34 (Erich) und 31 (Wilhelm) Jahre alt, wie Siegmund Zeisl im „Ansuchen um Genehmigung der Veräußerung" angeben musste. Allen vier Söhnen gelang die Flucht ins rettende Ausland.
Ende Mai, Anfang Juni 1938 sollte das Café Tegetthoff an den damals 47 Jahre alten langjährigen Zahlkellner des Cafés Edison im neunten Bezirk, Alser Straße 9, gehen. Zum Zeitpunkt des Antrags auf Genehmigung der „Arisierung" war dieser arbeitslos; zwecks Übernahme trat daher ein ebenfalls „arischer" (regimegenehmer) Investor aus der Lampigasse 17 im zweiten Bezirk auf. Der „Käufer" sollte laut „Kaufvertrag" vom 1. Juni 1938 in den Mietvertrag eintreten und das gesamte Inventar übernehmen, zugleich sollte Siegmund Zeisl seine Kaffeehauskonzession zugunsten des neuen Geschäftsinhabers zurücklegen. Der in den Akten einliegende Kaufvertrag, der Zeisl abgepresst worden war, musste jedoch noch amtlich

Flugpost-Brief des Vaters Siegmund Zeisl
von Wien an Erich und Gertrud Zeisl
nach Mamaroneck bei New York
Archiv des Exilarte Zentrum der mdw, Wien
(A-Weaz)

Der Brief des Vaters zur Zensur „Geöffnet"
und versehen mit dem Stempel „Oberkommando der Wehrmacht"
Archiv des Exilarte Zentrum der mdw, Wien
(A-Weaz)

genehmigt werden, von der Enteignungsbehörde – im spezifischen Jargon der Diktatur, das Unrecht gezielt verschleiernd, euphemistisch „Vermögensverkehrsstelle" genannt.

Daraus scheint laut „Arisierungs-Akt" (Behördenschrifttum) nichts geworden zu sein: Die Enteignungsbehörde setzte stattdessen am 24. Juni einen „kommissarischen Verwalter" für die Dauer der „Liquidierung" des Geschäftsbestands ein. Während Zeisl sein Café Tegetthoff noch am 12. Juli zum Verkauf an den Edison-Kellner melden musste (Formular der „Arisierungsstelle der Gast- und Schankgewerbeinnung, Wien 1, Regierungsgasse 1"), hatte der Liquidator seine Tätigkeit längst aufgenommen. Es handelte sich bei dem Mann ebenfalls um einen ehemaligen Kellner, doch hatte er einen entscheidenden Vorteil gegenüber seinen Konkurrenten: Er war nachweislich seit 1926 Mitglied der NSDAP – ein sogenannter Illegaler.[2] Im Zuge des Enteignungsverfahrens hatte einer der früheren Pächter zu intrigieren versucht, um seinerseits an einen Teil der Zeisl-Besitztümer heranzukommen, doch vergebens, der „Verwalter" setzte sich durch. Die „Arisierungen" waren ein ausgezeichnetes Geschäft für die Profiteure der Enteignungen. Ende September 1938 war die Zerschlagung des Betriebs abgeschlossen, die Firma „abgewickelt". Für ein Kaffeehaus bestand in dem Gebiet kein weiterer Bedarf. Sämtliche von der NS-Enteignungsbehörde aufgelisteten offenen Posten aus dem laufenden Geschäft (Mieten, Personalkosten und Ähnliches) waren durch den „kommissarischen Verwalter" bezahlt worden, der dafür die Betriebsmittel des Unternehmens abverkauft hatte. Der „kommissarische Verwalter" war ein viel beschäftigter Mann, er wickelte im selben Zeitraum auch noch das Café Abbazia in der Ausstellungsstraße 1 ab, weiters das Café Manny in der Ausstellungsstraße 5, das Café Jägerzeile in der Praterstraße 20 und das Café Buchsbaum in der Großen Sperlgasse 41.

Nach Auszahlung eines sehr geringen Restbetrags sollte Siegmund Zeisl aus einem bei der Länderbank eingerichteten „Sperrkonto" von der NS-Behörde einen monatlichen Betrag für seinen Lebensunterhalt erhalten. Siegmund Zeisl und seine zweite Ehefrau Malvine Zeisl (die Schwester von Siegmund Zeisls erster Frau Kamilla und Tante von Erich Zeisl) wurden am 14. Juli 1942 nach Theresienstadt und von dort am 21. September weiter ins Vernichtungslager Treblinka deportiert und ermordet. 1957 stellte Erich Zeisl als Erbe nach seinem Vater Entschädigungsansprüche an den österreichischen Staat. De facto hatte das Café Tegetthoff bereits 1939 nicht mehr existiert, ebenso wenig wie seine Stammkundschaft, und aus der nach dem genialen Dichter benannten Heinestraße war die nach einem radikalen Antisemiten benannte Schönererstraße geworden.[3]

Das ganze Stadtviertel erfuhr zwischen 1938 und 1945 eine brachiale und irreversible Veränderung, denn seine Bewohnerschaft wurde als jüdisch verfolgt, enteignet, zwangsumgesiedelt, vertrieben und umgebracht. Als Eigentümer des Gebäudes, in dem sich das Café Tegetthoff befand, gibt das zeitgenössische Adressbuch die sefardischen Familien „Brüder Asriel, Farchy und Mitbesitzer" an. Paula Asriel und Robert Asriel hatten in zwei Wohnungen im Haus gewohnt, Robert hatte auch die Hausverwaltung besorgt. Der Mietvertrag für das Geschäftslokal fiel unter die Mieterschutzbestimmungen; dies bewahrte Siegmund Zeisl jedoch nicht vor der Enteignung durch die NS-Behörden. Die Hausherren wurden genauso Opfer der Verfolgung durch das Regime. Paula Asriel fand im Haus Heinestraße 42 am 5. Oktober 1942 im Alter von 62 Jahren den Tod. Zu dem Zeitpunkt scheint Robert Asriel nicht mehr in der Heinestraße auf – möglicherweise war ihm noch 1939 die Flucht gelungen.[4]

Entwicklung des jüdischen Siedlungsschwerpunkts Nordbahnviertel

Seit den 1870er-Jahren waren über den Nordbahnhof massenweise Pogromflüchtlinge aus den Schtetln des Russischen Reichs nach Wien geströmt. Infolge des Zusammenbruchs der Habsburgermonarchie strandeten am gleichen Bahnhof weitere Flüchtlingswellen aus den ehemaligen Kronländern Galizien und Bukowina (heute Polen, Ukraine, Rumänien). Sie trafen auf eine bereits dichte jüdische Besiedlung aus Böhmen, Mähren, Ungarn und den Balkanländern im Nordbahnviertel, das im Zuge des Eisenbahnbaus westlich des Bahnhofsareals entstanden war (heute Volkertviertel und Alliiertenviertel). Die Prachtstraße des Viertels war die Heinestraße, jener Boulevard, der seit 1781 in Verlängerung der Prater-Hauptallee die Verbindung zum kaiserlichen Augarten herstellte und 1919 nach dem deutsch-jüdischen Autor benannt wurde. Südwestlich davon schloss sich das Kerngebiet der Türkisch-Israelitischen Kultusgemeinde Wien an.

Nach der Zerschlagung des Wohnviertels und seiner Infrastruktur wurde am nördlichen Rand ein Zwangsarbeiterlager eingerichtet.[5] Aus dem ehemaligen Kopfbahnhof der Kaiser-Ferdinands-Nordbahn des Freiherrn von Rothschild, dem einst größten und wichtigsten Bahnhof der Habsburgermonarchie, rollten ab 1943 die Deportationszüge in Richtung Vernichtungslager.

In der Kleinen Stadtgutgasse, Ecke Holzhausergasse, lag das Römische Bad. Nach der nationalsozialistischen Machtübernahme war es das einzige öffentliche Bad, das von Juden noch besucht werden durfte.

Der Nordbahnhof in Wien, zwischen 1865 und 1880
Wikipedia / Ferdinand Küss oder Michael Frankenstein, Galerie Bassenge, PD

Das jüdische Umfeld des Cafés Tegetthoff

Unweit des Cafés Tegetthoff, in der Heinestraße 35, befand sich das Bethaus des Rabbiners Israel Friedman (1854–1933) aus Czortków (nahe Tarnopol, Polen, heute Ukraine), des Czortkower Rebben. So wie er waren mehrere Gruppen von Chassidim unter Leitung ihres religiösen Oberhaupts Anfang des 20. Jahrhunderts nach Wien gekommen. Auf dem 2008 nach ihm benannten Rabbiner-Friedmann-Platz erinnert heute ein „Stolperstein" an die 24 Opfer der Schoah, die in diesem Haus gewohnt hatten: Rose Bass, Josef Delikat, Maria Goldmann, Jakob Goldmann, Friedrich Heyer, Sali Heyer, Hedwig Kaff, Adele Klausner, Leopold Klausner, Josefine Koch, Heinrich Markheim, Ludwig Mayer, Sara Reiss, Schaje Meier Reiss, Berta Schleicher, Hermann Schleicher, Chana Reisel Seliger, Rudolf Sonnenschein, Therese Sonnenschein, Henriette Steiner, Klara Margarete Steinitz, Leo Steinitz, Hanna Trager und Hugo Trager.

In der Heinestraße 27 war die spätere Kernphysikerin Lise Meitner (1878–1968, gestorben in Cambridge, UK) aufgewachsen. Da an Gymnasien keine Mädchen zugelassen waren, musste sie extern maturieren. Sie promovierte als zweite Frau an der Universität Wien im Hauptfach Physik und setzte ihre Arbeiten dann in Berlin fort. Die Erforscherin der Kernspaltung war zwar mehrmals für den Nobelpreis nominiert, erhalten hat sie ihn aber nie.

Das im historisierenden Stil gestaltete Wohnhaus Heinestraße 21 wurde 1874 von Wilhelm Stiassny (1842–1910), prominenter jüdischer Architekt der Ringstraßenära, errichtet.

Die Redaktion der jüdischen Wochenschrift *Die Wahrheit* befand sich in der Heinestraße 13. Die von Jakob Bauer (1852–1926) begründete Zeitung erschien zwischen 1885 und 1938 und verschrieb sich, ab den 1920er-Jahren als Organ der Österreichisch-Israelitischen Union, angesichts der zunehmenden Judenfeindschaft ganz der Integrationspolitik und der Förderung des Zusammenlebens von Juden und Nichtjuden. Als Herausgeber fungierten unter anderem Ludwig Hirschfeld (1873–1931) und sein Sohn Oskar Hirschfeld. Zu den bekanntesten Autoren zählte Max Grunwald (1871–1953), Rabbiner am Turnertempel, dann Leopoldstädter Tempel sowie Wissenschaftler und Mitgründer des ersten Jüdischen Museums Wien.

Lise Meitner, 1953
Wikipedia / ÖNB, USIS, PD

Der Rabbiner Max Grunwald
Wikipedia / Max Fenichel, ÖNB, PD

In der Heinestraße 4 lebte bis zu ihrer Delogierung durch das NS-Regime die Autorin Lili Grün (1904–1942)[6]; sie wurde 1942 deportiert und in Maly Trostinec ermordet.

Die Wohnung Tür 1 im selben Haus, Heinestraße 4, war auch die letzte Wiener Adresse des Theaterschriftstellers Jura Soyfer (1912–1939). Seine beklemmend präzis zutreffenden Beobachtungen als politisch aktiver Autor zur radikalisierten, volatilen innenpolitischen Situation schilderte er noch vor der Machtergreifung der Nationalsozialisten in Wien am 21. Februar 1938 in einem Brief an seine Familie, die zu dem Zeitpunkt bereits im Exil war. Kurz zuvor war er aus der Polizeihaft entlassen worden, nachdem er bereits 1937 irrtümlich anstelle des kommunistischen Parteifunktionärs Franz Marek festgenommen und, nach Klärung der Verwechslung, seinerseits als politischer Schriftsteller drei Monate gefangen gehalten worden war:

> Was aber war eigentlich mit mir los? Etwas fürchterlich Komisches. Ich wurde mit einem gewissen Herrn Seidel verwechselt! Infolgedessen mehrere Wochen beobachtet und auf der Straße verhaftet. Man fand in meinem Zimmer mehrere Exemplare der in Österreich verbotenen Baseler Rundschau und einen Artikel über die nationale Frage. Resultat: obwohl ich Herrn Dr. Hackel nach einigen Verhören zu beweisen vermochte, wie fatal er sich vergriffen hatte, bekam ich nicht nur 4 Wochen Polizeistrafe, sondern ein Untersuchungsverfahren auf Presse, Hochverrat und Staatsschutz § 4 & 5. Wahrscheinlich hätte der Staatsanwalt von alledem kaum etwas aufrechterhalten können, und nach weiteren 4–8 Wochen Untersuchung wäre die Sache schlimmstenfalls auf eine kleine Gerichtsstrafe hinausgelaufen; wozu es aber nicht kam, da ich amnestiert wurde. Voilà. Jeder Kommentar erübrigt sich und geht in einer abermaligen gellenden Lache unter. [...] Bedenke, Menschenskind, wie mir jetzt zumute ist: zum erstenmal im Leben werde ich von einer politischen Wendung nicht allein ideologisch, sondern materiell im armseligsten Sinn getroffen. Ich muß befürchten, persönlich in jene Probleme gedrängt zu werden, in jene Verteidigungsstellung, wo zu kämpfen uns so scheußlich mißbehagt. Ich werde mir vielleicht wirklich morgen die Frage vorlegen müssen: Was tut ein jüdischer Schriftsteller, wenn ...? Mensch, ist das nicht grauenhaft? [...] Ja, es gibt natürlich auch so einen anständigen Weg trotz wirtschaftlicher Emigration, etcetera, nämlich Heines Weg. Und den wird man ja auch einschlagen, wenn's soweit kommt. Aber mit wieviel gar nicht zu stillenden Selbstvorwürfen angesichts der Lage im Lande, angesichts jedes Franz! Mit wieviel Gefahren, den Geist, statt ihm zu dienen, in irgendwelchen erzwungenen Kuliarbeiten in Paris oder sonstwo erst recht zu verlieren![7]

Nach einem vereitelten Fluchtversuch am 13. März, unmittelbar nach der NS-Machtübernahme – auf Skiern vom vorarlbergischen Gargellen aus über die Berge in die Schweiz zu gelangen –, wurde der Autor noch im Juni 1938 ins KZ Dachau deportiert. Am 16. Februar 1939, nicht einmal ein Jahr nach dem zitierten Brief an die Familie, verstarb Soyfer im KZ Buchenwald, nachdem er mit Typhus infiziert worden war. Heute erinnert am Haus Heinestraße 4 eine Gedenktafel an ihn; „Steine der Erinnerung" am Trottoir vor demselben Gebäude nennen als Opfer stellvertretend auch noch Lili Grün, Oswald Levett, Alma Johanna Koenig und Ber Horowitz.

Jura Soyfer und Marika (Maria) Szècsi, 1930er-Jahre
Wikipedia / DÖW, PD

In der Taborstraße 72 wuchs der spätere Architekt Richard Neutra (1892–1970) als Sohn einer ungarisch-jüdischen Familie auf. Er emigrierte bereits 1923 in die USA und wurde vor allem durch seine Bauten in Kalifornien sehr bald international als prominenter Vertreter des dortigen modernen Baustils anerkannt.

Im Wohnhaus Am Tabor 2 hatte die Familie Körner gewohnt. Henry Körner (1915–1991) besuchte das Gymnasium in der Vereinsgasse, studierte Grafikdesign an der Höheren Graphischen Lehr- und Versuchsanstalt und arbeitete dann bei Victor Slama. 1938 wurde er ins Exil gezwungen; in den USA wurde der Maler ein bekannter Vertreter des magischen Realismus. Für *Time* gestaltete er unter anderem Coverseiten mit Porträts von Maria Callas, John F. Kennedy, Paul Getty oder Barbra Streisand. Aus dem Gedächtnis malte er *My Parents I*, ein berührendes Bild vom Wohnzimmer seiner Eltern, das die Atmosphäre der für immer untergegangenen jüdischen Welt um den Volkertmarkt einfing. Sein Sohn Joseph Leo Koerner, ein bekannter US-Kunsthistoriker, stellte es ins Zentrum seines familienbiografischen Films *The Burning Child* (2019).[8]

Der österreichisch-jüdische Maler Arik Brauer (1929–2021) gestaltete 1996 die Straßenfassade der römisch-katholischen Pfarrkirche Am Tabor 7. An die Schriftstellerin und Journalistin Else Feldmann, die, 1884 in Wien geboren, im Juni 1942 von den Nazis im Vernichtungslager Sobibor ermordet wurde, erinnert der nach ihr benannte Park neben der Kirche. Feldmann hatte unter anderem für die linksliberale Tageszeitung *Der Abend* gearbeitet, deren Herausgeber Carl Colbert (1855–1929)[9] ihr Schreiben förderte. Colberts Sohn Ernst Colbert (1891–1943), der die Zeitung 1928 übernommen hatte, wurde mit dem sogenannten Prominententransport vom 1. April 1938 ins KZ Dachau deportiert und am 2. Dezember 1943 in Auschwitz ermordet. Die sozialkritischen Reportagen eines weiteren von Colbert sen. unterstützten jungen Autors, Bruno Frei (1897–1988), sind eine wichtige Quelle für Informationen über die prekären Existenzbedingungen auch jüdischer Angehöriger der Unterschichten im Wien des 20. Jahrhunderts. Frei überlebte im Exil in Mexiko und kehrte 1947 nach Wien zurück.[10]

Synagogen, Bethäuser und Schulen

Die aschkenasische Synagoge des Stadtteils war in der Pazmanitengasse 6 und trug den Namen „Kaiser Franz Josef I. Huldigungstempel". Bauherr war der 1875 gegründete Bethausverein „Aeschel Awrachom" (Zelt Abrahams). Das markante Bauwerk aus dem modernen Baumaterial Stahlbeton für 500 Männer und 400 Frauen war 1911/12 vom bekannten jüdischen Architekten Ignaz Reiser (1863–1940) errichtet worden. Zu den hier tätigen Rabbinern zählten Armin Abeles (1872–1930) und Salomon Funk (1867–1928). Die Synagoge wurde im Novemberpogrom 1938 zerstört und nicht wieder errichtet.

Das sefardische Bethaus „Jeschuath Achim" (Brüderliche Hilfe) befand sich in der Darwingasse 21. Es war der Sitz eines jüdischen Bethaus- und Krankenunterstützungsvereins, der 1922 gegründet und 1939 vom NS-Regime aufgelöst wurde. Zu jenem Zeitpunkt hatte der Verein rund 100 (männliche) Mitglieder im Alter von 20 bis 50 Jahren. Der Obmann war Alexander Apter; der Vereinsrabbiner Chaim Pinter gehörte einer Rabbinerdynastie aus Bokovsko (Polen) an. Aus dem Gebäude wurden im Zuge des Terrors 30 Menschen deportiert, an sie erinnert heute eine Gedenktafel: Frida Bernstein, Natalie Biller, Anna Breindler, Rubin Breindler, Libe Brod, Marya Davidovitz, Emma Goldner, Isidor Goldner, Rosa Goldstein, Chaim Hausmann, Ides Hausmann, Walter Hennefeld, Ruchel Katz, Helene Knöpfelmacher, Otto Koretz, Hermann Launer, Hans Erich Löwy, Hugo Maier, Jankel Mandel, Maria Mandel, Hermine Markus, Margarethe Örtel, Eugenie Rechnitzer, Friedrich Schlesinger, Ottilie Schlesinger, Adolf Schubert, Ella Schubert, Katharina Schubert, Ferdinand Steiger und Rifka Weissglas.

In der Josefinengasse 7 lag seit 1890 das Bethaus des Wohltätigkeitsvereins „Meischisch Jeschuah" (Rasche Hilfe). Zum Zeitpunkt seiner gewaltsamen Auflösung 1938 hatte der Verein über 200 Mitglieder. Am 14. Oktober im ersten Jahr der NS-Herrschaft in Wien verübten junge Burschen einen Brandanschlag auf das Gotteshaus, der Verein wurde im darauffolgenden Jahr durch eine NS-Behörde, den beschönigend so genannten Stillhaltekommissar, enteignet und aufgelöst.

Der Verein „Achwa We Reuth" (Freundschaft und Brüderlichkeit) hatte sein Vereinsbethaus in der Taborstraße 59. Der Obmann war Salomon Reiss, Rabbiner war A. L. Arak.[11]

Das Gymnasium in der Vereinsgasse 21–23 wurde von vielen jüdischen Kindern besucht. 64 Schüler:innen wurden ab April 1938 vom Unterricht ausgeschlossen, die meisten von ihnen wurden in der Schoah ermordet. Aus einem Schulprojekt im Jahr 1990 entstanden eine Gedenktafel, die am Gebäude angebracht wurde, und das Buch *Begegnung mit Vergessenen, Verschollenen und Vertriebenen*, das Lebensläufe der Opfer enthält.

In der Castellezgasse 35 war jahrzehntelang die Zwi-Perez-Chajes-Schule untergebracht, benannt nach dem Rabbiner (1876–1927), der 1919 das erste jüdische Realgymnasium Wiens gegründet hatte. Chajes war ein Onkel des Pianisten und Komponisten Julius Chajes (1910–1985), mit dem Erich Zeisl in Wien über die Vereinigung „Junge Kunst" und später in den Vereinigten Staaten über die amerikanisch-jüdische Kunstmusikszene in Verbindung stand.

Weitere „Stolpersteine" finden sich in diesem Stadtviertel unter anderem in der Heinestraße 2 für die Familie Taussig, in der Heinestraße 20 für die „jiddische Omale" Maria Pecinovsky und in der Darwingasse 33 für die Familie Albin.

Zwi Perez Chajes, 1927
Wikipedia / Nella Katz, NLI, CC BY 3.0

Steine der Erinnerung für Josef Taussig, Olga Taussig, Helene Löffler und Oskar Weisz, Wien-Leopoldstadt, Heinestraße 2
Wikipedia / H. Wolfgang, 2022, CC BY-SA 4.0

1 Für Details zur „Arisierung" des Cafés Tegetthoff vgl. Österreichisches Staatsarchiv, Wien, AdR 06, Vermögensverkehrsstelle Zl. 202550; Unterlagen zur Verfügung gestellt von Karin Wagner.

2 Adolf Hitlers Nationalsozialistische Deutsche Arbeiterpartei Österreichs, gegründet 1926, war in Österreich von 1933 bis zur NS-Machtübernahme im März 1938 verboten, ihre Mitglieder wurden im NS-Regime retrospektiv lobend als „Illegale" hervorgehoben. Nach dem Ende des Zweiten Weltkriegs mussten sich alle Parteimitglieder gemäß dem „Verbotsgesetz" vom 8. 5. 1945 im Zuge der Entnazifizierung unter alliierter Kontrolle registrieren lassen. Später versuchten ehemalige Mitglieder – ebenso wie davon tangierte öffentliche Stellen –, solche Parteizugehörigkeiten zu verheimlichen oder zu vertuschen, um möglichen negativen Auswirkungen zu entgehen.

3 Georg Heinrich Ritter von Schönerer (1842–1921), Großgrundbesitzer und Politiker der deutschnationalen Bewegung, radikaler Antisemit und mit seiner rechtsextremen, rassistischen „deutsch-völkischen" Ideologie politisches Vorbild für den jungen Adolf Hitler.

4 Wiener Adreßbuch. Lehmanns Wohnungsanzeiger, 1938–1942, https://www.digital.wienbibliothek.at/wbrobv/periodical/titleinfo/5311 (abgerufen am 5. 10. 2024); Dokumentationsarchiv des österreichischen Widerstandes (DÖW), Wien, Erinnern, Personendatenbanken, Shoah-Opfer, https://www.doew.at/erinnern/personendatenbanken/shoah-opfer (abgerufen am 6. 10. 2024).

5 Nordbahnstraße 1–3.

6 Sie verfasste u. a. die Romane Herz über Bord (1933), Loni in der Kleinstadt (1935) und Junge Bürokraft übernimmt auch andere Arbeit ... (1936).

7 Jura Soyfer an seine Familie, 21. 2. 1938, zit. n. https://www.projekt-gutenberg.org/soyfer/misc/chap01.html (abgerufen am 23. 10. 2024).

8 The Burning Child (2019), 113 Min., Regie: Joseph Koerner und Christian D. Bruun, Produktion: Joseph Koerner, Christian D. Bruun und Bo-Mi Choi.

9 Nachlese: Alexander Emanuely, Das Beispiel Colbert. Fin de siècle und Republik oder die vergessenen Ursprünge der Zivilgesellschaft in Österreich, Wien 2020.

10 Bruno Frei, Der Strohhut. Jugenderinnerungen, hg. v. Evelyn Adunka, Wien 2024.

11 Israelitische Kultusgemeinde Wien, JJ32, KK37, IKG 1908/9, IKG36.

Siegmund Zeisl with his sons Eric, Egon, Walter and Wilhelm at the entry to the Café Tegetthoff, 1920s
Archiv des Exilarte Zentrum der mdw, Wien (A-Weaz)

Tina Walzer

CAFÉ TEGETTHOFF OF THE ZEISL FAMILY AT 42 HEINESTRASSE
Violent Upheaval in Vienna's Jewish Nordbahn Quarter, 1938

Café Tegetthoff was a long- and well-established Jewish family business located at 42 Heinestrasse, on the corner of the large Praterstern plaza. Siegmund Zeisl took over ownership of the popular café from his father, Emanuel Zeisl, on March 11, 1897, and managed it for nearly twenty-five years, until 1921. He then leased out the establishment until 1937. One of his tenants also lived in the building, as did the Zeisls themselves. When the café was expropriated in March 1938, it employed three non-Jewish staff. It had twenty-three booths furnished with marble tables, and there was a billiard table and a large chess set to entertain the guests. Neon signage and refrigeration were provided by the local Nussdorf Beer Brewery. Four large windows looked out onto Praterstern and Heinestrasse. In the spring of 1938, shortly after a major renovation, the establishment was seized and liquidated by the Nazi regime. The fate that befell the Zeisl family reflects the transition of an entire neighborhood.

42 Heinestrasse

Following the Nazi takeover in March 1938, Café Tegetthoff was "aryanized," meaning that Siegmund Zeisl lost his business license, his café was shut down by authorities, and its assets were seized.[1] At the time, Zeisl's four sons, Egon, Walter, Eric, and Wilhelm, were thirty-seven, thirty-six, thirty-four, and thirty-one years old, respectively—information he was required to detail in his official "Application for Approval for Sale." All four sons managed to escape to safety abroad.

In late May or early June 1938, the café was scheduled to be transferred to a then forty-seven-year-old former head-waiter from Café Edison at 9 Alser Strasse, in Vienna's ninth district. As he was, however, unemployed at the time of application for "Aryanization" approval, for the purposes of the takeover an "Aryan" investor (a regime supporter), from nearby 17 Lampigasse, stepped in. The "buyer," according to a "deed of purchase" dated June 1, 1938, would take over the rental contract and the whole inventory, while Siegmund Zeisl would surrender his café license in favor of the new owner. However, this coerced contract, extracted from Zeisl, still required official approval from the expropriation authority—named "Property Transaction Office" in the regime's euphemistic phraseology, a term designed to mask the true nature of the injustice.

According to the "Aryanization File" (official documentation), the proposed sale fell through. Instead, on June 24, the expropriation authority appointed an "acting administrator" to manage the "liquidation" of the business. While Zeisl was still required to report the sale of Café Tegetthoff to the Edison waiter by July 12 (on a form from the "Aryanization Office of the Hospitality and Pub Trade Association in Vienna 1, 1 Regierungsgasse"), the liquidator was already going about his business. He also was a former waiter but had a key advantage over his competitors: he had been a documented member of the Nazi Party since 1926—an "illegal" (member of the then illegal party).[2] During the expropriation process, one of the former tenants attempted to scheme his way into acquiring some of Zeisl's assets but failed; the "acting administrator" prevailed. "Aryanizations" were highly profitable for those benefitting from expropriations. The breaking-up of the business was completed, and the company "liquidated," by late September 1938. The neighborhood no longer needed a café. Any remaining expenses listed by the Nazi expropriation authority—rent, staff wages, etc.—were paid by the "acting administrator," who covered them by selling the café's assets. The "acting administrator" was a busy man; during this time, he also oversaw the liquidation of Café Abbazia on 1 Ausstellungsstrasse, Café Manny on 5 Ausstellungsstrasse, Café Jägerzeile on 20 Praterstrasse, and Café Buchsbaum on 41 Große Sperlgasse.

After the payout of the very small remaining amount of money, Siegmund Zeisl was to receive a monthly allowance from a "blocked account" held at Länderbank and managed by the Nazi authorities, for his living expenses. On July 14, 1942, Siegmund and his second wife, Malvine Zeisl (sister of his first wife Kamilla and aunt of Eric Zeisl), were deported to the Theresienstadt concentration camp. On September 21, they were transferred to the Treblinka extermination camp, where they were murdered. In 1957, Eric Zeisl, as his father's heir, filed claims for compensation from the Austrian state. In fact, Café Tegetthoff had already ceased to exist in 1939, along with its regular clientele. Heinestrasse, once named after the brilliant German-Jewish poet Heinrich Heine, had been renamed Schönererstrasse after the radically antisemitic Austrian politician Georg Ritter von Schönerer.[3]

Between 1938 and 1945, the entire neighborhood went through brutal and irreversible changes, as its Jewish residents were persecuted, dispossessed, forcibly relocated, deported, and killed. According to a contemporary address register, the building that housed Café Tegetthoff was owned by the Sephardic families "Brüder Asriel, Farchy, and Partners." Paula and Robert Asriel lived in two apartments in the building, with Robert also serving as property manager. Although the lease for the café was covered by tenant protection laws, Siegmund Zeisl was not shielded from expropriation by the Nazis. The building owners suffered similar persecution by the regime. Paula Asriel died in her apartment at 42 Heinestrasse on October 5, 1942, at the age of sixty-two. At that time, Robert Asriel's name no longer appeared in records for Heinestrasse—he may have managed to escape in 1939.[4]

Development of a Jewish Settlement Hub in Vienna's Nordbahn Quarter

Starting in the 1870s, waves of Jewish refugees fleeing pogroms in the shtetls of the Russian Empire poured into Vienna via the Nordbahnhof or North Railway station. After the collapse of the Habsburg monarchy, the same station saw new waves of refugees coming in from the former crown lands of Galicia and Bukovina (now parts of Poland, Ukraine, and Romania). These newcomers had to get a footing in an area already densely populated by Jews from Bohemia, Moravia, Hungary, and the Balkans in the "Nordbahn quarter" west of the station, which had been developed due to the expansion of the railroad (today known as the Volkert and Allied quarters). The neighborhood's grand boulevard, built in 1781, connected the Prater park with the imperial Augarten Palace and grounds; in 1919, it was renamed Heinestrasse after the German-Jewish writer and poet. Southwest of this area was the core neighborhood of Vienna's Sephardic "Turkish-Israelite Community."

After the destruction of the area's infrastructure and the expulsion of its Jewish population a forced labor camp was set up on its northern edge.[5] Starting in 1943, deportation trains left from the former terminal of the "Emperor Ferdinand Northern Railway," founded by Baron von Rothschild, once the largest and most important station in the Habsburg monarchy, now bound for extermination camps.

On the corner of Kleine Stadtgutgasse and Holzhausergasse, the "Roman Baths" were situated. After the Nazi takeover, this was the only public bathhouse in Vienna that Jews were still allowed to use.

"Stones of Memory" for Oswald Levett, Alma Johanna Koenig, Ber Horowitz and Lili Grün in Vienna's Leopoldstadt, Heinestrasse 4
Wikipedia / H. Wolfgang, 2022, CC BY-SA 4.0

The Jewish Neighborhood of Café Tegetthoff

Not far from Café Tegetthoff, at 35 Heinestrasse, was the prayer house of Rabbi Israel Friedman (1854–1933) from Czortków (near Ternopil, formerly Tarnopol, Poland, now Ukraine), known as the "Czortkow Rebbe." Like him, several groups of Hasidim led by their religious leaders had come to Vienna in the early twentieth century. On today's Rabbi Friedmann Square—named in his honor in 2008—a "stumbling stone" memorial plaque commemorates the twenty-four Shoah victims who once lived in this house: Rose Bass, Josef Delikat, Maria Goldmann, Jakob Goldmann, Friedrich Heyer, Sali Heyer, Hedwig Kaff, Adele Klausner, Leopold Klausner, Josefine Koch, Heinrich Markheim, Ludwig Mayer, Sara Reiss, Schaje Meier Reiss, Berta Schleicher, Hermann Schleicher, Chana Reisel Seliger, Rudolf Sonnenschein, Therese Sonnenschein, Henriette Steiner, Klara Margarete Steinitz, Leo Steinitz, Hanna Trager, and Hugo Trager.

Lise Meitner (1878–1968, died in Cambridge, UK), the nuclear physicist, grew up at 27 Heinestrasse. Since girls were not admitted to high schools, she had to complete her Matura exam externally. She became the second woman to gain a doctoral degree in physics at the University of Vienna and continued her work in Berlin. Although she was nominated several times for the Nobel Prize, she never received it.

The residential building at 21 Heinestrasse, designed in a historicist style, was built in 1874 by Wilhelm Stiassny (1842–1910), a prominent Jewish architect of Vienna's Ringstrasse era.

The editorial offices of the Jewish weekly *Die Wahrheit* (The truth) were located at 13 Heinestrasse. Founded by Jakob Bauer (1852–1926), the paper was published from 1885 to 1938. Beginning in the 1920s, as the organ of the

In exile: Lise Meitner teaching students at Bryn Mawr College, 1959
Wikipedia / Bryn Mawr College, CC BY-SA 2.0

Gravestone for Jura Soyfer, Hebrew Free Burial Association's Mount Richmond Cemetery
Wikipedia / Hebrew Free Burial Society, 2011, CC BY-SA 3.0

"Austrian-Israelite Union," it focused on promoting integration and advancing coexistence between Jews and non-Jews in response to rising antisemitism. Notable editors included Ludwig Hirschfeld (1873–1931) and his son, Oskar Hirschfeld. Among its best-known contributors was Max Grunwald (1871–1953), the rabbi of the Turner Temple and later of the Leopoldstadt Temple, a scholar and co-founder of Vienna's first Jewish Museum.

The writer Lili Grün (1904–1942) lived at 4 Heinestrasse until her eviction by the Nazi regime.[6] She was deported in 1942 and murdered at Maly Trostenets.

Apartment 1 in the same building, 4 Heinestrasse, was also the last Viennese residence of playwright Jura Soyfer (1912–1939). In a letter dated February 21, 1938, Soyfer, a politically active writer, conveyed his chillingly accurate observations on Vienna's increasingly radical and volatile political climate to his family, who had already gone into exile. Shortly before, he had been released from police detention after being mistakenly arrested in 1937 in place of Communist Party official Franz Marek. Even after the mix-up was clarified, he was held for three months for being an activist political writer.

> So, what exactly happened to me? Something horribly absurd. I was mistaken for one Mr. Seidel! Because of that, I was under surveillance for several weeks and arrested on the street. In my room, they found several issues of the Baseler Rundschau, which is banned in Austria, and an article about the national question. The result? Even though, after a few interrogations, I was able to prove to Dr. Hackel that he had made a fatal mistake, I was still given 4 weeks of police custody and an investigation on charges of press violations, high treason, and state security under § 4 & 5. Most likely the prosecutor couldn't have upheld most of it, and after another 4–8 weeks of investigation, the whole matter would, at worst, have come to a minor court sentence. But it didn't happen, because I received an amnesty. Voilà. There's really nothing left to say or do, except burst into yet another roaring laugh. [...] Goodness! Just think how I feel now: for the first time in my life, I'm personally affected by a political shift, not just ideologically but materially in the most miserable sense. I'm facing the prospect of being forced into exactly that defensive position from which to fight we dread so much. I may very well have to ask myself tomorrow: What does a Jewish writer do when ...? Boy, isn't that horrifying? [...] Sure, there's an "honorable" path, even if that means emigrating for work, et cetera—Heine's path. And, of course, we'd take it if it comes to that. But imagine the unending sense of guilt about the situation back home, about every "Franz" left behind! And what about the risk of losing the spirit altogether, instead of dedicating oneself to it, in some kind of forced work as a hack in Paris or who knows where![7]

Following a failed attempt to escape on skis over the mountains to Switzerland from Gargellen in Vorarlberg on March 13, right after the Nazi takeover, Jura Soyfer was arrested. By June 1938, he was deported to Dachau. On February 16, 1939, less than a year after the above letter to his family, Soyfer died of typhus in the Buchenwald concentration camp. He was twenty-seven years old. Today, a plaque on the house in 4 Heinestrasse honors him, while "Stones of Remembrance" on the pavement nearby commemorate more victims: Lili Grün, Oswald Levett, Alma Johanna Koenig, and Ber Horowitz.

At 72 Taborstrasse, future architect Richard Neutra (1892–1970) grew up with his Hungarian-Jewish family. He emigrated to the United States as early as 1923 and soon gained international recognition for his buildings in California as a prominent exponent of the local modernist building style.

The Körner family lived at 2 Am Tabor. Henry Körner (1915–1991) attended the high school in Vereinsgasse (see below) and studied graphic design at the renowned Higher Graphic Arts Education and Research Institute in Vienna before he went on to work for graphic designer Victor Slama. In 1938, Körner fled to the U.S., where later he became a well-known painter of magic realism. For *Time* magazine, he designed cover pages with his portraits of Maria Callas, John F. Kennedy, Paul Getty, and Barbra Streisand, among others. A painting he made from memory was *My Parents I*, a touching depiction of his parental living room that captures the atmosphere of the Jewish neighborhood around Volkertmarkt before it forever vanished. Körner's son, well-known art historian Joseph Leo Koerner, later placed his father's painting in the center of his 2019 autobiographical film *The Burning Child*.[8]

In 1996, Austrian-Jewish artist Arik Brauer (1929–2021) designed the façade of the Roman Catholic parish church at 7 Am Tabor. Adjacent is the Else Feldmann Park, named after the Viennese writer and journalist born in 1884 and murdered at the Sobibor extermination camp in 1942. Feldmann's writing career included work for the left-liberal daily *Der Abend* (The evening), published by Carl Colbert (1855–1929).[9] His son Ernst Colbert, who took over the paper in 1928, was deported to Dachau on April 1, 1938, on what came to be infamously known as the "celebrity transport" and murdered at Auschwitz in 1943. Another writer mentored by Carl Colbert was Bruno Frei (1897–1988). His socially critical reports are an important source of information about the precarious living conditions of Jewish members of Vienna's lower classes in the twentieth century. Frei survived in exile in Mexico and returned to Vienna in 1947.[10]

Richard Neutra on one of his self-designed chairs with a photograph of his prize-winning William and Melba Beard House in Altadena California, 1935
Wikipedia / Los Angeles Times, CC BY 4.0

Synagogues, Prayer Houses, and Schools

The Ashkenazi synagogue of the district, located at 6 Pazmanitengasse, was officially named "Emperor Francis Joseph I Memorial Temple." Commissioned by the prayer house association "Aeschel Awrachom" (Tent of Abraham), founded 1875, the landmark building, which used the modern construction material of reinforced concrete and seated five hundred men and four hundred women, was built by well-known Jewish architect Ignaz Reiser (1863–1940) in 1911/12. Among its rabbis were Armin Abeles (1872–1930) and Salomon Funk (1867–1928). The synagogue was destroyed during the November Pogrom in 1938 and never rebuilt.

21 Darwingasse was a Sephardic prayer house and seat of the welfare association "Jeschuath Achim" (Brotherly help), founded in 1922 and shut down by the Nazi regime in 1939. At the time, it had around one hundred members, all men between the ages of twenty and fifty. Its chairman was Alexander Apter, and Rabbi Chaim Pinter, a member of the Bokovsko rabbinic dynasty from Poland, served as the congregation's rabbi. A commemorative plaque now honors the thirty people deported from this building: Frida Bernstein, Natalie Biller, Anna Breindler, Rubin Breindler, Libe Brod, Marya Davidovitz, Emma Goldner, Isidor Goldner, Rosa Goldstein, Chaim Hausmann, Ides Hausmann, Walter Hennefeld, Ruchel Katz, Helene Knöpfelmacher, Otto Koretz, Hermann Launer, Hans Erich Löwy, Hugo Maier, Jankel Mandel, Maria Mandel, Hermine Markus, Margarethe Örtel, Eugenie Rechnitzer, Friedrich Schlesinger, Ottilie Schlesinger, Adolf Schubert, Ella Schubert, Katharina Schubert, Ferdinand Steiger, and Rifka Weissglas.

The prayer house of the charity association "Meischisch Jeschuah" (Swift help) had been located at 7 Josefinengasse since 1890. At the time of its violent dissolution by the Nazis in 1938, it had over two hundred members. On October 14, 1938, some teenage boys set fire to the building. The following year, the association was expropriated and dissolved by a Nazi authority with the euphemistic name of "Stillhaltekommissar" ("keep-still commissary," a supervisor for regime alignment and shutdown of organizations).

The association "Achwa We Reuth" (Friendship and brotherhood) was based at 59 Taborstrasse, with Salomon Reiss serving as chairman and Rabbi A. L. Arak as the officiating rabbi.[11]

The high school at 21–23 Vereinsgasse was attended by many Jewish children. In April 1938, sixty-four students were expelled, most of whom were murdered in the Shoah. A 1990 school project resulted in a commemorative plaque on the building and a book, *Begegnung mit Vergessenen, Verschollenen und Vertriebenen* (Encounters with the forgotten, missing, and displaced), documenting the lives of the victims.

The "Zwi Perez Chajes School" operated for decades at 35 Castellezgasse, named for Rabbi Zwi Perez Chajes (1876–1927), who founded Vienna's first Jewish secondary school in 1919. Chajes was the uncle of pianist and composer Julius Chajes (1910–1985), who had ties with Eric Zeisl through the "Young Art" association in Vienna and later through the American-Jewish music scene.

Additional commemorative "stumbling stones" can be found in the area, such as those at 2 Heinestrasse for the Taussig family, at 20 Heinestrasse for the "Yiddish granny" Maria Pecinovsky, and at 33 Darwingasse for the Albin family.

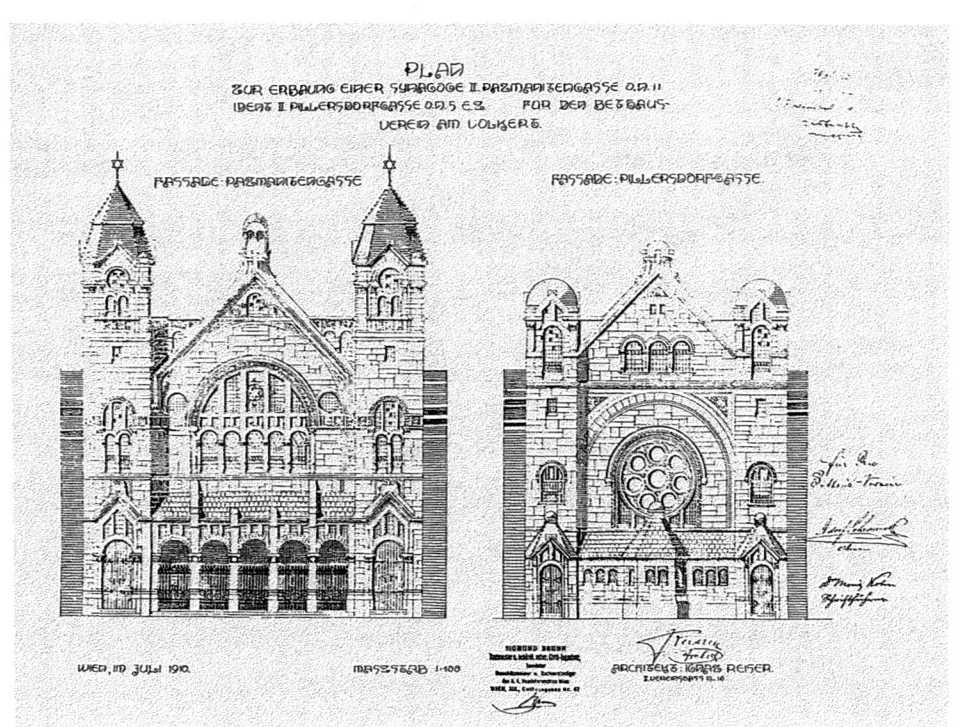

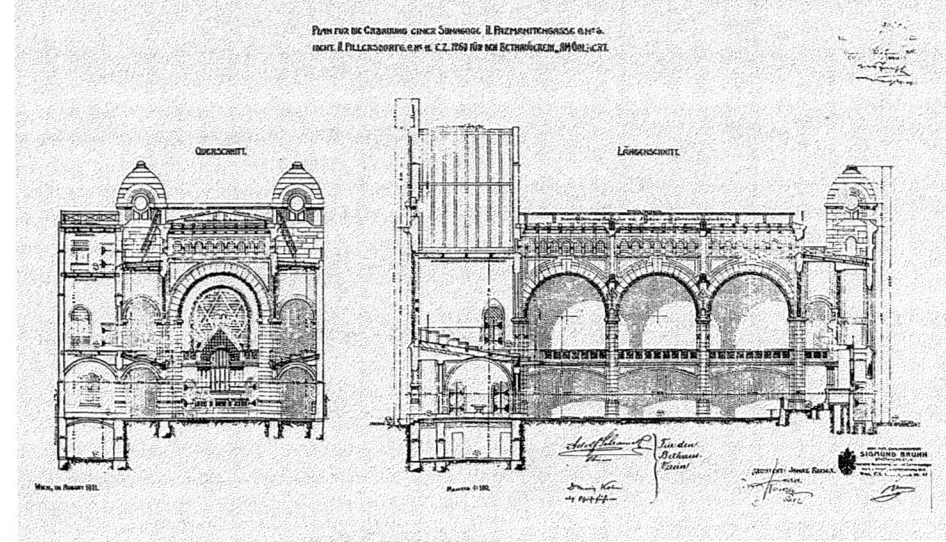

Plans for the Pazmaniten Temple by the architect Ignaz Reiser
Wikipedia / Pierre Genée, Wiener Synagogen 1825–1938, PD

1. For details for the expropriation of Café Tegetthoff see Austrian State Archives, Vienna, AdR 06, Vermögensverkehrsstelle Zl. 202550; documentation provided by Karin Wagner.

2. Adolf Hitler's National Socialist German Workers' Party of Austria, founded in 1926, was declared illegal in Austria from 1933 until the Nazi takeover in March 1938; retrospectively, its party members were praised by the Nazi regime as "illegals." After the end of the Second World War, all former party members had to register under Allied control in the course of the denazification process, pursuant to the "Verbotsgesetz" (Prohibition Act) of May 8, 1945. Later, former party members—as well as public institutions involved—deliberately tried to conceal or cover up any such party affiliations, in order to avoid possible negative consequences.

3. Georg Heinrich Ritter von Schönerer (1842–1921), landowner and one of the political leaders of the German-nationalist party. With his radically antisemitic views and racist Germanic ideology, he was idealized by Adolf Hitler when he first came to Vienna as a young man.

4. See *Wiener Adressbuch: Lehmanns Wohnungsanzeiger*, 1938–1942, https://www.digital.wienbibliothek.at/wbrobv/periodical/titleinfo/5311 (accessed Oct. 5, 2024); Documentation Centre of Austrian Resistance (DÖW), Vienna, Austrian Victims of the Holocaust, https://www.doew.at/english/austrian-victims-of-the-holocaust (accessed Oct. 6, 2024).

5. 1–3 Nordbahnstrasse.

6. Her works included the novels *Herz über Bord* (Heart overboard, 1933), *Loni in der Kleinstadt* (Small town Loni, 1935), and *Junge Bürokraft übernimmt auch andere Arbeit …* (Young office worker takes extra jobs …, 1936).

7. Jura Soyfer to his family, Feb. 21, 1938; https://www.projekt-gutenberg.org/soyfer/misc/chap01.html (accessed Oct. 23, 2024), trans. Michael Haas.

8. *The Burning Child* (2019), 113 min., directed by Joseph Koerner and Christian D. Bruun, produced by Joseph Koerner, Christian D. Bruun, and Bo-Mi Choi.

9. See Alexander Emanuely, *Das Beispiel Colbert: Fin de siècle und Republik oder die vergessenen Ursprünge der Zivilgesellschaft in Österreich* (Vienna, 2020).

10. Bruno Frei, *Der Strohhut: Jugenderinnerungen*, ed. Evelyn Adunka (Vienna, 2024).

11. Vienna's Jewish Community, JJ32, KK37, IKG 1908/9, IKG36.

Michael Haas

A TALE OF TWO VIENNESE JEWISH COMPOSERS
Eric Zeisl and Walter Bricht

Musical life in Vienna did not come to a halt with the fall of the Habsburg monarchy and the general re-location of the city's most creative spirits to Berlin. Franz Schreker and his composition class moved to Berlin in 1920 and Schoenberg followed in 1925. Other prominent Austrians who decided that Germany offered more opportunities than Vienna were Hans Gál who became director of the conservatory in Mainz (later Academy of Music) and Ernst Toch who after teaching in Mannheim and running various new-music initiatives moved to Berlin. Hanns Eisler abandoned his wife and son in Vienna for a more politically active life in Germany. Even the city's soloists and conductors had long decided that the future was to be found in Berlin rather than Vienna: Artur Schnabel, Fritz Kreisler and Emanuel Feuermann. Yet Vienna's musical life would still remain vibrant and active.

Berlin may have been the city to go to for fun, nightclubs and a vision of the future, but Vienna remained a city brimming with support for serious music with an enthusiastic public. The contrasts between the two cities is made most clearly in their attempts to engage the working classes with music. In Berlin, concerts for "the workers" were filled with agitprop and politically didactic stage works offering civic instruction. By contrast, David Josef Bach's "Arbeiterkonzerte" or "Workers' Concerts" in Vienna offered the opportunity for the newly enfranchised proletariat to hear Beethoven and Mahler.

Vienna's qualities of life and interest in new musical experiences was unique. This had much to do with the fact that the city's Jewish population had embraced music to a degree unknown in other European capitals such as London or Paris. Jews in the Habsburg realm saw music as the fast track to acceptance and assimilation. Jewish child prodigies became a cottage industry starting with the violinist Bronisław Huberman and the pianist Alfred Grünfeld, but continuing with countless others in their wake such as Rudolf Serkin, Erich Wolfgang Korngold and Erika Morini. Jews from the Habsburg eastern provinces came to Vienna and initially settled in the second district, known as Leopoldstadt or colloquially as the "Matzos Island". With ambition, education, and the ability to qualify within the professions, they were soon moving up the social ladder and relocating to Vienna's nobler, bourgeois districts.

With the eventual removal of restrictions on Jewish enterprise, following the Liberal Constitution of December 1867, antisemites were soon protesting at the pretentiousness of Jewish palatial homes along the Ringstrasse inhabited by industrialists and bankers, many of whom were wealthier than the Imperial family or the Empire's ancient aristocracy.

Where Jewish life became most dominant however was in the professions, and this included not just law and medicine, but also the press. Many of the city's important newspapers were Jewish owned and largely manned by Jewish journalists. By the time Gustav Mahler, a prominent Jewish convert to Catholicism noted that he could not imagine what he had in common with a group of newly arrived shtetl Jews from the East, it had already become clear that the Jews of Vienna had settled into two very separate tribes. One of bourgeois converts to Christianity and the other of traditional Jews, trying to build a life for themselves and a better life for their children.

This is the story of two composers, Walter Bricht (1904–1970) and Eric Zeisl (1905–1959) who came from these two very different Jewish tribes. It offers a stark representation of how opportunities and careers could vary. It also exposed the presumed privileges enjoyed by the wealthy Jewish population as a delusional sham as soon as Vienna fell to Nazi Germany.

For many of the city's ambitious Jews, the first and most important step towards acceptance was conversion to Christianity. Gustav Mahler remains emblematic for this development, but he was far from alone. Antisemitism in Austria was deeply ingrained in Viennese society. Indeed, it was so profound that Jews who converted discovered their acceptance into certain institutions and societies was offset by their exclusion from the personal and familial. As a result, converted Jews remained locked in a social circle of other converted Jews and found their opportunities to marry limited. Alma Schindler, later and better known as Alma Mahler must remain symbolic of the complicated free-spirited daughter from a successful artistic family who was happy to shock and break conventions. Her intimate relationships with Jewish men were expressions of the eroticism of the forbidden. At the same time, she remained bafflingly antisemitic in her own views, while simultaneously rejecting the antisemitism of those who disapproved of her relationships. She was a window into Vienna's bourgeois, non-Jewish soul.

The young Walter Bricht, c. 1924
Bricht Family Collection

Paul Amadeus Pisk referred to Eric Zeisl in an article for Radio Wien on 26. January 1934 as one of the "strongest personalities among Viennese composers not yet thirty years old". The photo was taken by Hermann Brühlmeyer.

Archiv des Exilarte Zentrum der mdw, Wien (A-Weaz)

For most wealthy and successful Jews, whether the Wittgensteins or the Gallias, conversion would never afford anything more than the appearance of acceptance. With the rise of Hitler and the National Socialists' seizure of power, the fragility of their acceptance would become painfully plain to see. The two tribes would soon find themselves amalgamated into a single community.

As noted, Walter Bricht and Eric Zeisl were born within a year of each other. They would go on to become two of the city's most productive and highly regarded composers. Bricht was born into a family not dissimilar to that of Erich Wolfgang Korngold, whose father Julius Korngold was arguably one of the most powerful music critics of the day. Bricht's father, Balduin Bricht was the cultural editor of the Österreichische *Volkszeitung*, a conservative-leaning, Catholic paper. He went on to found and become the head of Vienna's Association of Music Critics as well as the president of the Concordia Pension Fund, an umbrella organisation of Austrian journalists.[1] Walter Bricht's mother was Agnes Pyllemann, the daughter of the music journalist Franz Pyllemann. Agnes was a pianistic prodigy, admired by Brahms. She later developed into a noted singer and specialised in lied and oratorio. Franz Pyllemann would ultimately be revealed as the only member of the Bricht family not to have been born Jewish. Balduin, whose mother was Katharina Rosenfeld and father Samuel Bricht were both Jewish, though converted at some point after 1868.[2] Balduin and Agnes married in 1892. These appear to have been facts that were incidental to Walter Bricht, if indeed they were even known or viewed as relevant. By the time of Walter Bricht's birth, the Bricht/Pyllemann relationship represented the stereotypical Viennese middle-class family of former-Jews marrying other former Jews. Prior to Hitler's arrival and following the Constitution of 1867, conversion was merely the first step towards acceptance and assimilation. Marrying other converts to Christianity would not have seemed futile, but thought of as a further step towards greater social and professional acceptance.

Eric Zeisl, on the other hand came from a lower-middle-class Jewish family that ran a café near Vienna's Nordbahnhof or North Railway station, Vienna's entry point for shtetl Jews arriving from Poland and Ukraine. The family was also musical with the father singing in a men's chorus and brothers who would go on to become singers. Zeisl studied with Joseph Marx, Richard Stöhr and ultimately Hugo Kauder, who along with Stöhr became his most important influence. Bricht, on the other hand, was, according to the pianist Walter Robert, Franz Schmidt's favourite pupil and according to another Schmidt pupil, Walter Taussig, Schmidt even brought Bricht in for occasional outside advice concerning his own compositions.

The divergent paths became even more pronounced as demonstrated by their social circles. Bricht was a member of Vienna's haut-bourgeois attending the Akademisches Gymnasium, a high school that had educated much of Austria's intellectual elite. With a father who was a prominent cultural journalist and a mother who was a regular recitalist, (often accompanied by her son), Bricht's friends and acquaintances were nearly all musicians and nearly all devotees and students of Franz Schmidt.

Schmidt was a musical polymath who played the piano, organ and cello to concert performance levels while also composing and conducting with an ear so sensitive he could identify the pitch in the sounds of machinery or motors. Students admitted that his natural abilities were such that he was not the best teacher, incapable of explaining the means of achieving certain effects or addressing technical issues. This resulted in many of his students turning to outside advice within Schmidt's circle, chief of whom was Walter Bricht who offered additional tuition to any number of Schmidt pupils in both performance and composition.

It was in this circle of fellow Schmidt pupils that Bricht met his future wife, Ella Kugel, the daughter of Georg Kugel, one of Vienna's important concert agents and promoters. Ella was an accomplished pianist who went on to premiere Bricht's *First Piano Concerto* and was preparing for a performance of his *Second Piano Concerto* with the Vienna Philharmonic until its cancellation following Austria's annexation by Nazi Germany.

Eric Zeisl would also meet his future wife Gertrud Jellinek through his circle of friends, but unlike Bricht, Zeisl's circles were interdisciplinary including writers, painters, actors and musicians. Indeed, one was given the name of "Young Art". It included the composer Julius Chajes and the violinist Felix Galimir. The central figure in the group was the philosopher and writer Fred Hernfeld, known later in American exile as Alfred Farau. Zeisl and his wife also moved in another circle that included the writer Hilde Spiel, who described a fictional Zeisl in her novel *Kati auf der Brücke* (Kati on the bridge). The painter Lisel Salzer was also part of that group.

During the interwar years, Vienna was far from being a center of music modernism as found in Berlin, Frankfurt, Cologne or especially Mannheim. Even its more progressive elements were disinclined towards total anarchy and disruption. Developments in music, (apart from the Schoenberg circle), were largely organic. Kauder's departure from diatonic tonality tended towards the modal and Germany's "New Objectivity" movement was not a prominent feature. Nevertheless, "Modernism" in Viennese music was dynamic and affected by outside influences. Kauder's modal excursions found its echo in English composition while French Impressionism and neo-classicism also resonated throughout many inter-war compositions.

The dominant spirits, however, remained Brahms, Bruckner and Mahler with Schoenberg's Second Viennese School far more marginal that we tend to assume today. Nevertheless, Franz Schmidt would prepare and rehearse Schoenberg's *Pierre Lunaire*, while Alban Berg's compositions along with those of Egon Wellesz and other members of Schoenberg's circle were frequently heard in performance, not least at the State Opera.[3]

Austria remained for better or worse, a country torn between North and South and Vienna's two most prominent composers Joseph Marx and Franz Schmidt represented both poles. Schmidt was a pan-German, meaning he held to the common belief that Bismarck should have included Austria's German speaking regions in his unification of German states in 1871.[4] That they were excluded was a promise Hitler intended to make good many decades later. Schmidt looked to the North. Marx was half-Italian and the light and colour of his music suggests an Austrian answer to Respighi. The other prominent teacher at the time was the Brahmsian Richard Stöhr, born the same year as Arnold Schoenberg but inhabiting a very different musical age.

For that reason, it is important to understand that Zeisl's circle was not as progressive as one might have found in Mannheim or Berlin, but then, nor was Bricht's circle unremittingly conservative. Vienna continued to offer an aesthetic counterweight to developments taking place in Berlin, and even progressives such as Ernst Krenek, Egon Wellesz, Anton Webern and Alban Berg preferred life in Vienna to that in Berlin.

Walter Bricht and his fiancée,
Ella Kugel, c. 1930
Bricht Family Collection

Eric Zeisl and Gertrud Jellinek,
early 1930s
Archiv des Exilarte Zentrum der
mdw, Wien (A-Weaz)

Walter Bricht in the United States, c. 1960
Bricht Family Collection

Eric Zeisl, Los Angeles promotion photo
intended for the movie industry, 1940s
Archiv des Exilarte Zentrum, Wien (A-Weaz)

Given Bricht's natural entry into local musical life, it should come as no surprise that he was prominently featured almost weekly as either a conductor, pianist, chamber musicians or composer. He was a much sought after accompanist and his reputation would eventually cross borders at a time that was impossible for Zeisl, offering Bricht international credibility. Bricht would be championed by the German conductor Leopold Reichwein, a notorious antisemite who long before Hitler refused to conduct works by Mendelssohn. Through Franz Schmidt, Bricht had also become acquainted with the one-armed pianist Paul Wittgenstein. He would later be commissioned by Wittgenstein to compose works for the left hand. Bricht performed the orchestra accompaniment of Ravel's *Concerto for the Left Hand* in a demonstration of the score for the composer with Wittgenstein as soloist. Bricht was not consciously conservative, but as with the legendary former music critic Eduard Hanslick, he was a believer in the idea of "absolute music" meaning music not used in the employment of theatre or programmes. Music was intended to be composed and heard on its own merits and though there would always be a place for opera, especially in a city such as Vienna, Bricht showed no apparent desire in writing one.

Another difference in the two composer was their public profile with Bricht being mentioned in the press over 2000 times while Zeisl is only mentioned in 689 articles and reviews.[5] Nevertheless, by 1938 and coincidentally, just before Austria's annexation, Zeisl was given the sort of portrait coverage in the RAVAG journal, *Radio Wien*, that Bricht had long enjoyed.

This essay is not intended to be an extended biography of either composer, but rather to use the lives of these two very different, yet similar individuals to illustrate the social chasm that existed between Viennese Jews and how by 1938, this chasm was closed. Nothing illustrates this divergence and convergence better than their separate experiences of emigration. Bricht's *Second Piano Concerto* was to have been conducted by Clemens Krauss, performed by Ella Kugel and the Vienna Philharmonic. When Bricht was informed by Austrian Radio (RAVAG) that his services were no longer required following their research into his ancestry, Bricht was initially offered the status of "honorary Aryan", no doubt through the offices of Krauss and Baldur von Schirach, right up to Hitler himself. Bricht refused the offer and turning to contacts at the American Embassy swiftly managed an affidavit and visa to move to the United States.

Zeisl would also be negatively hit by the annexation of Austria into Hitler's Germany with the cancellation of the premiere of his opera *Leonce und Lena*. Initially, the Zeisl/Jellinek families left Vienna for neighbouring Baden only to be told by the local city council they needed to leave within forty-eight hours. There followed immigration to Paris. Beforehand, Gertrud and her mother wrote to every "Zeisl" and "Zeisel" they could find in various American telephone books. They then received an affidavit that took them to Paris, but it was insufficient for entry into the United States, and was subsequently replaced by another one.

What happened afterwards is of particular interest. Both composers would initially come to New York, but while Bricht who had enjoyed every advantage that musical Vienna could offer found it impossible to continue composing, Zeisl embraced new opportunities. His experience in Paris had exposed him to the idea of moving forward with his Jewish identity. In Paris, he composed incidental music for the play *Job* (*Hiob*) based on Joseph Roth's novel of the same name.

Zeisl was confronted with the reality that despite considering himself a child of German culture, Hitler had unilaterally declared him neither German nor Austrian. Stripped of such national identity, Zeisl realised through his work on *Job* that he still had his Jewish identity to fall back on.

Zeisl by force of circumstance would ultimately end up spending the war years in Hollywood carrying out the work of the hack studio musician. Afterwards, he felt sufficiently liberated to continue developing his ambitions to write music that was "Jewish" in character without resorting to obvious folkloric or liturgical models. Perhaps it was his experience with Kauder that opened the world of modal writing to him, though Zeisl would use modal colours while never actively departing from the diatonic.

The tragedy of Walter Bricht was his lack of cultural identity to turn to once he discovered that he like Zeisl, was no longer German nor Austrian and despite expectations, he was not regarded as American. His arrival in America, initially met with hope for his continued success would ultimately have more in common with his fellow non-Jewish refugee colleague, the composer Ernst Krenek who described America has "being without an echo". Like Krenek, Bricht's marriage would fall apart and he would go from a world of fame and instant recognition to being a musical luminary at a provincial college. Both Zeisl and Bricht were united in their love of art-song or lied. Once made to leave Austria, neither managed a significant return to the genre that reminded them of their loss of cultural identity. Bricht composed four lieder in 1940, though he did not give them opus numbers. He, like Zeisl never returned to the genre. There was a piano sonata in 1940 and a trio for Paul Wittgenstein in 1942, but these would be his last compositions until his return in his last years, writing chamber works for the flautist son of his ex-wife, Ella Kugel. Zeisl on the other hand had embraced his new opportunities and continued his journey in search of a synthesis of his new homeland and his individual Jewish identity.

---

1   https://data.onb.ac.at/nlv_lex/perslex/B/Bricht_Balduin.htm (viewed Dezember 8, 2024).
2   See Anna Staudacher, „… meldet den Austritt aus dem mosaischen Glauben" 18000 Austritte aus dem Judentum in Wien, 1868–1914: Namen, Quellen, Daten, New York-Frankfurt am Main 2009, ISBN 3-6315-5832-5, p. 81.
3   Arnold Schoenberg: *Gurrelieder*, performances at the State Opera on June 12 and June 13, 1920; Ernst Krenek: *Jonny spielt auf*, premiere at the State Opera on Dec. 31, 1927; Alban Berg: *Wozzeck*, premiere at the State Opera on April 4, 1930; Egon Wellesz: *Die Bakchantinnen*, world premiere at the State Opera on June, 20, 1931.
4   https://archive.org/details/handbuch-ns-musiker-prieberg, p. 6601 (accessed March 1, 2025).
5   https://anno.onb.ac.at/anno-suche/simple?query=%22Erich%20 Zeisl%22&from=1 (accessed March 1, 2025).

Michael Haas

EINE GESCHICHTE ZWEIER JÜDISCHER KOMPONISTEN AUS WIEN
Erich Zeisl und Walter Bricht

Das musikalische Leben in Wien kam nach dem Ende der Habsburgermonarchie und der Abwanderung vieler kreativer Köpfe nach Berlin keineswegs zum Stillstand. 1920 verlegte Franz Schreker seine Kompositionsklasse dorthin, 1925 erhielt Arnold Schönberg eine Berufung und übersiedelte 1926 nach Berlin. Auch andere bedeutende österreichische Musiker:innen erkannten, dass Deutschland mehr Chancen bot als Wien: Hans Gál wurde Direktor des Konservatoriums in Mainz, aus dem später die Hochschule hervorging, während Ernst Toch nach Mannheim und später nach Berlin zog, wo er sich in der neuen Musikszene engagierte. Hanns Eisler ließ Frau und Sohn in Wien zurück, um in Deutschland ein politisch aktiveres Leben zu führen. Selbst renommierte Solist:innen und Dirigent:innen wie Artur Schnabel, Fritz Kreisler und Emanuel Feuermann sahen ihre Zukunft in Berlin. Dennoch blieb Wien ein pulsierendes Musikzentrum.

Berlin mochte die Stadt sein, die man für Unterhaltung, Nachtclubs und visionäre Zukunftsideen besuchte, doch Wien blieb ein Zentrum der klassischen Musikszene – mit einer lebendigen Szene und einem leidenschaftlichen Publikum. Der Unterschied zwischen beiden Städten zeigte sich besonders in den Bemühungen, die Arbeiterschaft für Musik zu begeistern. Während „Arbeiterkonzerte" in Berlin oft mit Agitprop und politisch-didaktischen Bühnenwerken zur ideologischen Erziehung verbunden waren, boten die von David Josef Bach organisierten Wiener „Arbeiterkonzerte" dem erstarkenden Proletariat die Möglichkeit, Beethoven und Mahler zu erleben.

Die Lebensqualität und das musikalische Interesse Wiens waren einzigartig und eng mit der jüdischen Bevölkerung der Stadt verknüpft. Für viele Jüdinnen und Juden bot die Musik einen schnellen Weg zur gesellschaftlichen Akzeptanz und Assimilation. Jüdische Wunderkinder wie der Geiger Bronisław Huberman und der Pianist Alfred Grünfeld legten den Grundstein für ihre Karrieren, gefolgt von Talenten wie Rudolf Serkin, Erich Wolfgang Korngold und Erika Morini. Viele jüdische Zuwanderer aus den östlichen Provinzen der Habsburgermonarchie ließen sich in der Leopoldstadt, dem zweiten Bezirk Wiens, nieder – bekannt als „Matzesinsel". Mit Ehrgeiz, Bildung und beruflichen Qualifikationen gelang es zahlreichen von ihnen, in wohlhabendere bürgerliche Bezirke aufzusteigen.

Mit dem Wegfall der Beschränkungen für jüdische Geschäfte und Berufe nach der Verabschiedung der Dezember Verfassung 1867, blühte die jüdische Gemeinde wirtschaftlich auf – doch zugleich kam es zu antisemitischen Protesten gegen die prunkvollen jüdischen Paläste entlang des Ringstraßenboulevards. Diese imposanten Gebäude gehörten oft Industriellen und Bankiers, die mitunter wohlhabender waren als die kaiserliche Familie oder die alte Aristokratie der Monarchie. Besonders stark war die jüdische Präsenz in den freien Berufen – nicht nur in der Medizin und im Rechtswesen, sondern auch im Journalismus. Viele der bedeutendsten Wiener Zeitungen befanden sich in jüdischem Besitz und wurden von jüdischen Journalist:innen geleitet.

Gustav Mahler, selbst ein zum Katholizismus konvertierter Jude, erkannte, dass ihn wenig mit den jüngst aus dem Osten eingewanderten Schtetl-Juden verband. Diese soziale Kluft spiegelte sich auch innerhalb der jüdischen Gesellschaft Wiens wider, die sich zunehmend in zwei Gruppen teilte: Auf der einen Seite standen wohlhabende, häufig zum Christentum übergetretene und assimilierte Bürger:innen. Auf der anderen Seite, Juden aus traditionelleren Familien, die einfach nach einem besseren Leben für sich und ihre Kinder strebten.

Diese Geschichte handelt von den Komponisten Walter Bricht (1904–1970) und Erich Zeisl (1905–1959), die aus zwei sehr unterschiedlichen jüdischen Gemeinschaften stammten. Ihr Vergleich zeigt, wie unterschiedlich sich Karrieren entwickeln konnten – und wie schnell die vermeintlichen Privilegien wohlhabender jüdischer Familien mit der Machtübernahme der Nationalsozialisten zur Illusion wurden.

Wie erwähnt war für viele ambitionierte Wiener Jüdinnen und Juden die Konversion zum Christentum der erste und wichtigste Schritt zur gesellschaftlichen Akzeptanz. Ein prominentes Beispiel dafür war Gustav Mahler, der mit seiner Entscheidung keineswegs alleinstand. Der Antisemitismus war tief in der Wiener Gesellschaft verwurzelt: Während konvertierte Jüdinnen und Juden in bestimmten Institutionen willkommen waren, blieben sie in privaten und familiären Kreisen oft ausgeschlossen. Viele fanden sich in einem sozialen Umfeld anderer Konvertierter wieder, mit eingeschränkten Heiratsmöglichkeiten und begrenzter sozialer Durchlässigkeit.

Ein Sinnbild für diesen Widerspruch war Alma Schindler, die spätere Alma Mahler. Sie unterhielt intime Beziehungen zu jüdischen Männern, vertrat zugleich aber antisemitische Ansichten. Ihre Beziehungen spiegelten die Faszination des gesellschaftlich Verbotenen wider, während ihre Haltung tiefe Einblicke in die widersprüchliche Seele des Wiener Bürgertums gewährte.

Für wohlhabende jüdische Familien wie die Wittgensteins oder Gallias bedeutete die Konversion oft nur den Anschein von Akzeptanz. Mit Hitlers Aufstieg und der Machtübernahme der Nationalsozialisten zeigte sich jedoch die Fragilität dieser gesellschaftlichen Integration. Schon bald war die jüdische Gemeinschaft – ob konvertiert oder nicht – einem gemeinsamen Schicksal ausgeliefert.

Walter Bricht und Erich Zeisl waren im Abstand von nur einem Jahr geboren und entwickelten sich zu zwei der produktivsten und angesehensten Komponisten Wiens. Brichts familiärer Hintergrund ähnelte jenem von Erich Wolfgang Korngold, dessen Vater, Julius Korngold, einer der einflussreichsten Musikkritiker seiner Zeit war. Auch Walter Brichts Vater, Balduin Bricht, war eine prägende Figur im Wiener Kulturjournalismus: Er arbeitete als Kulturredakteur der konservativen, katholisch geprägten *Österreichischen Volkszeitung*, gründete und leitete den Verein der Musikkritiker Wiens und war zudem Präsident des Concordia-Pensionsfonds, einer Dachorganisation österreichischer Journalist:innen.[1]

Konzertbüro der Wiener Konzerthausgesellschaft

Kleiner Konzerthaus-Saal
Dienstag, den 17. April 1928, halb 8 Uhr abends

II. ABEND
des
KERSCHBAUMER-TRIOS

Edith Wachtel (Klavier)
Erwin Kerschbaumer (Violine)
Ernst Neumann (Cello)

Mitwirkend: **Franz Aschenbrenner** (Viola)

PROGRAMM:

Erich Zeisl . . . . Klavier-Trio-Suite in H-moll
  Präludium
  Adagio sostenuto
  Allegretto scherzando
  Finale (Thema mit Variationen)
  (Uraufführung)

Max Reger . . . . Streich-Trio in A-moll
  Sostenuto (Allegro agitato)
  Larghetto
  Scherzo
  Allegro con moto

Peter Tschaikowsky . . . Klavier-Trio in A-moll
  (Dem Andenken eines großen Künstlers)
  I. Pezzo elegioco
  II. a) Thema con variazioni
     b) Variazione Finale e Coda

Klavier: Bösendorfer

Verlag der Wiener Konzerthausgesellschaft, III., Lothringerstraße 20

Preis 50 GROSCHEN (inkl. Steuer).

Über behördliche Anordnung sind die Damen verhalten, die Hüte abzunehmen!

Ankündigung zur Uraufführung von
Zeisls *Klaviertrio-Suite* mit dem
Kerschbaumer Trio am 17. April 1928
im Wiener Konzerthaus
Archiv des Exilarte Zentrum der mdw,
Wien (A-Weaz)

Brichts Mutter, Agnes Pyllemann, stammte aus einer ebenfalls musikalisch geprägten Familie. Ihr Vater, Franz Pyllemann, war ein angesehener Musikjournalist, während Agnes selbst als hochbegabtes Wunderkind am Klavier galt und von Johannes Brahms geschätzt wurde. Später machte sie sich als Sängerin mit Spezialisierung auf Lied und Oratorium einen Namen. Erst später stellte sich heraus, dass Franz Pyllemann das einzige nicht-jüdische Mitglied der Familie Bricht war. Balduin Brichts Eltern, Katharina Rosenfeld und Samuel Bricht, stammten beide aus jüdischen Familien, konvertierten jedoch nach 1868 zum Christentum.[2] Balduin und Agnes heirateten 1892. Ob diese familiären Hintergründe Walter Bricht überhaupt bewusst waren oder für ihn eine Rolle spielten, bleibt ungewiss.

Zum Zeitpunkt von Walter Brichts Geburt repräsentierte die Verbindung der Familien Bricht und Pyllemann das typische Wiener Bürgertum ehemals jüdischer Familien, in dem Konvertierte meist untereinander heirateten. Vor Hitlers Machtergreifung und im Kontext der liberalen Verfassung von 1867 galt die Konversion als erster Schritt zur gesellschaftlichen Akzeptanz und Assimilation. Die Eheschließung mit anderen Konvertierten wurde nicht als Einschränkung, sondern als weiterer Schritt zu größerer sozialer und beruflicher Anerkennung gesehen.

Erich Zeisl hingegen stammte aus einer kleinbürgerlichen jüdischen Familie, die ein Café in der Nähe des Wiener Nordbahnhofs betrieb – jenem Ort, an dem Schtetl-Juden aus Polen und der heutigen Ukraine in die Stadt kamen. Auch in Zeisls Familie spielte Musik eine wichtige Rolle: Sein Vater sang in einem Männerchor, seine Brüder wurden Sänger. Zeisl studierte bei Joseph Marx, Richard Stöhr und Hugo Kauder, wobei insbesondere Kauder und Stöhr die prägendsten Einflüsse auf seinen musikalischen Werdegang ausübten. Im Gegensatz dazu war Walter Bricht Franz Schmidts bevorzugter Schüler, wie der Pianist Walter Robert berichtete. Der Schmidt-Schüler Walter Tausig erwähnte sogar, dass Schmidt gelegentlich Brichts Rat zu eigenen Kompositionen einholte.

Die unterschiedlichen sozialen Hintergründe der beiden Komponisten spiegelten sich auch in ihren Kreisen wider. Bricht gehörte zur gehobenen Wiener Bourgeoisie und besuchte das renommierte Akademische Gymnasium, das zahlreiche Mitglieder der österreichischen intellektuellen Elite ausgebildet hatte. Sein Vater war wie erwähnt ein prominenter Kulturjournalist, seine Mutter eine angesehene Sängerin, die regelmäßig Konzerte gab – oft begleitet von ihrem Sohn. Auch Brichts Freundes- und Bekanntenkreis bestand fast ausschließlich aus Musiker:innen sowie Anhänger:innen und Studierenden von Franz Schmidt.

Franz Schmidt war ein musikalisches Universalgenie: Er beherrschte Klavier, Orgel und Cello auf Konzertniveau, komponierte und dirigierte zugleich – und verfügte über ein derart feines Gehör, dass er selbst die Tonhöhe von Maschinengeräuschen oder Motoren bestimmen konnte. Seine Schüler:innen bestätigten seine außergewöhnlichen natürlichen Begabungen, doch gerade diese standen seiner Lehrtätigkeit im Weg. Oft war er nicht in der Lage, das Erreichen bestimmter musikalischer Effekte oder die Lösung musiktheoretischer Probleme verständlich zu erklären. Viele Studierende suchten daher Rat, und Walter Bricht wurde zu einem der wichtigsten Berater innerhalb des Schmidt-Kreises. Neben seinem eigenen Studium gab er Unterricht in Interpretation und Komposition.

In diesem Umfeld lernte Bricht seine spätere Frau Ella Kugel kennen. Sie war die Tochter von Georg Kugel, dem Inhaber einer bedeutenden Wiener Konzertdirektion, und eine talentierte Pianistin. Ella spielte die Uraufführung von Brichts *Erstem Klavierkonzert* und sollte auch sein *Zweites Klavierkonzert* mit den Wiener Philharmonikern aufführen. Nach dem „Anschluss" Österreichs wurde die geplante Aufführung jedoch abgesagt.

Auch Erich Zeisl lernte seine spätere Frau, Gertrud Jellinek, über seinen Freundeskreis kennen. Im Gegensatz zu Brichts eher musikzentriertem Umfeld bewegte sich Zeisl jedoch in interdisziplinären Kreisen, die Autor:innen, Maler:innen, Schauspieler:innen und Musiker:innen umfassten. Einer dieser Zirkel trug den Namen „Junge Kunst" und zählte unter anderem den Komponisten Julius Chajes sowie den Geiger Felix Galimir zu seinen Mitgliedern. Die zentrale Figur dieser Gruppe war der Philosoph und Autor Fred Hernfeld, der später im amerikanischen Exil als Alfred Farau bekannt wurde. Zeisl und seine Frau waren zudem Teil eines weiteren Kreises, dem auch die Schriftstellerin Hilde Spiel angehörte. In ihrem Roman *Kati auf der Brücke* verewigte sie Zeisl in einer fiktionalisierten Version. Auch die Malerin Lisel Salzer war Teil dieser intellektuellen Gemeinschaft.

Zwischen den Weltkriegen war Wien weit davon entfernt, ein Zentrum des musikalischen Modernismus zu sein – anders als Berlin, Frankfurt, Köln oder insbesondere Mannheim. Selbst die progressiveren Kräfte in Wien waren nicht darauf ausgerichtet, radikale Umwälzungen oder musikalische Anarchie zu fördern. Mit Ausnahme des Schönberg-Kreises verlief die musikalische Entwicklung weitgehend homogen. Hugo Kauders Abkehr von der diatonischen Tonalität tendierte eher zum Modalen, während die deutsche Bewegung der *Neuen Sachlichkeit* in Wien keine herausragende Rolle spielte. Dennoch war der Wiener „Modernismus" keineswegs statisch – er blieb dynamisch und offen für äußere Einflüsse. Kauders modale Exkursionen spiegelten sich beispielsweise in der englischen pastoralen Musik wider, während der französische Impressionismus und der Neoklassizismus ebenfalls deutliche Spuren in den Wiener Kompositionen der Zwischenkriegszeit hinterließen.

Die dominierenden Kräfte in der Wiener Musikszene blieben jedoch Brahms, Bruckner und Mahler, wobei Schönbergs Zweite Wiener Schule weniger Einfluss hatte, als man heute vielleicht annehmen würde. Dennoch arbeitete Franz Schmidt an Schönbergs *Pierrot lunaire* und probte das Stück, während die Kompositionen von Alban Berg regelmäßig zusammen mit denen von Egon Wellesz und anderen Mitgliedern des Schönberg-Kreises in Aufführungen zu hören waren – nicht zuletzt an der Staatsoper.[3]

Österreich blieb, ob zum Guten oder Schlechten, ein Land zwischen Norden und Süden. Joseph Marx und Franz Schmidt, die beiden prominentesten Komponisten Wiens, repräsentierten diese beiden Pole. Schmidt war ein überzeugter Pan-Germanist und vertrat die Ansicht, dass Bismarck die deutschsprachigen Regionen Österreichs in seine Reichseinigung von 1871 hätte einbeziehen sollen[4] – ein Vorgehen, das Hitler viele Jahrzehnte später zu „korrigieren" versuchte. Schmidt blickte daher nach Norden. Marx, der zur Hälfte Italiener war, brachte mit der Leichtigkeit und Farbigkeit seiner Musik eine österreichische Antwort auf Respighi und verband so den Süden mit dem Norden. Der andere prominente Lehrer jener Zeit, Richard Stöhr, ein

Eine Gastgarten-Runde in Österreich: Links von Zeisl sitzt der Pianist Fritz Kramer, der später Pianist der Comedy Harmonists war. Die Comedy Harmonists waren eine Splittergruppe der ehemaligen Comedian Harmonists.
Archiv des Exilarte Zentrum der mdw, Wien (A-Weaz)

Der angesehene Wiener Komponist
Walter Bricht, ca. 1930
Bricht Family Collection

Brahmsianer, wurde im selben Jahr wie Arnold Schönberg geboren, repräsentierte jedoch eine völlig andere musikalische Epoche.

Es ist wichtig zu verstehen, dass Zeisls Kreis nicht so fortschrittlich war wie die Gruppen in Mannheim oder Berlin, während Brichts Kreis jedoch auch nicht strikt konservativ war. Wien bot weiterhin ein ästhetisches Gegengewicht zu den Entwicklungen in Berlin, und selbst progressive Künstler wie Ernst Krenek, Egon Wellesz, Anton Webern und Alban Berg bevorzugten das Leben in Wien gegenüber dem in Berlin.

Angesichts von Brichts natürlichem Einstieg in das lokale Musikleben ist es nicht überraschend, dass er fast wöchentlich als Dirigent, Pianist, Kammermusiker oder Komponist gefragt war. Er war ein gefragter Begleiter, und sein Ruf wuchs über ein Maß hinaus, das für Zeisl zu dieser Zeit unerreichbar war. Dies verschaffte Bricht internationale Anerkennung. Besonders gefördert wurde er vom deutschen Dirigenten Leopold Reichwein, der jedoch für seine antisemitischen Ansichten bekannt war und sich bereits lange vor der Machtübernahme Hitlers geweigert hatte, Werke von Mendelssohn zu dirigieren. Durch Franz Schmidt lernte Bricht auch den einarmigen Pianisten Paul Wittgenstein kennen, der später bei ihm Kompositionen für die linke Hand in Auftrag gab. Bricht spielte die Orchesterbegleitung von Ravels Konzert für die linke Hand mit Wittgenstein als Solisten bei einer Aufführung des Werkes für den Komponisten selbst.

Bricht war nicht bewusst konservativ, aber er war ein leidenschaftlicher Verfechter der „absoluten Musik" – Musik, die nicht programmatische Intentionen verfolgte oder für das Theater komponiert wurde. Er glaubte – wie auch zuvor der legendäre Musikkritiker Eduard Hanslick –, dass Musik für sich selbst komponiert und gehört werden sollte. Obwohl es in einer Stadt wie Wien immer einen Platz für Oper gegeben hatte, zeigte Bricht kein nennenswertes Interesse daran, für dieses Genre zu schreiben.

Ein weiterer Unterschied zwischen den beiden Komponisten zeigte sich in ihrer öffentlichen Präsenz: Bricht wurde in der Presse über 2000 Mal erwähnt, während Zeisl nur etwa 689 Nennungen verzeichnen konnte.[5] Dennoch wurde Zeisl 1938, kurz vor dem „Anschluss", in der Zeitschrift der RAVAG, *Radio Wien*, mit einem Porträt gewürdigt – eine Medienpräsenz, an die Bricht längst gewöhnt war.

Dieser Essay ist keine ausführliche Biografie der beiden Komponisten, sondern soll die soziale Kluft innerhalb der Wiener jüdischen Gesellschaft anhand der Lebenswege zweier sehr unterschiedlicher, aber durchaus auch ähnlicher Persönlichkeiten verdeutlichen. Zudem zeigt diese Lebensläufe, wie diese Kluft im Jahr 1938 wieder geschlossen wurde. Nichts veranschaulicht diese Divergenz und Konvergenz besser als die unterschiedlichen Emigrationserfahrungen von Bricht und Zeisl. Brichts *Zweites Klavierkonzert* sollte von Clemens Krauss dirigiert und von Ella Kugel mit den Wiener Philharmonikern aufgeführt werden. Als Bricht jedoch vom österreichischen Rundfunk (RAVAG) darüber informiert wurde, dass seine Dienste aufgrund der Überprüfung seiner Abstammung nicht länger gewünscht waren, bot man ihm zunächst den Status eines „Ehrenariers" an – sicherlich vermittelt durch Krauss und Baldur von Schirach, bis hin zu Adolf Hitler persönlich. Bricht lehnte dieses Angebot jedoch ab und konnte dank seiner Kontakte zur amerikanischen Botschaft rasch ein Affidavit sowie ein Visum für die Einreise in die Vereinigten Staaten erhalten.

Auch Zeisl wurde vom „Anschluss" Österreichs an Hitler-Deutschland negativ betroffen, da die Uraufführung seiner

Erich Zeisl mit dem Dirigenten Hugo Strelitzer in der Big Bear Region in Kalifornien, 1953
Archiv des Exilarte Zentrum der mdw, Wien (A-Weaz)

Oper *Leonce und Lena* abgesagt wurde. Zunächst verließen die Familien Zeisl und Jellinek Wien und flüchteten in das benachbarte Baden, wo die Stadtgemeinde sie aufforderte, innerhalb von 48 Stunden die Stadt zu verlassen. Daraufhin emigrierten sie nach Paris. Vor ihrer Abreise schrieb Gertrud an alle „Zeisls" und „Zeisels", die sie in amerikanischen Telefonbüchern finden konnte. Sie erhielten zwar ein Affidavit, das sie nach Paris brachte, aber für die Einreise in die Vereinigten Staaten war es zu schwach, sodass ein weiteres Affidavit beantragt werden musste.

Was danach geschah, ist besonders aufschlussreich. Beide Komponisten gelangten zunächst nach New York, doch während Bricht, der in Wien alle Vorteile des musikalischen Lebens genossen hatte, das Weiterkomponieren als unmöglich empfand, ergriff Zeisl neue Möglichkeiten. Seine Zeit in Paris hatte ihn dazu angeregt, seine jüdische Identität weiterzuentwickeln. In Paris komponierte er eine Bühnenmusik zu *Hiob*, einem Stück basierend auf Joseph Roths gleichnamigem Roman. Zeisl wurde mit der schmerzhaften Realität konfrontiert, dass Hitler ihn, obwohl er sich selbst als Kind der deutschen Kultur betrachtete, weder als Deutschen noch als Österreicher anerkannte. Dieser Verlust einer nationalen Identität führte dazu, dass Zeisl, als er an *Hiob* arbeitete, erkannte, dass er dennoch auf seine jüdische Identität zurückgreifen konnte – ein Rückhalt, den er zuvor nicht in dieser Weise wahrgenommen hatte.

Zeisl verbrachte die Kriegsjahre in Hollywood, wo er als Studiomusiker arbeitete. Nach dem Krieg fühlte er sich befreit genug, um seine künstlerischen Ambitionen weiterzuentwickeln und Musik zu komponieren, die einen „jüdischen" Charakter trug, ohne dabei auf offensichtliche folkloristische oder liturgische Modelle zurückzugreifen. Vielleicht war es seine Erfahrung mit Kauder, die ihm die Welt des modalen Komponierens näherbrachte, auch wenn Zeisl modale Elemente verwendete, ohne aktiv von der Diatonik abzuweichen.

Für Walter Bricht war es tragisch, dass ihm eine Identität fehlte, auf die er hätte zurückgreifen können. Er erkannte, dass er, ähnlich wie Zeisl, weder als Deutscher noch als Österreicher wahrgenommen wurde und auch nicht als Amerikaner galt, obwohl er dies erwartet hatte. Seine Ankunft in den USA, die zunächst mit der Hoffnung auf weiteren Erfolg verbunden war, spiegelte schließlich mehr Parallelen zur Situation seines nicht-jüdischen Exilkollegen Ernst Krenek wider, der Amerika als „ohne Echo" erlebte. Wie bei Krenek zerbrach auch Brichts Ehe, und der ehemals gefeierte Musiker, der als Komponist von Ruhm und sofortiger Anerkennung geprägt war, wurde zu einer musikalischen Koryphäe an einem Provinzcollege.

Zeisl und Bricht teilten die Liebe zum Kunstlied, doch nach ihrer Vertreibung aus Österreich kehrten beide nie wieder signifikant zu diesem Genre zurück, da es für sie den Verlust ihrer kulturellen Identität symbolisierte. Bricht komponierte 1940 vier Lieder, doch verzichtete er darauf, ihnen Opuszahlen zuzuweisen. Wie Zeisl kehrte er nie zu diesem Genre zurück. In den Jahren 1940 und 1942 entstanden noch eine Klaviersonate und ein Trio für Paul Wittgenstein – seine letzten Kompositionen, bis er in den letzten Jahren seines Lebens Kammermusik für den Sohn seiner ehemaligen Frau Ella Kugel, einen Flötisten, schrieb. Zeisl hingegen nahm die neuen Möglichkeiten wahr und setzte seinen Weg fort, auf der Suche nach einer Synthese zwischen seiner neuen Heimat und seiner persönlichen jüdischen Identität.

1 https://data.onb.ac.at/nlv_lex/perslex/B/Bricht_Balduin.htm (abgerufen am 8.12.2024).
2 Siehe Anna Staudacher, „... meldet den Austritt aus dem mosaischen Glauben". 18000 Austritte aus dem Judentum in Wien. 1868–1914: Namen, Quellen, Daten, New York-Frankfurt/Main 2009, S. 81.
3 Arnold Schönberg: *Gurrelieder*, Aufführungen an der Staatsoper am 12. und 13. Juni, 1920; Ernst Krenek: *Jonny spielt auf*, Premiere an der Staatsoper am 31. Dez. 1927; Alban Berg: *Wozzeck*, Premiere an der Staatsoper am 4. April 1930; Egon Wellesz: *Die Bakchantinnen*, UA an der Staatsoper am 20. Juni 1931.
4 https://archive.org/details/handbuch-ns-musiker-prieberg, S. 6601 (abgerufen am 1. 3. 2025).
5 https://anno.onb.ac.at/anno-suche/simple?query=%22Erich%20Zeisl%22&from=1 (abgerufen am 1. 3. 2025).

Erich Zeisl, 1950er-Jahre
Archiv des Exilarte Zentrum der mdw, Wien (A-Weaz)

Barbara Zeisl-Schoenberg, E. Randol Schoenberg (the grandson of Arnold Schoenberg and Eric Zeisl) and Ronald Schoenberg in Brentwood, Los Angeles, 2016
Photo © E. Randol Schoenberg

E. Randol Schoenberg

THE CONVERGENCE OF SCHOENBERG AND ZEISL

As I was named after both my grandfathers—Eric being my legal first name, but called Randy after my middle name, Randol, an anagram of Arnold—I felt a strong desire to come closer to them, to listen to their music and learn about their stories. Born in 1966, years after both men had died, I of course never had a chance to form any individual firsthand impressions of my grandfathers. My parents Barbara Zeisl-Schoenberg and Ronald Schoenberg were only teenagers when their fathers died and therefore also weren't in much of a position to pass on more than anecdotes. This forced me to seek further information from experts and scholars, and especially from the music and other works that my grandfathers had left behind. Whereas Schoenberg naturally was a dominant presence in our household, especially after we moved into the family's Spanish tile-roofed house in Brentwood Park in 1972, the fact that I only had one remaining grandparent, my maternal grandmother Gertrud Zeisl[1], served as a counterbalance of sorts. Unlike so many musical adherents, I felt no need to pick sides, and as a result I developed a relatively open ear, able to appreciate all their music, regardless of the style of composition.

This attitude I may have inherited (or been taught) by my parents and especially my maternal grandmother, who was herself an admirer of Schoenberg's music, as well as her husband's. In her diary entry of November 2, 1945, she recounted the first meeting between my two grandfathers, on an evening at the home of the Berlin-born violin dealer and collector Erich Lachmann[2] and his Belgian wife Nora:

> We met Schoenberg during an evening at the Lachmanns'. It was really an event about which I was so excited that I had dreamed about it the night before. I was incredibly eager to see in person the man who has sparked so much controversy, even between Eric and me. It was a big surprise, and meeting him in person completely changed both of our perspectives on this "phenomenon" (because that is what he actually is). He is a good man. He burns with an electricity that flickers like a flame and naturally pulls you closer, though he also delivers shocks that only fools find terrible. Yet these shocks are invigorating, perhaps even healing, like a force of nature. He is a fascinating person who speaks with a strong Viennese or rather, more Austrian accent, and in both his manner and appearance, he does not come across as Jewish at all. The exaggerated quality in him is not, as one might assume, Talmudic scholarship, but rather the abundant patience of a woodcarver who painstakingly whittles out delicate ornaments and designs from the densest materials. He is communicative and shares his wealth of knowledge gen-

erously, without reservation. The price of this is that he also says things that he probably doesn't really mean. Why people don't understand this is beyond me. Norman Wright and some other Americans felt antagonized and offended. When someone pours out their heart so freely, their bitterness inevitably spills out as well. That is why he rants critically about America. Yet he is not as conceited as they think, when he says, "You do not understand my music, and you do not deserve that I appear before you." Yet, only moments earlier, he said about himself, "I don't know anything; with every work I have to start over again." When Eric asked him, "Why do you compose a fourfold double canon if it can't even be heard?" he replied, "In order to satisfy my internal logic." What a statement! Eric went home deeply inspired by this encounter and began a ballet based on Maurice Dekobra's text Uranium 235. For six weeks, the magical electric force emanating from this man helped him overcome every emotional obstacle and self-doubt until his new work was complete. It was a work in which he managed to shed many weaknesses and created large structural arcs. It displays a level of accomplishment that if he continues on this path, will undoubtedly place him among the masters.[3]

Although both were born in Vienna, and even attended the same school in the second district, my grandfather Zeisl had little chance of meeting Schoenberg before coming to Los Angeles. Schoenberg was a generation older, just three years younger than Zeisl's father Siegmund (who also attended the Realschule in Vereinsgasse 21 at the same time as Schoenberg). From 1920, when Zeisl enrolled at age fifteen, his principal composition teacher in the Vienna State Academy was Richard Stöhr[4], a conservative proudly in the anti-modern camp. In 1905, Stöhr had proclaimed, "I'm a composer of the present time, I don't understand the modern development [...]."[5] Stöhr, who later called Zeisl "without any exaggeration the most gifted student I ever had,"[6] clearly would not have encouraged Zeisl to go in Schoenberg's direction, even if the teenage lieder-composer had been so inclined, which he clearly was not. When Schoenberg finally left Vienna for Berlin in January 1926, Zeisl was only twenty years old. After a brief period studying with Joseph Marx[7], Zeisl approached Hugo Kauder[8], formerly a violinist with Schoenberg's Society for Private Musical Performances, to gain confidence writing chamber music. This resulted in the completion of his *First String Quartet* (ca. 1930–1933). However, by the time Zeisl began to get some recognition in Vienna—for example, the comprehensive and very favorable review in *Radio Wien*[9] by Paul Amadeus Pisk[10], founding secretary of Schoenberg's Society, concerning a broadcast of Zeisl's *First String Quartet* by the Galimir Quartet[11]—Schoenberg had already fled to America. Apparently, some tactless comments against twelve-tone music led to Zeisl being dismissed by Universal Edition's Erwin Stein[12], a loyal Schoenberg pupil, but the publisher did ultimately relent, approving the appearance of Zeisl's string orchestra arrangement of his first quartet's *Scherzo and Fugue* in 1937, just months before on March 12, 1938, the Nazi annexation of Austria or "Anschluss" eliminated all further possibilities for publications or performances.[13]

It was only after his escape from Vienna the day after surviving the "Kristallnacht" pogrom of November 9, 1938, that Zeisl began to encounter people who could bring him closer to Schoenberg and his circle. The first of these was Alma Mahler-Werfel[14], who saw Zeisl writing music in a Paris café

Getrud Zeisl's diary entry from November 2, 1945 in which she relates the first encounter between Arnold Schoenberg and Eric Zeisl at the home of the former Berlin violin dealer and collector, Erich Lachmann.
Archiv des Exilarte Zentrum der mdw, Wien (A-Weaz)

November 5

und naturgemäss Schläge versetzt, die man die Summen als schmerzhaft empfinden, denn [strikethrough] ohne schlag belehrend und vielleicht sogar heilend wie Naturkräfte. Eine faszinierende

November 6

Mensch. Er spricht sehr stark mit Wiener bezw. mehr Oesterreichischem Akzent und wirkt in seiner ganzen Erscheinung überhaupt nicht jüdisch. Das Hervorspringende an ihm ist nicht

November 7

eigentlich wie man vermutet talmudische Gelehrsamkeit sondern viel mehr die unselige Geduld des Holzschnitzers der aus dem spröden Material die feinsten Zierate und Falten weiss herausbastelt. Er ist mitteilsam

November 8

und gibt von den Schicksalen seines Erdenlebens rückhaltslos. Der Preis ist, dass es einerlei ob ich zu sagen habe, was er gar nicht meint. Diese die Menschen dies nicht verstehen. Norman wusste es

November 9

einige andere (Amerikaner) waren prompt antagonisiert und beleidigt. Wenn eines seiner Verse so freigebig ausschüttet, kommt eben auch die Bitterheit der Jahre mit heraus. Deshalb schimpft er auch

November 10

Amerika. Sonst ist es nicht ungebildet wie sie meinen, wenn er sagt: Sie verstehen meine Musik nicht. Sie verdienen nicht das ich vor ihnen erscheine. Denn wenige Augenblicke vorher sagt er auf sich selbst: Ich kann gar nichts, jedes Werk muss ich von neuem beginnen

November 11

Als Erich ihn fragt Warum machen Sie einen 4 fachen Doppelkanon wenn man ihn doch nicht hören kann. Das ist zur Befriedigung der inneren Logik

November 12

sagt er. Welch ein Wort Erich ging nach beschenkt damit nach Hause. Er begann ein Ballet nach Maurice Schobes's Text Manuskript 235 Durch 6 Wochen hielt die

November 13

magische elektrische Kraft die von diesem Manne ausgeht an. Er machte über sehen alle Klippen und Zweifel Gefühle bis sein neues Grosses Werk fertig entstanden war. Ein

November 14

Werk in dem viele Schönheiten aufgespeichert sind, Die Grosse Bogen in der Form Gesang und ein Können tritt jetzt hast ihn wenn er auf diesem Wege fortschreitet in die November Gruppe endgültig Aufnahme finden lassen wird.

November 16

Arnold Schoenberg in Brentwood, Los Angeles, 1948
Photo: Richard Fish, Arnold Schönberg Center
Privatstiftung, Wien (A-Was)

Eric Zeisl in Los Angeles, c. 1955
Archiv des Exilarte Zentrum der mdw, Wien (A-Weaz)

and immediately befriended him. According to my grandmother, Alma said after hearing Zeisl play some of his music, "You are a tonal nature, just like Schoenberg is an atonal one." Through Mahler-Werfel, the Zeisls were introduced to the French composer Darius Milhaud[15], who had visited Schoenberg with Francis Poulenc in Mödling, a small town just outside Vienna, already in 1922. The Schoenbergs had spent the evening of October 21, 1933, in Paris with the Milhauds just three days before their departure to New York. Now, five years later, Milhaud found Zeisl a piano, offered him concert tickets, protected his refugee status, and opened many doors for work and social engagement during his time in Paris. Later, after settling in Oakland near San Francisco, the Milhauds often visited Southern California, where they would spend time with both the Zeisls and the Schoenbergs, sometimes one for lunch and the other for dinner.

In New York since October 1939, Zeisl's search for work opportunities led him to write to Erwin Piscator (1893–1966) at the New School for Social Research. A reply letter came from the composer Hanns Eisler[16], a former Schoenberg pupil, who soon became a friend and encouraged Zeisl to move to Hollywood. On May 28, 1942 Eisler even wrote a letter of introduction for Zeisl to give to Schoenberg. "Mr Eric Zeisl, a truly talented composer (refugee from Vienna), wishes to work with you. Allow me to introduce him to you."[17] Zeisl didn't use the letter of introduction. The war years between 1941 and 1944 were consumed with a battle for work in the studios, where Zeisl never gained a real foothold despite contributing music for at least twenty films.

In 1944, Zeisl wrote a disturbing essay against Schoenberg and atonal music. We do not know what led him to write the piece, which was never published. He sent a copy to his old

Darius Milhaud in exile in California. The photo carries the inscription
„To Trudi, Erich and Barbara
Souvenir de Vienne Paris
Hollywood. San Francisco
Milhaud"
Archiv des Exilarte Zentrum der mdw, Wien (A-Weaz)

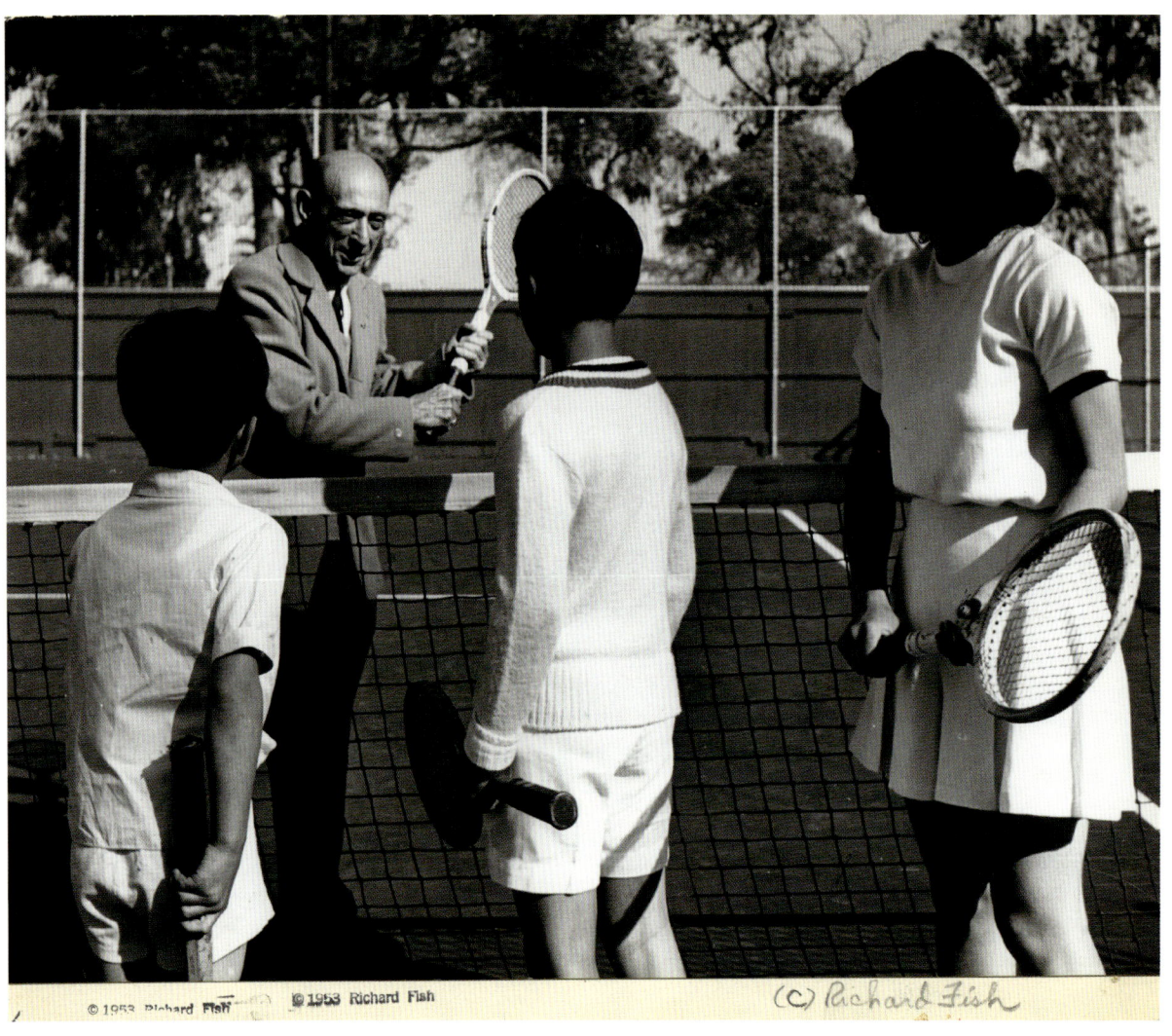

Arnold Schoenberg at the tennis court with his children Lawrence, Ronald and Nuria, Santa Monica, 1948
Photo: Richard Fish, Arnold Schönberg Center Privatstiftung, Wien (A-Was)

professor Richard Stöhr, by then living in exile in Vermont. Stöhr's response was disapproving, reminding Zeisl that there are different perspectives and that a person's attitude to a particular composition, even one's own, can change over time. Perhaps experience had also softened Stöhr's attitude toward modern music. It also appears from the letter that my grandparents had had an argument about Schoenberg's music, and Stöhr was defending my grandmother's position.

> As long as you believe in a single possible perspective for viewing a work of art, Trude's standpoint must appear to you either 1.) as hypocrisy or 2.) as a lack of "understanding." Both are incorrect. Now, this is my view based on my experiences of 35 years of teaching, particularly regarding the attitudes of the younger generation toward the new, Schoenbergian direction. Among the progressive-minded, I found two groups (excluding here those who already were inclined towards the "classical"): The radical group tolerated music from the past purely from an intellectual perspective, as a necessary but now outdated stage of development. Their hearts, however, belonged entirely to the new direction. The other group was more conservatively inclined. For them, Beethoven and Brahms still meant something for their emotional lives. But, in contrast to the first group, they were never intellectually drawn to Schoenberg and his artistic intentions. You see, then, two different perspectives. I believe your wife firmly belongs to the latter group, because through her marriage to you and your own music, she is more deeply rooted emotionally than a radical admirer of Schoenberg (such as Erw [Erwin] Stein at U.[niversal] E.[dition] for instance).—But in no case should you speak here of right and wrong.[18]

Although Stöhr's letter is undated, his subsequent letter of March 20, 1945, refers to the previous letter as having been sent around Christmas, although Zeisl had failed to respond to it when he sent Stöhr a copy of his newly completed *Requiem Ebraico*. So this dispute over Schoenberg in 1944 was clearly in the background when the two composers first met one year later in November 1945.

Zeisl's *Requiem Ebraico, Psalm 92* of 1944/45 also offers another point of contact between the two composers. The work was commissioned by Rabbi Jacob Sonderling (1878–1964), the same rabbi who had commissioned Schoenberg's *Kol Nidre* in 1938. Sonderling was born in Silesia and emigrated to the United States in 1923 after serving as a German army chaplain in the First World War. In Los Angeles, he founded the Society for Jewish Culture-Fairfax Temple, which catered to the German-speaking immigrant community. Along with Schoenberg and Zeisl, he commissioned a *Passover Psalm* from Erich Wolfgang Korngold[19] and the *Cantata of the Bitter Herbs* from Ernst Toch[20]. The premiere of the *Requiem Ebraico* (organ version) took place on April 18, 1945, as part of an interfaith forum led by Rabbi Sonderling, with the Fairfax Temple choir under the direction of Hugo Strelitzer[21] with Norman Söreng Wright[22] (1905–1982) on the organ. Zeisl's younger brother William (1907–1972), who was the cantor of the Fairfax Temple, sang the baritone part.[23]

The *Requiem Ebraico* is Zeisl's most performed work. It holds a singular place as the very first musical work dedicated to the victims of the Holocaust. The work's title is certainly unusual (from a Jewish perspective) and led to objections from Zeisl's publisher, Joseph Freudenthal of Transcontinental Music Publishers. But Zeisl insisted, arguing in a letter of October 16, 1945, "The Jews need a requiem so let's try to give

Three composers in Hollywood exile: Eric Zeisl, Alexandre Tansman and Mario Castelnuovo-Tedesco, c. 1945
Archiv des Exilarte Zentrum der mdw, Wien (A-Weaz)

it to them." Zeisl had never converted from Judaism but had early in his composing career occupied himself with a *Kleine Messe* (1932) and then a *Requiem Concertante* (1934). The title therefore reflects Zeisl's belief that, despite the absence of a Latin Catholic text, his Hebrew psalm setting fit into the great musical tradition in the same manner as Brahms's *Ein deutsches Requiem*.

The orchestral version of the *Requiem Ebraico*[24] was performed in Los Angeles on April 17, 1949, conducted by Adolf Heller[25] with the choir of the First African Methodist Episcopalian Church and soloists Ruth Henry, Susan Corey, and Stephen Kemalyan. The texts were sung in English. Radio station KFWB broadcast the performance as part of the Contemporary Chamber Music Series, and it is preserved on record with an introduction by an American radio announcer. It was very likely this performance that led to an anecdote involving Julius Toldi and my two grandfathers.

Julius Toldi (1891–1965) studied violin with Vienna Philharmonic concertmaster Arnold Rosé (1863–1946) and composition with Franz Schreker (1878–1934). He was one of a number of students who celebrated Schoenberg's birthday (and the engagement of his daughter Trudi to Felix Greissle) in Traunkirchen in September 1921. In May 1940, Schoenberg wrote a recommendation letter for Toldi to lecture at Occidental College, calling him "one of my best and talented former pupils."[26] Toldi ultimately worked for the classical music radio station KFWB and was friendly with both the Schoenbergs and the Zeisls. His radio program "Music of Today" was broadcast on Sunday afternoons, and the members of the émigré music community were of course avid listeners. The story told by my grandmother was that one day Toldi came over to the Zeisls so full of excitement he could hardly speak. He said he had just come from Brentwood and that Schoenberg had heard the *Requiem Ebraico* and said that he liked it very, very much. Toldi was beside himself, "completely flustered and flabbergasted" as my grandmother recalled, because he did not understand how Schoenberg could have said something so unexpected about a tonal work. The moral of the story, as my grandmother relayed it to us, was that Schoenberg's disciples were often much more doctrinaire than their master, unwilling to even consider the possibility that a tonal work could be worthwhile, whereas Schoenberg himself, the true master, understood that it was the musical idea, not the style, that was important. Schoenberg had recognized in Zeisl's *Requiem Ebraico* the music of an accomplished composer. At the very least, the counterpoint in the concluding fugue must have impressed him greatly.

Later that year, the Zeisls were among the many who sent a congratulatory telegram to Schoenberg on his seventy-fifth birthday on September 13, 1949: "Many happy returns on this historic day to one of the most fascinating appearances of the spiritual world in great admiration."[27] In return Schoenberg sent his mimeographed birthday letter "To become recognized only after one's death ...!" That same month Zeisl was appointed to teach the composition classes at Los Angeles City College. The appointment was announced in the *Los Angeles Times* on September 18, 1949, on the same page as an article previewing the Schoenberg birthday concert that kicked off the twelfth season of the city's premiere contemporary music venue Evenings on the Roof with *Pierrot Lunaire*. Zeisl had his only appearance at Evenings on the Roof just the previous year, playing his *Kinderlieder* (1930/31) with the soprano Brunetta Mazzolini. The songs were the hit of the evening, singled out during the concert by a call for an encore performance, as well as in the glowing review by *Los Angeles Times* music critic Albert Goldberg ("As always in such programs a few numbers seemed to stand out well above the rest")[28]. The fact that Zeisl was never programmed again on Evenings on the Roof was attributed to jealousy by my grandmother.

In May 1950, Goldberg published a three-part series on "The Transplanted Composer," which discussed the question whether emigration had hindered the compositional process. The first article featured Igor Stravinsky (1882–1971), Schoenberg, and Mario Castelnuovo-Tedesco (1895–1968).[29] Stravinsky, whose social circle Zeisl had joined, rejected the question out of hand. Schoenberg is quoted tersely responding "If immigration to America has changed me—I am not aware of it." But Castelnuovo-Tedesco, with whom Zeisl, upon his arrival in Hollywood, had lived through the sufferings of unnamed studio composers at MGM, answered more fulsomely that the difficulty of overcoming the obstacles of "expatriation (and under tragic circumstances) was a bitter test, from which I suffered, at the beginning, almost physically." After the middle installment,[30] featuring Ernst Krenek[31] and Eugene Zádor[32], Goldberg's final contribution focused on Zeisl, the film composer Miklós Rózsa (1907–1995; no friend of Zeisl, he later managed to strip away a film commission for *A Time to Love and a Time to Die* that Korngold had helped Zeisl to obtain), and Béla Bartók (1881–1945), the source being a letter from Bartók to Zádor of July 1, 1945. Zeisl's response to Goldberg's prompt is quite the opposite of Schoenberg's:

> Speaking for myself, I find that the events of my life and the consequent strife caused by my immigration to America had indeed a *very deep* effect on my work, but one which I feel has brought me the strongest possible artistic impulses rather than frustrations; to the point that I feel that I might never have written my best were it not for the great emotional strife of my uprooting.[33]

Searching through the news archives from those years (see newspapers.com) reveals further examples of the parallel lives of the two composers: On March 6, 1948, an announcement appeared in the *Los Angeles Evening Citizen News* of the plan of Egon Newman (1894–1950, born Neumann in Mödling, a second cousin once removed of my grandmother Gertrud Schoenberg) to establish a graduate music school: "Arnold Schoenberg, Erich Zeisl and Norman Soreng Wright will be among the faculty members, while Erich Korngold and Fritz Reiner may also teach at the school when it opens." (Nothing came of the plans, and Newman apparently committed suicide in Mexico City soon thereafter.) In the following year, the same page of the Sunday, November 27, 1949, edition of the *Los Angeles Times* included articles on both Schoenberg's upcoming lecture "My Evolution" at UCLA and the world premiere of Zeisl's *Songs for the Daughter of Jephtha* (1948), along with the West-Coast premiere of Stravinsky's *Mass* (1948) at the Wilshire Ebell Theater. The announcement of Zeisl's *Requiem Ebraico* broadcast on April 17 of that same year was placed next to an article on the revival of the Los Angeles Chapter of the International Society for Contemporary Music chaired by Ernst Krenek, which was already planning an all-Schoenberg concert for the composer's seventy-fifth birthday, featuring the *Ode to Napoleon Bonaparte*, op. 41. On June 10, 1950, the news was about upcoming radio broadcasts of Schoenberg's *Herzgewächse*, op. 20, by the young soprano Marni Nixon

Music

Los Angeles Times — SUNDAY, MAY 14, 1950 — Part IV — 5

The SOUNDING BOARD
By ALBERT GOLDBERG

The Transplanted Composer

[This is the first article in a series of three].

A distinguished composer of European birth who has been working in the United States for some 10 years recently made the statement to this department that he believed the work of most European composers had changed since they lost contact with their native countries and the music the majority of them had written here did not equal that which they had previously composed.

He further made the statement that, although he was sincerely grateful for the opportunities he had had in the United States, he felt that here he was "a little below his proper level."

Wondering if this feeling was common among European composers who have settled here a request was sent to a number of prominent composers asking them to state frankly the difficulties they have experienced in adjusting themselves to life in a new country—taking into consideration the different attitude toward creative musicians, the difficulty of obtaining performances, whether separation from the homeland has affected the character and quality of their work, or any other pertinent factors.

The replies received form an interesting symposium of opinion on a subject that has sometimes been widely debated but upon which the composers, to our knowledge, have not previously expressed themselves.

Igor Stravinsky writes:

"I think that your conversationalist, who felt himself 'a little below his proper level' in composing music out of his native country, would better abstain from generalizations. Besides, this argument, used mostly by the Soviets against their emigrants, is anything but new and was in the history of art brilliantly refuted by such famous names as Poussin, Handel, Gogol, Chopin, Picasso and a number of others.

"So, contrary to your feeling, I do not think that this subject is really worth a column of your pen."

Arnold Schoenberg writes:

"When for eight months I lived in Barcelona, finishing the second act of my opera, 'Moses and Aaron,' a Spanish musician wondered whether climate and character of this country might not refresh my mind to replace the somber aspect of my music by lively, gay and light colors.

"I asked whether he would expect me to write another style as often as I live in a different country; extremely cold in Alaska or Siberia, very hot near the equator, damp in the jungles and so forth.

"If immigration to America has changed me—I am not aware of it. Maybe I would have finished the third act of 'Moses and Aaron' earlier. Maybe I would have written more when remaining in Europe, but I think; nothing comes out, what was not in. And two times two equals four in every climate. Maybe I had four times four times harder to work for a living. But I made no concessions to the market."

Mario Castelnuovo-Tedesco writes:

"When your letter arrived I was just reading in Albert Einstein's recent book 'Out of My Later Years' the following words:

"'The bitter and the sweet come from the outside, the hard from within, from one's own efforts. For the most part I do the thing which my own nature drives me to.'

"This answers, as far as I am concerned, your very interesting inquiry about the problem of adjustment for the European composers now living in this country; a problem of which I have thought many times and of which I have had experience myself.

"I cannot speak for any of my colleagues but (in spite of what your informer stated) I wouldn't say that the works which the leading European composers (here resident for the last decade or more) have written during this period are in any sense different from or inferior to those which they wrote 10 or 15 years ago.

Personal Reasons Seen

"If sometimes they are of a lesser quality I don't think it is because of the change of environment, but for personal, intimate, aesthetic reasons. And, after all, even the greatest composers of the past (with the exception of perhaps Palestrina, Bach, Mozart and Chopin) had their ups and downs, including the great Beethoven and the divine Schubert.

"As for my own experience, expatriation (and under tragic circumstances) was a bitter test from which I suffered, at the beginning, almost physically. But morally I never felt 'cut off;' my Jewish ancestry and my Latin culture were a wealth which I had acquired once and for all; which were within me forever, which I never tried to forget, to dismiss or to minimize.

"On the other hand America gave me something I didn't have before (or perhaps I hadn't fully developed); a greater sense of freedom and a better understanding of social conditions and of community life.

Adjustment Takes Time

"Adjustment, of course, is a slow and difficult process, which requires patience, good will and (above all) time! From the practical standpoint I had some hard times getting organized; I had often to deal, as everybody else, I believe, with the difficult temper of conductors, with the vanity of performers, with the superficiality of critics, with the inconsistency of agents, with the erratic policies of publishers, and (here in Hollywood) with the peculiar requirements of the movie industry.

"Yet these, no matter how unpleasant, are just minor factors as far as creative life is concerned; the artist can't overlook them but he has to 'overlive' them! And I don't think they affected my personality as a composer or my beliefs in any sense.

Natural Trend Rules

"'Adjustment,' artistically speaking, shouldn't mean 'opportunism' or obedience to transitory fashions. I believe that only by following sincerely and honestly my natural trend can I bring some contribution, no matter how modest, to musical art; and it is in this direction that all my efforts are concentrated.

"All in all today (at 55) I can sincerely tell you that I feel perfectly at peace with myself and with my environment; mainly because, no matter how difficult the external circumstances were, I remained faithful to myself and to my own beliefs."

Other composers to be heard from in this series will include Ernst Krenek, Eugene Zador, Miklos Rozsa, Eric Zeisl, as well as a hitherto unpublished letter of Bela Bartok bearing on the subject.

COMPOSERS IN SYMPOSIUM—Igor Stravinsky, Arnold Schoenberg and Mario Castelnuovo-Tedesco (from left to right) express opinions on situation of emigre composers, in first of a series of articles in adjoining Sounding Board column.

1950

On May 14, 1950, Albert Goldberg wrote about Igor Stravinsky, Arnold Schoenberg and Mario Castelnuovo-Tedesco in his article for the *Los Angeles Times*, "The Transplanted Composer".
Archiv des Exilarte Zentrum der mdw, Wien (A-Weaz)

Music

4 Part IV—SUNDAY, MAY 28, 1950 · Los Angeles Times

The SOUNDING BOARD

By ALBERT GOLDBERG

The Transplanted Composer
(The last of a series of three articles)

The problems of the European composer who has settled in this country have already been discussed in this series from various viewpoints by Igor Stravinsky, Arnold Schoenberg, Mario Castelnuovo-Tedesco, Ernst Krenek and Eugene Zador.

Today two more composers of European origin add their comments and by way of conclusion we publish for the first time a letter from the late Bela Bartok expressing his longing to return to his native Hungary, a wish that was never to be gratified.

Miklos Rozsa writes:

"The problem you raise is certainly interesting and vital for us composers of European descent. Let me try to explain what the composer of European background is lacking in the new humus in which he finds himself transplanted.

"I agree that something is missing on the musical scene of this country; something of the bubbling, fertile and germinating artistic atmosphere of prewar Europe, that gave inspiration to so many masterpieces. Many great works came into being as a result of spurning commissions and from the sheer impetus that one derives from the fact of being wanted.

Composer Isolated

"In no country have I found the contemporary and progressive composer more apart from the public than in this one. There is virtually no public demand for new music and the public is entirely satisfied with the thousand-times-heard old warhorses, where it feels comfortable and doesn't have to strain its brains in hearing something new. This negative attitude naturally reflects on the performer will perform a few new works—for political reasons preferably of American-born composers or well-established 'names'—and with this their duty toward new music is done.

Works' Lives Differ

"A successful new performance in Europe meant immediate offers from several publishers and a great number of follow-up performances in all the capital cities, radios and also smaller orchestras in every country. In America, each work dies after each performance, no matter how well the public or critics liked it. To find a publisher is a great rarity, and to secure a new performance you need to know the conductor personally and 'work on him' until he succumbs and promises a performance—providing you have the stomach and energy to do so!

"The impetus derived from the feeling that one is in demand is completely missing here and the inner urge of creation must completely replace the outward rewards of clamorous success. For the composer of European background this naturally means a complete readjustment of mental attitude toward his art, but I don't really think that it should impair the quality of his work. One might write less, but one might become more critical as every work and every performance starts to count.

"I could not change this even if I wanted to; it would only mean that I was trying to create from the surface rather than the core of my memories.

"I state this frankly in the face of recent tendencies in this country, in which America looks only for the image of her own features in art. America can find in my work not her own image mirrored, but she can find there strong medicines against the ills of fate, which I have learnt to brew and which she may need one day. They are hers."

A Bela Bartok Letter:

The letter from Bela Bartok is published by courtesy of Eugene Zador, to whom the composer wrote from Lake Saranac, N.Y., under date of July 1, 1945. This was less than three months before Bartok's death in New York on Sept. 26 of that year. He died in neglect and straitened circumstances just as he was on the threshold of the universal recognition which has since been accorded his work, and the letter is a poignant work, but one which I feel has brought me the strongest possible artistic impulses rather than frustrations; to the point that I feel that I might never have written my best were it not for the great emotional strife of my uprooting.

"I am generally of the opinion that the artist as an individual is always unhappy and maladjusted to his society and that it is this very maladjustment and despair which prompts him to dig so deeply into the hidden resources of his soul, to find there new faith and strength for his weaknesses.

"The more harassed he is, the stronger the medicines with which he will come up for his own benefit and the benefit of mankind. (See Beethoven, Mozart, Wagner, etc.) Longing, nostalgia, loneliness and strife, I would know of no better nourishment for the artist's soul, and we have in proof the fact that the world's most beautiful works of art and music have frequently been created in exile and far from home. (Wagner, Chopin, Stravinsky, Hindemith, etc.)

Restriction Felt

"There is to be felt, however, a definite restriction not in quality but in quantity of creative output because of lesser opportunities as against the old world.

"In other respects the difference of environment should not be overrated in its effect on an artist of maturity. As old as he may grow the artist will usually be tapping the emotional resources of his memory of early childhood and youth for his creative work.

"They will forever be decisive factors in his work. I came to America in my early thirties; that is probably still young enough to undergo subtle changes of my personality. On the whole, however, I was a finished product of the old world..."

COMPOSERS EXPRESS VIEWS—Eric Zeisl, left, and Miklos Rozsa comment on situation of European composer in America, in adjoining Sounding Board column.

MUSIC MAIL BOX

...for the image of her own features in art. America can find in my work not her own image mirrored, but she can find there strong medicines against the ills of fate, which I have learnt to brew and which she may need one day. They are hers."

A Bela Bartok Letter:

The letter from Bela Bartok is published by courtesy of Eugene Zador, to whom the composer wrote from Lake Saranac, N.Y., under date of July 1, 1945. This was less than three months before Bartok's death in New York on Sept. 26 of that year. He died in neglect and straitened circumstances just as he was on the threshold of the universal recognition which has since been accorded his work, and the letter is a poignant reminder of the composer's unhappiness and his nostalgia for his native land.

Bela Bartok writes:

"The news coming from Hungary is extremely depressing: there's awful destruction, poverty, and the threat of chaos. A local Hungarian Communistic newspaper gets—obviously through the Russian embassy—a number of Hungarian papers which they reprint in facsimile; other people get news through private sources).

"As I see the situation today, we can't think of going home. It wouldn't even be possible: no transportation and no (Russian) permission. But, even if there were a possibility, in my opinion it is more advisable to await developments. God knows how many years it will last until the country can recover, if at all. And how much I would like to go home, but forever..."

Works' Lives Differ

"A successful new performance in Europe meant immediate offers from several publishers and a great number of follow-up performances in all the capital cities, radios and also smaller orchestras in every country. In America, each work dies after each performance, no matter how well the public or critics liked it. To find a publisher is a great rarity, and to secure a new performance you need to know the conductor personally and 'work on him' until he succumbs and promises a performance—providing you have the stomach and energy to do so!

Many Dilute Art

"There is, however, a danger, a pitfall, into which many European composers now living in this country have fallen. In order to achieve sucess at any price he lowers his own standards and 'writes down' to the American public taste, thereby diluting his own art. Real art can only be produced with full conviction, and compromise is synonymous with the ruin of all artistic endeavor.

"In spite of all these odds, I think that I am not immodest in stating that everything I have composed in this country is superior to my former European output. I write considerably less, but I think, at least, that I write better. As a result of more critical writing my works have become more introspective."

Eric Zeisl writes:

"Speaking for myself, I feel that the events of my life and the consequent strife caused by my immigration to America had It seems to me that position on the music an extremely untenable idea that starvation, strife, etc., are the basis tions for composing g is repugnant to me.

Psychiatry teaches us great men of music and an outlet that produce nacles" of happiness un and unfelt by the rest o kind.

That Schubert had to co on the backs of menus caused more suffering a illettantes than he probably people have not only writte he backs of old menus but h also eaten them and, when th are extremely hungry, ea other.

I believe that the great men all ages are the only ones wh have ever really inhabited th earth and the rest of mankin has had an aphislike existence taking time out from aiming a each other to nibble at th greenery these men produced.

Study Reveals Peace

A study of the writings of great men reveal an inner peace not attained by others. Irwin Edman, in his introduction to "The Philosophy of Schopenhauer," says: "Schopenhauer offers us the choice of two ways out of the suffering and disillusions of life. One, the amiable, transient way of the fine arts; two, the sanctified and eternal way of the saint."

Let's try to cheer up Mr. Zeisl. After all, if he is correct and proves that the proper incubation of a composer lies in "unhappiness, maladjustment and being harassed," we would soon have too many composers and no audiences (composers seldom go to concerts). So, let's keep Mr. Zeisl's formula a secret.

THEODORE NORMAN
Los Angeles

On May 21, 1950, Albert Goldberg wrote about Eric Zeisl, Miklós Rózsa and Béla Bartók in his article for the *Los Angeles Times*, "The Transplanted Composer".
Archiv des Exilarte Zentrum der mdw, Wien (A-Weaz)

(1930–2016) and *Friede auf Erden*, op. 13, by the Roger Wagner Chorale, as well as a concert in Beverly Hills featuring Zeisl's *Brandeis Sonata* for violin and piano (1949/50) performed by Israel Baker (1919–2011) and Yaltah Menuhin (1921–2001), the sister of the violinist Yehudi Menuhin.

Zeisl's increasing success and compositional activity in the immediate postwar period led to his first professional recordings with the Society of Professional Artists (SPA) label founded by F. Charles Adler (1889–1959). Adler was a conductor who had worked with and for various publishers, including Bote & Bock and Heinrichshofen, while in Berlin, and G. Schirmer after his emigration to New York in 1934. He had corresponded with Schoenberg about the publication of the *Begleitungsmusik zu einer Lichtspielszene*, op. 34—a performance of which he conducted in Vienna in 1953—and the *Cello Concerto in D Major after Monn* (1933). In 1949, Zeisl wrote to Adler to suggest performances of his works. Adler responded encouragingly, and the correspondence led ultimately to two recordings of Zeisl's music in 1951 under the brand-new SPA label. The first record (SPA-5) featured Zeisl's *Kinderlieder* (1930/31), sung in English, and *Pieces for Barbara* (1944) with Zeisl on the piano. On the second record (SPA-10) were two recently composed sonatas, the *Brandeis Sonata* performed by Baker and Menuhin, and the *Viola Sonata* (1950) performed by two former Schoenberg pupils, Sven Reher (1918–1979) and Eda Schlatter (1919–2012). (Baker later recorded Schoenberg's *Violin Concerto*, op. 36, and *Phantasy for Violin and Piano*, op. 47, with Glenn Gould.) Schlatter had become a trusted advocate of Zeisl's music, who also performed his opulent *Sonata Barocca* (1948/49) and commissioned his *Piano Concerto* (1951/52), which was written for her. Another Schoenberg pupil, pianist Natalie Limonick (1920–2007), similarly championed Zeisl's works, performing the *Sonata Barocca* and the *Kinderlieder* with Nixon (who also recorded Schoenberg's *Brettl-Lieder* with Leonard Stein).

When in May 1952 the *Los Angeles Evening Citizen News* interviewed Zeisl ahead of the premiere performance of his opera *Leonce und Lena* (1937),[34] the conversation turned to Schoenberg. Perhaps it was because the opera was based on a play by Georg Büchner, also the author the drama underlying Alban Berg's *Wozzeck*.

> Zeisl admires Schoenberg and Alban Berg, although he is no follower of the 12-tone school of composition. He believes there is an increasing trend back toward tonality in music. He says: 'As long as you have something to say which is your own, you can say it in any idiom. The creative mind can take any material, triads, atonality, tonality and it becomes meaningful.' But among the atonalists, he acknowledges only Schoenberg and Berg. 'Whether or not Schoenberg is accepted, he showed us how far we can go. And he crucified himself for the young composer. He was a saint. But he knew better than anyone else that the creator creates his own world—it is the technician who always wants a system!'[35]

Following Schoenberg's death in 1951, the Zeisls became closer friends with his widow, my other grandmother Gertrud. For Zeisl's fiftieth birthday in 1955, she dedicated to him a rare copy of the *Sonderheft der Musikblätter des Anbruch* published for Arnold Schoenberg's fiftieth birthday.[36] When Zeisl was suddenly felled by a heart attack on February 18, 1959, Gertrud Schoenberg was the first to come console my other grandmother, bringing with her a bottle of cognac, which was much appreciated. My parents did not know each other at that time. My father says that his mother would often ask him to drive her to a friend, promising he would be meeting one of the friend's daughters there. But after several of those turned out to be too old or too young, he declined and never took her up on the offer to come with her to the Zeisls. My parents met only later, when my father returned home on leave from the Army and found my mother house-sitting with his grandmother Henriette Kolisch in the family's Brentwood home.

I became interested in the music of my grandfathers when I was still a teenager, after my bar mitzvah in 1979, during which choral and organ works by both of my grandfathers were performed. I recall a big brouhaha the year before when Lionel Rolfe, a nephew of Yehudi and Yaltah Menuhin, wrote a large article in the *Los Angeles Times* entitled "An Odd Couple and the Lure of the Southland." Accompanying the far less than accurate article was a large illustration of Schoenberg and Zeisl's heads close together with the caption "Composers Arnold Schoenberg and Eric Zeisl became fast friends in the late '40s, early '50s." I remember everyone being outraged by the fabricated "fast friends" story. Schoenberg's pupil Leonard Stein (1916–2004), then director of the Arnold Schoenberg Institute at the University of Southern California, wrote a letter to the editor correcting some of the many mistakes. And my grandmother also wrote, "There are far too many things wrong in the article by Mr. Rolfe to go into detail but I must especially point out that my husband, Eric Zeisl, though he admired Schoenberg, met him person to person only very few times, never belonged to the inner circle of Schoenberg's friends and family while he was alive and that this is not his claim to fame."

At my grandmother's house I listened to the old, often scratchy Zeisl recordings, which we then transferred from records or tape reels onto cassette tapes. My favorites were the *Second String Quartet* and the *Requiem Ebraico*. While a student at Princeton University in the mid-1980s, I received a call from composer Milton Babbitt (1916–2011)—who once proudly told me he had greeted my Schoenberg grandparents as they descended from the ship upon first arriving in New York in 1933—asking if I would give a tour to a prospective student from Los Angeles whose parents, Robina Young and René Goiffon, had produced a recording by Robert Taub of Babbitt's solo piano music for their label Harmonia Mundi USA. During the tour I mentioned that I had another composer grandfather named Eric Zeisl. Robina was interested, or polite, enough to ask me to send her some of Zeisl's music. After graduating in 1988, I returned to Los Angeles for law school at the University of Southern California and moved into the home of my grandmother, who had passed away the year before. I decided to follow up with Robina and sent her a tape recording of Zeisl's chamber music from performances in the 1950s. In May 1989, my mother and I met with Robina at the Harmonia Mundi USA office just below the Santa Monica Freeway in Culver City. Robina suggested a recording of some of Zeisl's chamber music, namely his *Second String Quartet*, the *"Arrowhead" Trio* for flute, viola and harp, and the early *Piano Trio Suite*, op. 8, which had recently been rediscovered in a Santa Barbara music archive.

To perform the works, I turned to some friends of mine. Harpist Marcia Dickstein was best friends with my law school classmate, and had recently formed her Debussy Trio, named after the first composer to use the combination of flute, viola, and harp. Violinists Mitch Newman and René Mandel, violist Evan Wilson and cellist David Low had put together a group called the Brandeis-Bardin Ensemble after the American Jewish University's campus retreat north of Los Angeles in Simi Valley, where David was music director and where Zeisl had been composer in residence over four decades earlier. Mitch and David invited their friend pianist Daniel Shapiro to join them in the Zeisl trio. The recording took place on October 15 to 17, 1990, in the beautiful and acoustically exquisite Bridges Hall of Music (known as Little Bridges) at Pomona College in Claremont, California, where my mother taught German language and literature.

The resulting Harmonia Mundi recording issued in 1991, the first Zeisl recording in forty years, garnered some good reviews. "Sometimes it's the projects from left field that catch the ear," wrote the New York Times. "The two young ensembles give polished, focused performances that serve the music wonderfully."[37] Gramophone magazine was equally impressed. "It's always stimulating to discover a composer whose name you've never heard before and of whose music you've never heard a note [...] all who enjoy the music of the early part of this century will appreciate such craftsmanship as is demonstrated by the fine performances of Eric Zeisl's music on this disc. May it bring him many more admirers."[38]

Around this time my aunt Nuria Schoenberg-Nono, who had been living in Los Angeles while working on her Schoenberg document biography Arnold Schönberg, 1874–1951: Lebensgeschichte in Begegnungen (1992), met the young record producer Michael Haas. Michael was just starting his "Entartete Musik" series for Decca/London Records, and Nuria must have suggested that Michael contact me to ask about Zeisl. Fortunately, Michael was already aware of the Harmonia Mundi chamber music recording. In 1994, I sent him a number of cassette tapes of Zeisl recordings, including the 1952 performance of Leonce und Lena and the Requiem Ebraico. I had lost hope that something would come of it when out of the blue I received word from Michael that he would be including Zeisl's Requiem Ebraico as the companion piece to the planned recording of Franz Waxman's Song of Terezin. My mother and I traveled to Berlin in early 1997 to attend the recording sessions. It was my first trip back to Berlin since I had studied there in 1987, but I became very ill after the first days and didn't see much beyond the Jesus-Christus-Kirche in Dahlem, where the recording sessions took place. The conductor was Lawrence Foster, who recounted the story that his mother had brought him to take composition lessons with Zeisl, only to be told that the boy had no talent for composition. Foster went on to study with Waxman, whose music he was now keen to champion. Luckily, Foster didn't hold a grudge against Zeisl and the resulting CD was another big success for all parties involved.

With two modern recordings accomplished, more soon followed.[39] I quickly learned that each new recording could plant the seed for the next, and by now we have a large portion of Zeisl's oeuvre available to be heard and enjoyed by the public. There are still some large gaps, notably the operas, and most of the choral and ballet music. But with time those, too, will certainly be discovered and recorded. The recordings also spur performances, which continue in fits and starts. My friend Gabor Lukin, a great-grandson of the Hungarian playwright Franz Molnar, years ago began assisting Zeisl's biographer Prof. Malcolm Cole (1936–2017) with the preparation of Zeisl scores for publication or performance. During the pandemic he transcribed all of Zeisl's one hundred lieder, and those are now being issued in a series of recordings on the Naxos label. A performance of Zeisl's Mond-

bilder (1928) in the version for orchestra and his massive ballet *Uranium 235* (1945/46), the first significant musical work inspired by the atom bomb, is planned for this year.

In this article, I have recounted the limited, but to me very meaningful, relationship between my grandfathers, and the history which led the two families to come together after the two protagonists had died. I am the product of that union of traditions. I have tried in my life to keep my foot in both camps, and to use that perspective to understand each of my grandfathers as he was. There was never a need for me to overestimate one at the expense of the other.

1   Gertrud S. Zeisl, née Jellinek (1906 Vienna - 1987 Salzburg), studied law at the University of Vienna. After a long courtship opposed by her father Hermann Jellinek (1867–1933), she married Eric Zeisl on Dec. 29, 1935. After emigrating via Paris and New York to Los Angeles, she became a high school teacher of Latin, French, and German. Her oral history conducted by Prof. Malcolm Cole is a primary source for much information about her husband: http://zeisl.com/archive/gertrud-zeisls-oral-history.htm (accessed Dec. 8, 2024).

2   Erich (1886–1961) and Nora (1891–1974) Lachmann. A book describing the Lachmann instrument collection was published in 1950: *Erich Lachmann Collection of Historical Stringed Musical Instruments* (Los Angeles: Allan Hancock Foundation, University of Southern California, 1950). The collection was purchased by UCLA around 1960, and many instruments were deaccessioned and auctioned off at Christie's in 2009. According to the Christie's catalogue, Lachmann relocated to Los Angeles in 1932 and "became regarded as the most influential dealer on the West Coast prior to World War II." See https://www.christies.com/presscenter/pdf/09142009/14263.pdf (accessed Nov. 14, 2024).

3   Gertrud Zeisl, diary entry, Nov. 2, 1945, Eric Zeisl Estate, Exilarte Center, Vienna.

4   Karin Wagner, *Fremd bin ich ausgezogen: Eric Zeisl; Biografie* (Vienna, 2005), p. 35.

5   "Ich bin Komponist der Gegenwart, verstehe die moderne Richtung nicht [...]." Quoted in ibid. See also Alban Berg to Arnold Schoenberg, Mar. 18, 1912: "diese Schweine, Stöhr vor allem" ("those pigs, Stöhr above all"), ASCC 19761 (= Arnold Schönberg Center Correspondence).

6   Richard Stöhr, recommendation letter, May 22, 1938, Eric Zeisl Estate, Exilarte Center, Vienna.

7   Joseph Marx (1882–1964), composer and music professor. In 1922, Marx succeeded Ferdinand Löwe as director of the Academy of Music and Performing Arts in Vienna. On Dec. 26, 1922, Schoenberg wrote a letter to Marx reacting cautiously to an offer of a teaching position at the Academy, which, however, did not materialize. See http://www.joseph-marx-gesellschaft.org/english/joseph-marx.html (accessed Dec. 8, 2024).

8   Hugo Kauder (1888 Tovačov, Moravia - 1972 Bussum, Netherlands) was a violist, violinist, composer, and music professor. See https://www.hugokauder.org/ (accessed Dec. 8, 2024). He performed in two concerts of the Society on Mar. 30 and June 6, 1919. See also Karin Wagner, *Hugo Kauder (1888–1972). Komponist – Musikphilosoph – Theoretiker. Eine Biographie* (Vienna, 2018).

9   "Eine der stärksten Persönlichkeiten der noch nicht dreißigjährigen Wiener Komponisten ist Erich Zeisel [sic]." Paul A. Pisk, "Erich Zeisel" [sic], *Radio Wien*, no. 18 (Jan. 26, 1934), pp. 2-3. See https://anno.onb.ac.at/cgi-content/anno?aid=raw&datum=19340126&seite=4&zoom=33 (accessed Dec. 8, 2024).

10 Paul Amadeus Pisk (1893 Vienna - 1990 Los Angeles) earned his doctorate in musicology from the University of Vienna in 1916 under Guido Adler. He also studied with Franz Schreker and Arnold Schoenberg (1917–1919). He served as board member, secretary, and pianist for Schoenberg's Society for Private Musical Performances. After his emigration he taught at the University of Redlands in Southern California.

11 The Galimir Quartet was led by violinist Felix Galimir (1910 Vienna - 1999 New York) and his three sisters Clara (1905–1985), Renée (1908–1973), and Adrienne (1912–1997). The quartet made the premiere recording of Alban Berg's *Lyric Suite* in 1935. The youngest Galimir sister Adrienne married the American violinist Louis Krasner (1903–1995), who commissioned and premiered Alban Berg's 1935 *Violin Concerto*. Krasner also premiered Schoenberg's *Violin Concerto*, op. 36, in 1940 under the direction of Leopold Stokowski.

12 Erwin Stein (1885 Vienna - 1958 London) studied with Schoenberg between 1906 and 1910. He worked closely with Schoenberg in the Society for Private Musical Performances and made several arrangements (Gustav Mahler's *Symphony No. 4* and Anton Bruckner's *Symphony No. 7*) that were performed at the Society's concerts. He worked for Schoenberg's principal publisher Universal Edition from 1924 to 1938, after which he emigrated to England and joined the publisher Boosey & Hawkes.

13 The *Scherzo and Fugue* was scheduled to be performed on Mar. 10, 1938, by the Wiener Konzertorchester. *Reichspost*, Mar. 10, 1938, p. 11.

14 Alma Mahler-Werfel (1879–1964), a student of Alexander Zemlinsky and widow of Gustav Mahler, lastly married the writer Franz Werfel, who was Arnold Schoenberg's third cousin (although it is likely that neither of them was aware of the relationship). Alma was Schoenberg's most long-term close friend living in Los Angeles, as the two had been closely acquainted for over fifty years when Schoenberg died in 1951. See Haide Tenner, *"Ich möchte so lange leben, als ich Ihnen dankbar sein kann": Alma Mahler – Arnold Schönberg; Der Briefwechsel* (St. Pölten, 2012); Elizabeth L. Keathley and Marilyn L. McCoy, *Schoenberg's Correspondence with Alma Mahler* (Oxford, 2019). Alma often found herself in the middle of disputes involving Schoenberg, as in the 1923 exchange of letters with Wassily Kandinsky concerning anti-Semitism at the Bauhaus, or the 1948 conflict with Thomas Mann over *Doktor Faustus*. She was also a friend of the Zeisls in Los Angeles, and my grandmother recalled in her oral history that Alma was once very jealous because Stravinsky had come over to the Zeisls' house for a party but had declined her invitation. On Zeisl's death she sent a telegram to my grandmother: „I am very very sad about your loss. I felt his great talent but also his deep disappointment about his life which did not bring him the success due to his significance." Alma Mahler-Werfel to Gertrud Zeisl, Mar. 21, 1959, Eric Zeisl Estate, Exilarte Center, Vienna.

15 The prolific French composer Darius Milhaud (1879 Marseille - 1964 Geneva) was a member of "Les Six." He conducted the first English performance of Schoenberg's *Pierrot Lunaire* in London in 1923. Milhaud emigrated in 1940 to Oakland, California, where he taught music at Mills College and at Music Academy of the West in Santa Barbara.

16 Composer Hanns Eisler (1898 Leipzig - 1962 Berlin) was a student of Arnold Schoenberg from 1919 to 1923. Like Zeisl, he moved to Los Angeles in 1942 to write film music. The two composed music for competing films on the 1942 assassination of Reinhard Heydrich. Fritz Lang's *Hangmen Also Die* (1943), which was released first, earned Eisler an Oscar nomination. Zeisl's contributions went uncredited in Douglas Sirk's *Hitler's Madman* (1943), released several months later.

17 "Herr Erich Zeisl, ein wirklich begabter Komponist (Refugee aus Wien) möchte gerne mit Ihnen arbeiten. Ich erlaube mir ihn hiemit vorzustellen." Hanns Eisler to Arnold Schoenberg, May 28, 1942, Eric Zeisl Estate, Exilarte Center, Vienna.

18 Richard Stöhr to Eric Zeisl, undated, quoted in Karin Wagner (ed.), *… es grüsst Dich Erichisrael: Briefe von und an Eric Zeisl, Hilde Spiel, Richard Stöhr, Ernst Toch, Hans Kafka u. a.* (Vienna, 2008), p. 166. Translation Michael Haas.

19 Composer Erich Wolfgang Korngold (1897 Brno - 1957 Los Angeles) was a child prodigy, son of the conservative music critic Julius Korngold (1860 Brno - 1945 Los Angeles) and a pupil of Alexander Zemlinsky. As a teenager, he was close friends with Maria (Mitzi) Kolisch, the older sister of my grandmother, and dedicated a love song to her. In Hollywood, he was the most successful of the émigré composers, defining what came to be known as the "Hollywood sound" while scoring sixteen films, winning two academy awards and two more nominations. Upon arriving in Los Angeles, the Zeisls became friends with the Korngolds through their mutual friends Fritz and Maria Reitler. Maria's father was the music critic Josef Reitler (1883 Vienna - 1948 New York), an early music theory pupil of Schoenberg from 1902 to 1905. Schoenberg and Julius Korngold had been in separate camps in Vienna, and only came to know each other personally in Los Angeles, where they exchanged several warm letters, culminating in a personal condolence letter from Schoenberg to Korngold's children upon his death in September 1945. „I had the opportunity—unfortunately only late in our lives—of having contact with your father and I must say that I regret it has not happened earlier. A man like he, whose knowledge and judgement of music was based upon a profound love for this art, such a man should have lived earlier and longer in this country." Arnold Schoenberg to Erich Wolfgang and Luzi Korngold, Sept. 3, 1945, ASCC 23956. The deep and very close friendship between Korngold and Zeisl is evidenced by a dedication of a score of Korngold's opera *Die tote Stadt*: "Erich Zeisl – dem alten Freund der 'toten Stadt' mit allen guten Wünschen: Erich Wolfgang Korngold (der neue Freund in der ganz 'toten Stadt'!) Hollywood, Weihnachten 1946." ("To Eric Zeisl— the old friend from the 'Dead City' with all good wishes: Erich Wolfgang Korngold [the new friend in the very 'Dead City'!] Hollywood, Christmas 1946.") Eric Zeisl Estate, Exilarte Center, Vienna.

20 The composer Ernst Toch (1887 Vienna - 1964 Santa Monica, CA) appears not have had much contact with Schoenberg until the two were living in Berlin after 1929. With the rise of the Nazis, both fled in spring 1933 and were together in Paris in May 1933, when Schoenberg began thinking seriously about means to rescue the Jews of Europe with the establishment of a Jewish state, writing to Toch, "Darum will ich eine Bewegung hervorrufen, welche die Juden wieder zu einem Volk macht und sie in einem geschlossenen Land zu einem Staat vereinigt." ("For that reason, I want to start a movement that makes the Jews a people again, uniting them as a nation in a self-contained country.") Arnold Schoenberg to Ernst Toch, May 1933, ASCC 6587. In Los Angeles from 1936, Toch taught at the University of Southern California. He remained on good terms with Schoenberg, and their daughters became friends. When they were introduced at a New Year's party in 1942, Zeisl also became friends with Toch. From Gertrud Zeisl's oral history: "Now, on this New Year's Eve, he had invited Eric, and there was Ernst Toch, and the two became friends almost immediately. And they sat down at the piano, and without talking about it they began to play four hands, in a kind of funny way, and went through the waltzes of Vienna and so on and had this kind of New Year's Eve mood. And it was very funny." The two were composers in residence together at Brandeis Camp in Simi Valley in 1948, and later at the Huntington Hartford Foundation in Rustic Canyon in Santa Monica in 1957.

21 Hugo Strelitzer (1896 Berlin - 1981 Los Angeles) was the head of the opera department at Los Angeles City College. On Nov. 18, 1945, he was chorusmaster for Werner Janssen's premiere of Nathaniel Shilkret's *Genesis Suite*, which consisted of compositions by Shilkret and composers he commissioned (Alexandre Tansman, Darius Milhaud, Ernst Toch, Igor Stravinsky, Mario Castelnuovo-Tedesco, and Arnold Schoenberg). Shilkret converted Schoenberg's *Prelude to Genesis*, op. 44, to a postlude for the performance and the 1946 recording, as he feared Schoenberg's music would make a negative impression on the audience. It is unknown whether the Zeisls attended the concert, but it seems very likely, as Zeisl was by that time on very friendly terms with Tansman and Castelnuovo-Tedesco, whom he had met through his film studio work, as well as Milhaud and Stravinsky, whom he had met through Tansman. Strelitzer also became a very close friend of the Zeisls. In 1952, Strelitzer's opera workshop at Los Angeles City College premiered Zeisl's opera *Leonce und Lena*. At my parents' wedding on Nov. 23, 1965, Hugo Strelitzer stood in for my mother's father as he walked her down the aisle (actually a staircase in their Miler Drive home).

22 Following this introduction to Zeisl, Wright became a tireless advocate for his music. He led the choir at the Eric Zeisl memorial concert on Nov. 23, 1959.

23 According to Gertrud Zeisl's oral history, Strelitzer had recommended William Zeisl to be cantor of the Fairfax Temple, and it was through this connection that Rabbi Sonderling met Zeisl and suggested he compose

a setting of Psalm 92. See Jonathan L. Friedmann and John F. Guest, *Songs of Sonderling: Commissioning Jewish Émigré Composers in Los Angeles, 1938–1945*, Modern Jewish History (Lubbock, TX, 2021).

24 The orchestral version of the *Requiem Ebraico* had been premiered Jan. 23, 1948, under Jacques Rachmilovich with the Santa Monica Little Symphony. See *Los Angeles Times*, Jan. 26, 1948, p. 10.

25 Conductor Adolf Heller (1901 Prague - 1954 Santa Barbara, CA) taught for five years at Los Angeles City College, where he led the opera workshop with Hugo Strelitzer. Heller was engaged as assistant conductor of the San Francisco Opera (under Kurt Herbert Adler) at the time of his death in a car accident in 1954. See https://www.imdb.com/name/nm0375265/ (accessed Nov. 19, 2024). Heller, Strelitzer, and Zeisl vacationed and taught together in Lake Arrowhead, California, at the Arrowhead Music Camp affiliated with the Los Angeles Conservatory of Music. See *Los Angeles Times*, June 4, 1950, p. 104. Besides the *Requiem Ebraico*, Heller also conducted the 1952 premiere of Zeisl's opera *Leonce und Lena* at Los Angeles City College.

26 Arnold Schoenberg to the President of Occidental College Remsen DuBois Bird, May 22, 1940, ASCC 23646.

27 Eric Zeisl to Arnold Schoenberg, Sept. 13, 1949, ASCC 19345.

28 *Los Angeles Times*, Dec. 7, 1948, p. 42: "Mr. Zeisl is that curiosity among modern composers, one who writes as he feels without regard to formulas or fashions. His brief songs were all quick and definite impressions of childhood [...]. Their main interest lay more in the accompaniments Mr. Zeisl played so expertly and feelingly [...]. [T]hey are varied and attractive songs which should win a place in the repertoire."

29 *Los Angeles Times*, May 14, 1950, p. 107.

30 *Los Angeles Times*, May 21, 1950, p. 116.

31 Ernst Krenek, a pupil of Franz Schreker, who was married briefly to Gustav and Alma Mahler's daughter Anna, visited Southern California in 1937, and in 1938 took up an appointment at the Malkin Conservatory in Boston (where Schoenberg had also first taught after arriving in the United States in 1933). Krenek returned to live in Los Angeles in 1947, teaching alongside Zeisl at the Southern California School of Music and Arts and at Los Angeles City College. A 1950/51 college brochure listed five music classes: "Contemporary Music" and "Brief History of Opera" taught by Krenek; "Analysis & Composition" and "Chromatic Harmony" taught by Zeisl; and the "Opera Workshop" taught by Heller and Strelitzer. Zeisl would often take over Krenek's classes when Krenek was traveling. See, e.g., Eric Zeisl to Richard Stöhr, Dec. 12, 1951, and Eric Zeisl to Hilde Spiel, undated, in Wagner, *... es grüsst Dich Erichisrael*, p. 264, 271. At Ronald Schoenberg's confirmation ceremony in May 1950, Krenek agreed (reluctantly, at Arnold Schoenberg's request) to be the boy's sponsor.

32 Eugen(e) Zádor (1894 Bátaszék, Hungary - 1977 Hollywood, CA) was a composer who studied in Vienna and in Leipzig with Max Reger. From 1921 he taught at the Neues Wiener Konservatorium. After emigration, he wrote much uncredited music for MGM, and worked in close collaboration with Miklós Rózsa.

33 *Los Angeles Times*, May 28, 1950, p. 90.

34 The premiere of *Leonce und Lena*, composed in 1937, was supposed to take place at the Schönbrunn Palace Court Theatre in Spring 1938, conducted by Kurt Herbert Adler (1905–1988; later conductor of the San Francisco Opera), but the Nazi "Anschluss" made any performance impossible. It was performed in Linz, Austria, in 2017 and most recently at the Eduard-von-Winterstein-Theater in Annaberg-Buchholz, Germany, in fall 2021.

35 *Los Angeles Evening Citizen News*, May 3, 1952, p. 5.

36 Gertrud Schoenberg was listed among the Committee of Friends who organized the May 22, 1955, gala festival concert in honor of Zeisl's fiftieth birthday. Other committee members were Kurt Herbert Adler, Erich Wolfgang Korngold, Alma Mahler-Werfel, Darius Milhaud, Edward Muhl, Igor Stravinsky, Hugo Strelitzer, Alexandre Tansman, Ernst Toch, John Vincent, Eugene Zádor, and Fritz Zweig. Malcolm S. Cole and Barbara Barclay, *Armseelchen: The Life and Music of Eric Zeisl* (Westport, CT, 1984), p. 70.

37 *New York Times*, Mar. 22, 1992, sect. 2, p. 32.

38 *Gramophone*, Sept. 1992.

39 See http://www.zeisl.com/books-and-recordings/recordings.htm (accessed Dec. 8, 2024).

Arnold Schönberg mit seiner Frau Gertrud und der Tochter Nuria vor dem Haus in Brentwood, Los Angeles, 1937
Arnold Schönberg Center Privatstiftung, Wien (A-Was)

Erich Zeisl mit seiner Tochter Barbara vor dem Haus am West Knoll Drive, Los Angeles, ca. 1945
Archiv des Exilarte Zentrum der mdw, Wien (A-Weaz)

E. Randol Schoenberg

DIE KONVERGENZ ZWISCHEN SCHÖNBERG UND ZEISL

Da ich nach meinen beiden Großvätern benannt wurde – Eric ist mein offizieller Vorname, mein Rufname aber Randy nach Randol, meinem zweiten Vornamen, einem Anagramm von Arnold –, verspürte ich den starken Wunsch, ihnen näherzukommen, ihre Musik zu hören und mehr über ihr Leben zu erfahren. Ich wurde natürlich erst 1966, nach dem Tod beider Männer, geboren und hatte daher nie die Möglichkeit, mir aus erster Hand ein Bild von meinen Großvätern zu machen. Meine Eltern Barbara Zeisl-Schoenberg und Ronald Schoenberg waren Teenager, als ihre Väter starben. Mehr als Anekdoten konnten sie daher auch nicht weitergeben. So war ich gezwungen, mich für weiterführende Erkenntnisse an Expert:innen und Wissenschaftler:innen und insbesondere auch an die Musik und andere Werke zu halten, die meine Großväter hinterlassen hatten. Während Schönberg in unserem Haus natürlich eine dominante Präsenz war, vor allem nachdem wir 1972 in das Haus der Familie mit dem spanischen Ziegeldach in Brentwood Park gezogen waren, bildete der Umstand, dass ich nur noch einen Großelternteil hatte, nämlich Gertrud Zeisl[1], meine Großmutter mütterlicherseits, eine Art Gegengewicht. Anders als so viele einseitige Verfechter:innen einer musikalischen Richtung hatte ich nicht das Bedürfnis, mich für eine Seite zu entscheiden. Ich entwickelte daher ein relativ offenes Ohr und schätzte die Musik meiner Großväter unabhängig von jeder stilistischen Zuordnung.

Diese Einstellung habe ich vielleicht von meinen Eltern und speziell von meiner Großmutter mütterlicherseits übernommen (oder man brachte sie mir bei). Meine Großmutter war selbst genauso eine Bewunderin der Musik Schönbergs wie der ihres Mannes. In ihrem Tagebucheintrag vom 2. November 1945 berichtete sie von der ersten Begegnung zwischen meinen beiden Großvätern an einem Abend im Haus des aus Berlin stammenden Geigenhändlers und Sammlers Erich Lachmann[2] und seiner belgischen Frau Nora:

> Bei einem Abend bei Lachmanns haben wir Schönberg kennengelernt. Es war ein Ereignis. Ich träumte schon die Nacht davor davon so aufgeregt war ich darüber. Ich war so riesig gespannt diesen Mann der so viele Kontroversen auslöst sogar zwischen mir und Erich leibhaftig zu sehen. Es war eine große Überraschung für mich und es änderte meinen und auch Erichs Standpunkt diesem Phenomen gegenüber (denn so muß man ihn nennen) vollkommen, daß wir ihn persönlich kennenlernten. Er ist ein guter Mensch. Er brennt in einem elektrischen Feuer, daß ihn selbst zucken macht wie eine Flamme und naturgemäß Schläge versetzt die nur die Dummen als schrecklich empfinden, denn diese Schläge die sind belebend und vielleicht sogar heilend wie Naturkräfte. Ein faszinierender Mensch. Er spricht sehr stark mit Wiener bzw. mehr Oesterreichischem Akzent und wirkt in Wesen ja selbst

Erscheinung überhaupt nicht jüdisch. Das überspitzte an ihm ist nicht eigentlich wie man vermutet talmudische Gelehrsamkeit sondern viel mehr die unselige Geduld des Holzschnitzers der aus dem spröden Material die feinsten Zierate und Faltenwürfe herausbastelt. Er ist mitteilsam und gibt von den Schätzen seiner Erkenntnis rückhaltslos. Der Preis ist, daß er auch ab und zu sagen darf, was er gar nicht meint. Wieso die Menschen dies nicht verstehen. Norman Wright und einige andere Amerikaner waren derart antagonisiert und beleidigt. Wenn einer sein Herz so freigebig ausschüttet, kommt eben auch die Bitterkeit die darin ist mit heraus. Deshalb spricht er schlecht / schimpft er auf Amerika. Auch ist er nicht eingebildet, wie sie meinen, wenn er sagt. Sie verstehen meine Musik nicht und verdienen nicht daß ich vor ihnen erscheine. Denn wenige Augenblicke vorher sagt er auf sich selbst. Ich kann gar nichts jedes Werk muß ich von neuem beginnen. Als Erich ihn fragte Warum machen Sie einen 4 fachen Doppelkanon wenn man ihn doch nicht hören kann. „Das ist zur Befriedigung der inneren Logik" sagte er. Welch ein Wort Erich ging reich beschenkt damit nach Hause und er begann ein Ballet nach Maurice Dekobra's Text Uranium 235. Durch 6 Wochen hielt die magische elektrische Kraft die von diesem Manne ausgeht an und brachte ihn über alle Klippen und Unlust Gefühle bis sein neues großes Werk fertig entstanden war. Ein Werk in dem viele Schwächen abgestreift sind, der große Bogen in der Form gelang und ein Können sich zeigt dass ihn wenn er auf diesem Wege fortschreitet in die Meistergruppe endgültig Aufnahme finden lassen wird.[3]

Obwohl beide in Wien geboren wurden und sogar die gleiche Schule im zweiten Bezirk besuchten, hatte mein Großvater Zeisl vor Los Angeles kaum je Gelegenheit, mit Schönberg zusammenzutreffen. Schönberg war eine Generation älter, nur drei Jahre jünger als Zeisls Vater Siegmund (der zur gleichen Zeit wie Schönberg die Realschule in der Vereinsgasse 21 besuchte). Ab 1920, als Zeisl sich mit 15 Jahren an der Akademie für Musik und darstellende Kunst einschrieb, war sein wichtigster Kompositionslehrer Richard Stöhr[4], ein bekennend konservativer Komponist aus dem antimodernen Lager, der 1905 erklärt hatte: „Ich bin Komponist der Gegenwart, verstehe die moderne Richtung nicht [...]."[5] Stöhr, der Zeisl später „ohne jede Übertreibung den begabtesten Schüler, den ich je hatte"[6], nannte, hätte Zeisl sicherlich nicht zur Avantgarde ermutigt, selbst wenn der jugendliche Liederkomponist dazu geneigt gewesen wäre. Als Schönberg schließlich im Jänner 1926 Wien in Richtung Berlin verließ, war Zeisl gerade 20 Jahre alt. Nach einer kurzen Studienzeit bei Joseph Marx[7] wandte er sich, um beim Schreiben von Kammermusik sicherer zu werden, an Hugo Kauder[8], ehemals Geiger in Schönbergs Verein für musikalische Privataufführungen. Dies führte zur Fertigstellung des *Ersten Streichquartetts* (ca. 1930–1933). Doch zu der Zeit, als Zeisl in Wien erste Anerkennung fand, etwa durch die ausführliche und sehr positive Besprechung des *Ersten Streichquartetts* in der Interpretation des Galimir Quartetts[9] in *Radio Wien*[10], verfasst von Paul Amadeus Pisk[11], dem Gründungssekretär von Schönbergs Verein, war Schönberg bereits in die Vereinigten Staaten geflüchtet. Offenbar führten einige taktlose Kommentare gegen die Zwölftonmusik dazu, dass Zeisl von dem treuen Schönberg-Schüler Erwin Stein[12] von der Universal Edition ausgemustert wurde. Doch der Verlag lenkte ein und edierte 1937 Zeisls *Scherzo und Fuge für Streichorchester*, eine Bearbeitung zweier Sätze des *Ersten Streichquartetts*. Dies geschah, nur wenige Monate bevor der „Anschluss" Österreichs an Nazideutschland am 12. März 1938 alle weiteren Möglichkeiten für Veröffentlichungen oder Aufführungen zunichtemachte.[13]

Nach der Pogromnacht des 9. November 1938 („Kristallnacht") flüchtete Zeisl aus Wien. Erst danach traf er auf Menschen, die ihn Schönberg und seinem Kreis näherbrachten. Die erste darunter war Alma Mahler-Werfel[14]: Sie entdeckte Zeisl beim Notieren von Musik in einem Pariser Café und freundete sich sofort mit ihm an. Meine Großmutter berichtete, dass Alma, nachdem sie Zeisl einige seiner Stücke spielen gehört hatte, sagte: „Sie sind eine tonale Natur, so wie Schönberg eine atonale ist." Durch Mahler-Werfel lernten die Zeisls den französischen Komponisten Darius Milhaud[15] kennen, der Schönberg gemeinsam mit Francis Poulenc bereits 1922 in Mödling bei Wien besucht hatte. Nur drei Tage vor ihrer Abreise nach New York hatten die Schönbergs den Abend des 21. Oktober 1933 in Paris bei den Milhauds verbracht. Nun, fünf Jahre danach, organisierte Milhaud für Zeisl ein Klavier, bot ihm Konzertkarten an, sicherte seinen Aufenthaltsstatus als Flüchtling und vermittelte ihm Arbeit und Sozialkontakte während der Zeit in Paris. Später reisten die Milhauds von ihrer neuen Heimat Oakland nahe San Francisco oft nach Südkalifornien, wo sie Besuche sowohl bei den Zeisls als auch bei den Schönbergs machten, manchmal zu Mittag bei der einen Familie und zum Abendessen bei der anderen.

Seit Oktober 1939 war Zeisl in New York, in der Suche nach Arbeitsmöglichkeiten schrieb er an den an der New School for Social Research tätigen Erwin Piscator (1893–1966). Eine Antwort kam von Schönbergs ehemaligem Schüler Hanns Eisler[16], der bald zum Freund wurde und Zeisl zur Übersiedlung nach Hollywood ermutigte. Am 28. Mai 1942 verfasste Eisler sogar ein Empfehlungsschreiben für Zeisl, dieser er

Darius Milhaud in „Selbstdarstellung", ein Geschenk an die Zeisls: „to Trudy und Eric affectionately Milhaud"
Archiv des Exilarte Zentrum der mdw, Wien (A-Weaz)

Schönberg übergeben sollte. („Herr Erich Zeisl, ein wirklich begabter Komponist (Refugee aus Wien) möchte gerne mit Ihnen arbeiten. Ich erlaube mir ihn hiermit vorzustellen."[17]) Zeisl verwendete das Schreiben nie. Die Kriegsjahre 1941 bis 1944 waren bestimmt vom Kampf um Arbeit in den Filmstudios, wo Zeisl trotz seiner Musik für mindestens 20 Filme nie richtig Fuß fassen konnte.

1944 schrieb Zeisl einen irritierenden Essay gegen Schönberg und die atonale Musik. Wir wissen nicht, was ihn zu diesem nie veröffentlichten Aufsatz veranlasste. Zeisl schickte eine Kopie des Texts an seinen ehemaligen Lehrer Richard Stöhr, der zu dieser Zeit im Exil in Vermont lebte. Stöhr reagierte ablehnend auf Zeisls Ausführungen und wies ihn darauf hin, dass es unterschiedliche Sichtweisen gebe und jemandes Einstellung einer bestimmten Komposition gegenüber, sogar einer eigenen, sich ändern könne. Vielleicht hatten Stöhrs eigene Erfahrungen seine Haltung zur modernen Musik gemildert. Aus dem Brief geht auch hervor, dass meine Großeltern sich über Schönbergs Musik stritten und Stöhr die Haltung meiner Großmutter verteidigte.

> Solange Sie an einen einzig möglichen Standpunkt in der Kunstwerk-Betrachtung glauben, muss Ihnen Trude's Standpunkt entweder 1.) als Heuchelei oder 2.) als Mangel an „Verständnis" erscheinen. Beides ist falsch. Nun werde ich Ihnen von meinen Erfahrungen im Berufe 35jähriger Lehrtätigkeit, in Bezug auf die Einstellung der heranwachsenden Jugend zu der neuen, Schönberg'schen Richtung erzählen. Ich fand zwei Gruppen unter den fortschrittlich Gesinnten. (Die anderen „klassisch" eingestellten schließe ich hier aus.) Die Radikalen unter ihnen duldeten die vergangene Musik vom intellektuellen Standpunkt als notwendiges, aber nun vergangenes Entwicklungsstadium, ihr Herz gehörte aber ganz der neuen Richtung. Die andere Gruppe war mehr konservativ eingestellt, Beethoven und Brahms bedeutete immer noch etwas für ihr Gefühlsleben, aber umgekehrt zur ersten Gruppe wurden Sie nie intellektuell durch Schönberg und seinen Kunstwillen angezogen. Sie sehen also zwei verschiedene Standpunkte. Ich glaube, dass Ihre Frau sehr der letzteren Gruppe angehört, weil sie doch durch ihre Ehe mit Ihrer eigenen Musik inniger verwurzelt ist als der radikale Schönberganbeter (z.b. Erw [Erwin] Stein, U.[niversal] E.[dition]) – Aber in keinem Fall dürfen Sie hier von Recht u Unrecht sprechen.[18]

Stöhrs Brief ist undatiert, ein späterer Brief aus seiner Hand vom 20. März 1945 bezieht sich jedoch auf den vorangegangenen, um Weihnachten herum gesendeten Brief, auf den Zeisl jedoch nicht reagierte, auch nicht als er Stöhr eine Kopie des eben fertiggestellten *Requiem Ebraico* schickte. Als die beiden Komponisten einander im November 1945 erstmals wieder trafen, war der Streit um Schönberg aus dem Jahr 1944 eindeutig abgeflaut.

Zeisls *Requiem Ebraico, Psalm 92* (1944/45) markiert einen weiteren Berührungspunkt zwischen den beiden Komponisten. Das Werk wurde von Rabbi Jacob Sonderling (1878–1964) in Auftrag gegeben, der auch der Auftraggeber von Schönbergs *Kol Nidre* (1938) war. In Schlesien geboren, emigrierte Sonderling 1923 in die Vereinigten Staaten, nachdem er im Ersten Weltkrieg als deutscher Militärseelsorger gedient hatte. In Los Angeles gründete er die Society for Jewish Culture-Fairfax Temple, die die deutschsprachige Exilgemeinde betreute. Sonderling beauftragte auch Erich Wolfgang Korngold[19] zu *Passover Psalm* und Ernst Toch[20] zur *Cantata of the Bitter Herbs*. Die Uraufführung des *Requiem*

Erich Zeisl und Tochter Barbara am Will Rogers Beach, um 1947
Archiv des Exilarte Zentrum der mdw, Wien (A-Weaz)

Ebraico (Orgelfassung) fand am 18. April 1945 im Rahmen eines interreligiösen Forums unter der Leitung von Rabbiner Sonderling statt. Hugo Strelitzer[21] dirigierte den Fairfax-Temple-Chor, Norman Söreng Wright[22] (1905–1982) spielte die Orgel, Zeisls jüngerer Bruder William (1907–1972) war Kantor des Fairfax-Tempels und sang den Baritonpart[23].

Das *Requiem Ebraico* ist Zeisls meistaufgeführtes Werk. Als erste Komposition, die den Opfern des Holocausts gewidmet ist, nimmt es eine Sonderstellung ein. Der Titel ist (aus jüdischer Sicht) sicherlich ungewöhnlich, Zeisls Verleger Joseph Freudenthal (Transcontinental Music Publishers) hatte vorerst Einwände, Zeisl bestand jedoch auf dieser Titelgebung und argumentierte in einem Brief vom 16. Oktober 1945: „Die Juden brauchen ein Requiem, also versuchen wir, ihnen eines zu geben." Zeisl war nie vom Judentum konvertiert, verfasste aber schon früh eine *Kleine Messe* (1932) und das *Requiem Concertante* (1934). Der Titel spiegelt also Zeisls Überzeugung wider, dass seine Vertonung eines hebräischen Psalms sich auch ohne einen lateinisch-katholischen Text in gleicher Weise in die musikalische Tradition einfügt wie Brahms' *Deutsches Requiem*.

Die Orchesterfassung des *Requiem Ebraico*[24] wurde am 17. April 1949 in Los Angeles unter der Leitung von Adolf Heller[25] mit dem Chor der First African Methodist Episcopalian Church und den Solist:innen Ruth Henry, Susan Corey und Stephen Kemalyan aufgeführt. Die Texte wurden in englischer Sprache gesungen. Im Rahmen einer Reihe zeitgenössischer Kammermusik strahlte der Radiosender KFWB die Aufführung aus, sie ist mit der Werkeinführung eines amerikanischen Radiosprechers auf Schallplatte erhalten. Vermutlich führte genau dieses Konzert zu einer Anekdote über Julius Toldi und meine beiden Großväter.

Julius Toldi (1891–1965) studierte Violine bei Arnold Rosé (1863–1946), dem Konzertmeister der Wiener Philharmoniker, und Komposition bei Franz Schreker (1878–1934). Er gehörte zu jenen Studierenden, die Schönbergs Geburtstag (und die Verlobung seiner Tochter Trudi mit Felix Greissle) im September 1921 in Traunkirchen feierten. Schönberg verfasste für Toldi im Mai 1940 eine Empfehlung für einen Lehrauftrag am Occidental College und nannte ihn darin „einen meiner besten und talentiertesten ehemaligen Schüler"[26]. Toldi arbeitete schließlich für den Klassik-Radiosender KFWB und war sowohl mit den Schönbergs als auch mit den Zeisls befreundet. Seine Sendung „Music of Today" wurde sonntagnachmittags ausgestrahlt, die Musik-Exilcommunity bildete dabei eine höchst begeisterte Zuhörerschaft. Meine Großmutter erzählte folgende Geschichte: Einmal kam Toldi ganz aufgeregt zu den Zeisls, er konnte kaum sprechen und meinte, er sei gerade in Brentwood gewesen und Schönberg habe das *Requiem Ebraico* gehört. Tatsächlich sei Schönberg von dem Stück sehr, sehr begeistert gewesen. Toldi war außer sich, „komplett verwirrt und verblüfft", wie meine Großmutter sich erinnerte, denn die unerwartete Äußerung Schönbergs über ein tonales Werk war ihm völlig unverständlich. Die Moral von der Geschichte, wie meine Großmutter sie uns überlieferte, war, dass die Jünger Schönbergs oft doktrinärer waren als ihr Meister und nicht gewillt, auch nur die Möglichkeit zu erwägen, dass ein tonales Werk Wert haben könnte, während Schönberg selbst, der wahre Meister, wusste, dass nicht der Stil von Bedeutung war, sondern die musikalische Idee. Schönberg erkannte in Zeisls *Requiem Ebraico* das Werk eines vollendeten Komponisten. Zumindest der Kontrapunkt in der abschließenden Fuge muss ihn sehr beeindruckt haben.

Arnold Schönberg mit seinen Söhnen Ronald und Lawrence im Garten in Brentwood, März 1945
Arnold Schönberg Center Privatstiftung, Wien (A-Was)

Später in diesem Jahr zählten die Zeisls zu den vielen Personen, die Schönberg am 13. September 1949 zum 75. Geburtstag ein Glückwunschtelegramm sendeten: „Herzlichen Glückwunsch zu diesem historischen Tag an eine der faszinierendsten Erscheinungen der geistigen Welt in großer Bewunderung."[27] Im Gegenzug schickte Schönberg seinen vervielfältigten Geburtstagsbrief: „Erst nach dem Tode erkannt zu werden ...!" Im selben Monat wurde Zeisl als Lehrer für Komposition an das Los Angeles City College berufen. Die Los Angeles Times berichtete über die Ernennung am 18. September 1949, auf derselben Seite las man von einem Geburtstagskonzert für Schönberg, einer Aufführung von Pierrot Lunaire zur Eröffnung der zwölften Saison der Veranstaltungsreihe „Evenings on the Roof", der ersten Adresse der Stadt für Konzerte zeitgenössischer Musik. Zeisl hatte seinen einzigen Auftritt bei den „Evenings on the Roof" gerade ein Jahr zuvor erlebt, als er die Kinderlieder (1930/31) mit der Sopranistin Brunetta Mazzolini interpretierte. Die Lieder waren der Hit des Abends, das Publikum forderte eine Zugabe und Albert Goldberg, der Musikrezensent der Los Angeles Times, verfasste eine glühende Kritik („Wie immer bei solchen Programmen schienen manche Nummern weit über den übrigen zu stehen"[28]). Dass Zeisl bei „Evenings on the Roof" nie mehr wieder auf dem Programm stand, war laut meiner Großmutter auf Eifersucht zurückzuführen.

Unter dem Titel „The Transplanted Composer" schrieb Goldberg im Mai 1950 eine dreiteilige Serie, in der er den Einfluss der Emigration auf den Kompositionsprozess hinterfragte. Der erste Artikel war Igor Strawinsky (1882–1971), Schönberg und Mario Castelnuovo-Tedesco (1895–1968) gewidmet.[29] Strawinsky, dessen Kreis sich auch Zeisl angeschlossen hatte, wies die Frage schlichtweg zurück. Schön-

Die „Zeisls" in Los Angeles, 1950er-Jahre
Archiv des Exilarte Zentrum der mdw, Wien (A-Weaz)

berg wurde mit der lapidaren Antwort zitiert: „Wenn die Einwanderung nach Amerika mich verändert hat – so bin ich mir dessen nicht bewusst." Castelnuovo-Tedesco aber, mit dem Zeisl nach der Ankunft in Hollywood die Leiden ungenannter Komponisten bei MGM durchlebt hatte, antwortete ausführlicher: Für ihn war die Schwierigkeit bei der Überwindung der Hindernisse der „Expatriierung (und das unter tragischen Umständen) [...] eine bittere Prüfung, unter der ich anfangs beinahe körperlich litt". In der zweiten Folge[30] stellte Goldberg Ernst Krenek[31] und Eugene Zádor[32] vor, im letzten Beitrag behandelte er Zeisl, Miklós Rózsa (1907–1995) – kein Freund von Zeisl, dem er später den Auftrag für die Filmmusik zu *A Time to Love and a Time to Die* abjagte, zu dem Korngold Zeisl verholfen hatte – und Béla Bartók (1881–1945; die Quelle war ein Brief Bartóks an Zádor vom 1. Juli 1945). Zeisls Antwort auf Goldbergs Aufforderung fiel anders aus als jene Schönbergs:

> Ich für meinen Teil finde, dass die Ereignisse meines Lebens und die daraus resultierenden Erschwernisse, die durch meine Einwanderung nach Amerika verursacht wurden, in der Tat eine sehr tiefe Auswirkung auf meine Arbeit hatten, aber eine, von der ich das Gefühl habe, dass sie mir eher die stärksten künstlerischen Impulse als Frustrationen brachte; es geht sogar so weit, dass ich das Gefühl habe, ich hätte vielleicht niemals mein Bestes geschrieben, wenn ich nicht den emotionalen Tumult der Entwurzelung erlebt hätte.[33]

Die Suche in den Nachrichtenarchiven jener Jahre (siehe newspapers.com) bringt weitere Beispiele für Parallelen im Leben der beiden Komponisten zutage. Die *Los Angeles Evening Citizen News* berichtete am 6. März 1948 über den Plan von Egon Newman (1894–1950, in Mödling als Egon Neumann geboren; ein Cousin zweiten Grades meiner Großmutter Gertrud Schönberg) zur Gründung einer Musikhochschule: „Arnold Schoenberg, Erich Zeisl und Norman Soreng Wright werden dem Lehrkörper angehören, aber auch Erich Korngold und Fritz Reiner könnten an der Schule unterrichten, sobald sie eröffnet." (Die Pläne wurden nicht realisiert, Newman beging offenbar kurz darauf in Mexiko-Stadt Selbstmord.) Im Jahr darauf finden sich auf einer Seite der Sonntagsausgabe der *Los Angeles Times* vom 27. November 1949 gleich drei Artikel: einer zu Schönbergs bevorstehendem Vortrag „My Evolution" an der UCLA, ein anderer zur Uraufführung von Zeisls *Songs for the Daughter of Jephtha* (1948) und ein dritter zur Westküstenpremiere von Strawinskys *Mass* (1948) im Wilshire Ebell Theater. Die Ankündigung von Zeisls *Requiem Ebraico*, das am 17. April 1949 ausgestrahlt wurde, fand sich neben einem Artikel über die Wiederbelebung des kalifornischen Verbandes der International Society for Contemporary Music in Los Angeles unter dem Vorsitz von Ernst Krenek. Die Society plante bereits ein reines Schönberg-Konzert zum 75. Geburtstag des Komponisten mit der *Ode to Napoleon Bonaparte*, op. 41. Am 10. Juni 1950 waren Rundfunkübertragungen von Schönbergs Werken *Herzgewächse*, op. 20, mit der jungen Sopranistin Marni Nixon (1930–2016) und *Friede auf Erden*, op. 13, mit dem Roger Wagner Chorale angekündigt; außerdem ein Konzert in Beverly Hills mit einer Aufführung von Zeisls *Brandeis Sonata* für Violine und Klavier (1949/50) mit Israel Baker (1919–2011) und Yaltah Menuhin (1921–2001), der Schwester des Geigers Yehudi Menuhin.

Zeisls zunehmender Erfolg und seine kompositorische Tätigkeit in der unmittelbaren Nachkriegszeit führten zu ersten professionellen Aufnahmen bei dem von F. Charles Adler

(1889–1959) gegründeten Label Society of Professional Artists (SPA). Der Dirigent Adler war in Berlin für verschiedene Verlage tätig, darunter Bote & Bock und Heinrichshofen; nach seiner Emigration nach New York im Jahr 1934 arbeitete er für G. Schirmer. Mit Schönberg korrespondierte er über die Veröffentlichung der *Begleitungsmusik zu einer Lichtspielszene*, op. 34, deren Aufführung er 1953 in Wien dirigierte, und des *Cellokonzerts D-Dur nach Monn* (1933). 1949 schrieb Zeisl an Adler und schlug die Aufführung seiner Werke vor. Adler antwortete positiv, die Korrespondenz hatte schließlich zwei Aufnahmen von Zeisls Musik im Jahr 1951 unter dem neuen Label SPA zur Folge. Die erste Aufnahme (SPA-5) enthielt Zeisls *Kinderlieder* (1930/31), auf Englisch gesungen, und *Pieces for Barbara* (1944) mit Zeisl am Klavier. Die zweite Aufnahme (SPA-10) brachte die beiden kürzlich komponierten Sonaten: Die *Brandeis Sonata* in der Interpretation von Baker und Menuhin und die *Viola Sonata* (1950), gespielt von den zwei ehemaligen Schönberg-Schüler:innen Sven Reher (1918–1979) und Eda Schlatter (1919–2012). (Baker nahm später Schönbergs *Violinkonzert*, op. 36, und die *Phantasy for Violin and Piano*, op. 47, mit Glenn Gould auf.) Schlatter war zu einer treuen Fürsprecherin von Zeisls Musik geworden, sie führte auch die opulente *Sonata Barocca* (1948/49) auf und gab das eigens für sie geschriebene *Piano Concerto* (1951/52) in Auftrag. Eine andere Schülerin Schönbergs, die Pianistin Natalie Limonick (1920–2007), setzte sich ebenfalls für Zeisls Werke ein. Sie führte die *Sonata Barocca* und die *Kinderlieder* mit Nixon auf (die auch die *Brettl-Lieder* von Schönberg mit Leonard Stein auf Platte einspielte).

Als die *Los Angeles Evening Citizen News* Zeisl im Mai 1952 vor der Uraufführung seiner Oper *Leonce und Lena* (1937) interviewte,[34] kam das Gespräch auf Schönberg. Grund dafür mag gewesen sein, dass die Oper auf einem Theaterstück Georg Büchners basiert, der ja auch der Autor der Vorlage zu Alban Bergs *Wozzeck* war.

Zeisl bewundert Schönberg und Alban Berg, obwohl er kein Anhänger der Zwölfton-Kompositionslehre ist. Er glaubt, dass es in der Musik einen zunehmenden Trend zurück zur Tonalität gibt. Er meint: „Solange man etwas zu sagen hat, das einem zu eigen ist, kann es in jedem Idiom ausgedrückt werden. Der kreative Kopf kann jedes Material formen, gleich ob Dreiklänge, Atonalität, Tonalität, es wird bedeutungsvoll." Aber unter den Atonalisten respektiert er nur Schönberg und Berg. „Ob Schönberg nun akzeptiert wird oder nicht, er hat uns gezeigt, wie weit wir gehen können. Und er hat sich für die jungen Komponisten geopfert. Er war ein Heiliger. Aber er wusste besser als alle anderen, dass der Schöpfer seine eigene Welt erschafft – es ist der Techniker, der immer nach einem System verlangt!"[35]

Nach Schönbergs Tod im Jahr 1951 freundeten die Zeisls sich enger mit seiner Witwe, meiner anderen Großmutter Gertrud, an. Zu Zeisls 50. Geburtstag 1955 widmete Gertrud Schönberg ihm ein seltenes Exemplar des *Sonderhefts der Musikblätter des Anbruch*, erschienen zu Arnold Schönbergs 50. Geburtstag.[36] Als Zeisl am 18. Februar 1959 plötzlich einem Herzinfarkt erlag, war Gertrud Schönberg die Erste, die meine andere Großmutter tröstete. Sie brachte eine Flasche Cognac mit, die dankbar entgegengenommen wurde. Zu diesem Zeitpunkt kannten meine Eltern einander noch nicht. Mein Vater erzählt, dass seine Mutter ihn oft bat, sie zu einem Freund zu fahren, mit dem Versprechen, er könne dann die Tochter dieses Freundes kennenlernen. Aber nachdem

Arnold Schönberg, 1948
Foto: Richard Fish, Arnold Schönberg Center Privatstiftung, Wien (A-Was)

mehrere von diesen Töchtern sich als zu alt oder zu jung herausgestellt hatten, verweigerte mein Vater und nahm das Angebot, seine Mutter zu den Zeisls zu begleiten, nicht wahr. Meine Eltern lernten einander erst später kennen, als mein Vater auf Urlaub von der Armee nach Hause kam und bei seiner Großmutter Henriette Kolisch auf meine Mutter als Haushüterin im Haus der Familie in Brentwood traf.

Ich begann mich als Teenager für die Musik meiner Großväter zu interessieren, genauer gesagt nach meiner Bar-Mizwa im Jahr 1979, bei der Chor- und Orgelwerke meiner beiden Großväter aufgeführt wurden. Ich erinnere mich an einen großen Aufruhr im Jahr zuvor, als Lionel Rolfe, ein Neffe von Yehudi und Yaltah Menuhin, in der Los Angeles Times einen großen Artikel unter dem Titel „An Odd Couple and the Lure of the Southland" veröffentlicht hatte. Eine groß aufgemachte Illustration begleitete den durchaus nicht zutreffenden Artikel: Die Köpfe von Schönberg und Zeisl dicht beieinander, der Bildtext lautete: „Ende der 40er, Anfang der 50er wurden die Komponisten Arnold Schoenberg und Eric Zeisl rasch Freunde." Ich erinnere mich, dass alle über die erfundene Geschichte von den „raschen Freunden" entrüstet waren. Der damalige Direktor des Arnold Schoenberg Institute an der University of Southern California und Schönberg-Schüler Leonard Stein (1916–2004) schrieb einen Leserbrief und korrigierte einige der vielen Fehler. Und auch meine Großmutter widersprach dem Artikel: „Es finden sich zu viele Dinge, die in dem Artikel von Mr. Rolfe falsch sind, um diese im Detail darzulegen. Aber ich muss vor allem darauf hinweisen, dass mein Mann, Eric Zeisl, Schoenberg nur wenige Male persönlich begegnete, obwohl er ihn sehr bewunderte. Er zählte zu Schoenbergs Lebzeiten nie zu dessen innerem Kreis von Freunden und Familie und erhob darauf auch nicht Anspruch, um Ruhm zu ernten."

Im Haus meiner Großmutter hörte ich die alten, oft kratzigen Zeisl-Aufnahmen, die wir dann von Schallplatten oder Tonbandspulen auf Kassetten überspielten. Meine Lieblingsstücke waren das *Zweite Streichquartett* und das *Requiem Ebraico*. Als ich Mitte der 1980er-Jahre an der Princeton University studierte, erhielt ich einen Anruf des Komponisten Milton Babbitt (1916–2011), der mir einmal stolz erzählte, er habe meine Schönberg-Großeltern begrüßt, als sie bei der Einreise 1933 in New York vom Schiff kamen. Babbitt fragte mich, ob ich einem angehenden Studenten aus Los Angeles eine Führung geben würde, dessen Eltern, Robina Young und René Goiffon, eine Aufnahme von Robert Taub mit Babbitts Solo-Klaviermusik für ihr Label Harmonia Mundi USA produziert hatten. Während der Tour sprach ich von meinem anderen Komponisten-Großvater namens Erich Zeisl. Robina war interessiert oder höflich genug, mich zu bitten, ihr einige Werke von Zeisl zu schicken. Nach meinem Abschluss 1988 kehrte ich nach Los Angeles zurück, um an der University of Southern California Jus zu studieren, und zog ins Haus meiner Großmutter, die im Jahr zuvor verstorben war. Ich beschloss, mich mit Robina in Verbindung zu setzen, und schickte ihr eine Tonbandaufnahme von Aufführungen von Zeisls Kammermusik aus den 1950er-Jahren. Im Mai 1989 trafen meine Mutter und ich Robina im Büro von Harmonia Mundi USA in Culver City, direkt unter dem Santa Monica Freeway. Robina schlug vor, Zeisls Kammermusik aufzunehmen, genauer sein *Zweites Streichquartett*, das „Arrowhead"-Trio für Flöte, Bratsche und Harfe und die frühe *Klaviertrio-Suite*, op. 8, die erst kurz zuvor in einem Musikarchiv in Santa Barbara wiederentdeckt worden war.

Um die Werke aufzuführen, wandte ich mich an einige meiner Freunde. Die Harfenistin Marcia Dickstein war die beste Freundin einer Studienkollegin von mir an der juristischen Fakultät und hatte gerade ihr Debussy Trio gegründet, benannt nach dem ersten Komponisten, der die Kombination Flöte, Viola und Harfe verwendete. Die Geiger Mitch Newman und René Mandel, der Bratschist Evan Wilson und der Cellist David Low hatten ein Quartett gebildet, das sich Brandeis-Bardin Ensemble nannte, nach dem Campus der American Jewish University in Simi Valley nördlich von Los Angeles, wo David Musikdirektor war und Zeisl mehr als vier Jahrzehnte zuvor als „composer in residence" gewirkt hatte. Mitch und David luden ihren Freund, den Pianisten Daniel Shapiro, ein, dem Zeisl-Trio beizutreten. Die Aufnahme fand vom 15. bis 17. Oktober 1990 in der wunderschönen und akustisch exquisiten Bridges Hall of Music (bekannt als Little Bridges) am Pomona College in Claremont, Kalifornien, statt. Meine Mutter lehrte dort Germanistik.

Die daraus resultierende Harmonia-Mundi-Aufnahme von 1991, die erste Zeisl-Einspielung seit 40 Jahren, erhielt einige gute Kritiken. „Manches Mal sind es die aus dem Rahmen fallenden Projekte, die aufhorchen lassen", schrieb die *New York Times*. „Die beiden jungen Ensembles bieten ausgefeilte, konzentrierte Aufführungen, die der Musik wunderbar dienen."[37] Die Zeitschrift *Gramophone* war ebenfalls beeindruckt. „Es ist immer anregend, einen Komponisten zu entdecken, dessen Namen man nie und von dessen Musik man nie eine Note gehört hat […] alle, die an Musik aus der ersten Hälfte dieses Jahrhunderts Freude haben, werden ein Können zu schätzen wissen, wie es in den glänzenden Darbietungen der Musik Eric Zeisls auf dieser Platte demonstriert wird. Möge sie ihm viele weitere Bewunderer bringen."[38]

Um diese Zeit lernte meine Tante Nuria Schoenberg-Nono, die in Los Angeles lebte und an ihrer dokumentarischen Schönberg-Biografie *Arnold Schönberg. 1874–1951. Lebensgeschichte in Begegnungen* (1992) arbeitete, den jungen Plattenproduzenten Michael Haas kennen. Michael war gerade dabei, seine Reihe „Entartete Musik" für Decca/London Records zu starten, und Nuria muss ihm vorgeschlagen haben, sich bei mir nach Zeisl zu erkundigen. Glücklicherweise kannte Michael bereits die Kammermusikaufnahme von Harmonia Mundi. 1994 schickte ich ihm eine Reihe von Kassetten mit Zeisl-Aufnahmen, darunter *Leonce und Lena* von 1952 und das *Requiem Ebraico*. Ich hatte die Hoffnung auf eine positive Reaktion bereits aufgegeben, als ich aus heiterem Himmel von Michael erfuhr, dass er Zeisls *Requiem Ebraico* als Begleitstück zur geplanten Aufnahme von Franz Waxmans *Song of Terezin* einspielen würde. Anfang 1997 reisten meine Mutter und ich nach Berlin, um den Aufnahmesitzungen beizuwohnen. Es war dies meine erste Reise zurück nach Berlin, seit ich 1987 dort studiert hatte. Nach den ersten Tagen wurde ich sehr krank und sah bis auf die Jesus-Christus-Kirche in Dahlem, wo die Aufnahmen stattfanden, nicht viel anderes. Es dirigierte Lawrence Foster, der erzählte, dass seine Mutter ihn zum Kompositionsunterricht zu Zeisl gebracht hatte, von dem sie nur hörte, der Junge habe kein Talent zum Komponieren. Foster studierte dann weiter bei Waxman, für dessen Musik er sich nun eifrig einsetzte. Zum Glück hegte Foster keinen Groll gegen Zeisl und die aus diesem Projekt hervorgegangene CD war ein weiterer großer Erfolg für alle Beteiligten.

Als einmal zwei moderne Aufnahmen fertiggestellt waren, folgten bald weitere.[39] Ich lernte schnell, dass jede neue Aufnahme den Grundstein für die nächste legen kann, und inzwischen steht ein großer Teil von Zeisls Œuvre für den Hörgenuss des Publikums zur Verfügung. Es gibt immer noch große Lücken, insbesondere bei den Opern und dem Großteil der Chor- und Ballettmusik. Aber mit der Zeit werden sicherlich auch diese Werke entdeckt und eingespielt werden. Die Aufnahmen geben auch Anlass für Aufführungen, die sporadisch, aber immer wieder stattfinden. Mein Freund Gabor Lukin, ein Urenkel des ungarischen Dramatikers Franz Molnar, begann vor Jahren, Zeisls Biografen Malcolm Cole (1936–2017) bei der Aufbereitung von Zeisl-Partituren zu unterstützen. Während der Pandemie transkribierte er alle 100 Lieder von Zeisl, die nun in einer Serie bei Naxos veröffentlicht werden. Für dieses Jahr geplant sind Aufführungen der *Mondbilder* (1928) in der Fassung für Orchester und des gewaltigen Balletts *Uranium 235* (1945/46), des ersten bedeutenden Musikwerks, das von der Atombombe inspiriert wurde.

In diesem Artikel habe ich die begrenzte, aber für mich sehr bedeutende Beziehung zwischen meinen Großvätern beschrieben und über das Zusammenkommen der beiden Familien nach dem Tod der zwei Protagonisten berichtet. Ich bin das Produkt dieser Verbindung von Traditionen. In meinem Leben versuchte ich, in beiden Lagern verankert zu sein und diese Perspektive zu nutzen, um jeden meiner Großväter genau so zu verstehen, wie er eben war. Es gab niemals die Notwendigkeit, den einen höher zu schätzen als den anderen.

1   Gertrud S. Zeisl geb. Jellinek (1906 Wien – 1987 Salzburg) studierte Rechtswissenschaften an der Universität Wien. Ihr Vater Hermann Jellinek (1867–1933) war lange Zeit gegen die Verbindung mit Erich Zeisl, den sie am 29. 12. 1935 heiratete. Sie emigrierte über Paris und New York nach Los Angeles und wurde Highschool-Lehrerin für Latein, Französisch und Deutsch. Das Oral-History-Interview, das Malcolm Cole mit ihr führte, ist eine wichtige Quelle zu ihrem Ehemann: http://zeisl.com/archive/gertrud-zeisls-oral-history.htm (abgerufen am 8. 12. 2024).

2   Erich (1886–1961) und Nora (1891–1974) Lachmann. 1950 erschien ein Buch, das die Lachmann-Instrumentensammlung beschreibt: *Erich Lachmann Collection of Historical Stringed Musical Instruments*, Los Angeles: Allan Hancock Foundation, University of Southern California, 1950. Die Sammlung wurde um 1960 von der UCLA erworben, viele Instrumente wurden deakzessioniert und 2009 bei Christie's versteigert. Laut dem Auktionskatalog zog Lachmann 1932 nach Los Angeles und „wurde vor dem Zweiten Weltkrieg zum einflussreichsten Händler an der Westküste". Siehe https://www.christies.com/presscenter/pdf/09142009/14263.pdf (abgerufen am 14. 11. 2024).

3   Gertrud Zeisl, Tagebucheintrag, 2. 11. 1945, Erich-Zeisl-Nachlass, Exilarte Zentrum, Wien.

4   Karin Wagner, *Fremd bin ich ausgezogen. Eric Zeisl. Biografie*, Wien 2005, S. 35.

5   Zit. n. ebd. Siehe auch Alban Bergs Brief vom 18. 3. 1912 an Schönberg: „diese Schweine, Stöhr vor allem", ASCC 19761 (= Arnold Schönberg Center Correspondence).

6   Richard Stöhr, Empfehlungsschreiben, 22. 5. 1938, Erich-Zeisl-Nachlass, Exilarte Zentrum, Wien.

7   Joseph Marx (1882–1964), Komponist und Musikprofessor. Marx trat 1922 die Nachfolge von Ferdinand Löwe als Direktor der Akademie für Musik und darstellende Kunst in Wien an. Schönberg schrieb am 26. 12. 1922 einen Brief an Marx, in dem er mit vorsichtiger Zurückhaltung auf ein Angebot für eine Lehrtätigkeit an der Akademie reagierte; sie kam jedoch nicht zustande. Siehe http://www.joseph-marx-gesellschaft.org/english/joseph-marx.html (abgerufen am 8. 12. 2024).

8   Hugo Kauder (1888 Tovačov, Mähren - 1972 Bussum, Niederlande) war Bratschist, Geiger, Komponist und Musikprofessor. Siehe https://www.hugokauder.org/ (abgerufen am 8. 12. 2024). Er nahm an zwei Konzerten des Vereins teil, am 30. 3. und 6. 6. 1919. Siehe Karin Wagner, *Hugo Kauder (1888–1972). Komponist – Musikphilosoph – Theoretiker. Eine Biographie*, Wien 2018.

9   Das Galimir Quartett bestand aus dem Geiger Felix Galimir (1910 Wien – 1999 New York) und seinen drei Schwestern Clara (1905–1985), Renée (1908–1973) und Adrienne (1912–1997). Es spielte 1935 erstmals Alban Bergs *Lyrische Suite* ein. Die jüngste Galimir-Schwester, Adrienne, heiratete den amerikanischen Geiger Louis Krasner (1903–1995), der 1935 das *Violinkonzert* von Alban Berg in Auftrag gab und uraufführte. Krasner brachte 1940 auch Schönbergs *Violinkonzert*, op. 36, unter der Leitung von Leopold Stokowski zur Uraufführung.

10 „Eine der stärksten Persönlichkeiten der noch nicht dreißigjährigen Wiener Komponisten ist Erich Zeisel [sic]." Paul A. Pisk, „Erich Zeisel [sic]", in: *Radio Wien*, 26. 1. 1934, S. 2-3. Siehe https://anno.onb.ac.at/cgi-content/anno?aid=raw&datum=19340126&seite=4&zoom=33 (abgerufen am 8. 12. 2024).

11 Paul Amadeus Pisk (1893 Wien – 1990 Los Angeles) promovierte 1916 bei Guido Adler an der Universität Wien in Musikwissenschaft. Von 1917 bis 1919 studierte er auch bei Franz Schreker und Arnold Schönberg. Er war Vorstandsmitglied, Sekretär und Pianist in Schönbergs Verein für musikalische Privataufführungen. Nach seiner Emigration lehrte er an der University of Redlands in Südkalifornien.

12 Erwin Stein (1885 Wien – 1958 London) studierte zwischen 1906 und 1910 bei Schönberg. Er arbeitete im Verein für musikalische Privataufführungen eng mit ihm zusammen und schuf mehrere Bearbeitungen (Gustav Mahlers *Symphonie Nr. 4* und Anton Bruckners *Symphonie Nr. 7*), die in Konzerten des Vereins aufgeführt wurden. Von 1924 bis 1938 arbeitete er bei Schönbergs Hauptverlag Universal Edition, danach emigrierte er nach England und wechselte zum Verlag Boosey & Hawkes.

13 Die Aufführung von *Scherzo und Fuge* mit dem Wiener Konzertorchester war für 10. 3. 1938 angekündigt. Siehe *Reichspost*, 10. 3. 1938, S. 11.

14 Alma Mahler-Werfel (1879–1964), eine Schülerin von Alexander Zemlinsky und Witwe von Gustav Mahler, heiratete zuletzt den Schriftsteller Franz Werfel, der Arnold Schönbergs Cousin dritten Grades war (obwohl das wahrscheinlich keiner der beiden wusste). Alma war die langjährigste enge Freundin Schönbergs, die in Los Angeles lebte. Als er 1951 starb, waren die beiden über 50 Jahre eng befreundet gewesen. Siehe Haide Tenner, *„Ich möchte so lange leben, als ich Ihnen*

dankbar sein kann". Alma Mahler – Arnold Schönberg. Der Briefwechsel, St. Pölten 2012; Elizabeth L. Keathley, Marilyn L. McCoy, *Schoenberg's Correspondence with Alma Mahler*, Oxford 2019. Alma fand sich oft inmitten von Streitigkeiten wieder, in die Schönberg verwickelt war, wie jene im Briefwechsel mit Wassily Kandinsky 1923 über den Antisemitismus am Bauhaus oder im Konflikt mit Thomas Mann 1948 über *Doktor Faustus*. Sie war auch mit den Zeisls in Los Angeles befreundet, und meine Großmutter erinnerte sich in ihrer Oral History, dass Alma einmal sehr eifersüchtig war, weil Strawinsky zu einer Party ins Haus der Zeisls gekommen war, ihre Einladung aber abgelehnt hatte. Nach Zeisls Tod schickte sie ein Telegramm an meine Großmutter: „I am very very sad about your loss. I felt his great talent but also his deep disappointment about his life which did not bring him the success due to his significance." Alma Mahler-Werfel an Gertrud Zeisl, 21. 3. 1959, Erich-Zeisl-Nachlass, Exilarte Zentrum, Wien.

15   Der profilierte französische Komponist Darius Milhaud (1879 Marseille – 1964 Genf) war Mitglied von „Les Six". Er dirigierte 1923 die erste englische Aufführung von Schönbergs *Pierrot Lunaire* in London. Milhaud emigrierte 1940 nach Oakland, Kalifornien, wo er am Mills College und an der Music Academy of the West in Santa Barbara Musik lehrte.

16   Der Komponist Hanns Eisler (1898 Leipzig – 1962 Berlin) war von 1919 bis 1923 Schüler von Arnold Schönberg. Wie Zeisl zog er 1942 nach Los Angeles, um Filmmusik zu komponieren. Die beiden schrieben Musik für konkurrierende Filme über die Ermordung von Reinhard Heydrich im Jahr 1942. Fritz Langs Film *Hangmen Also Die* (1943), der einige Monate früher herauskam, brachte Eisler eine Oscar-Nominierung ein. Zeisl blieb für seine Beiträge zu *Hitler's Madman* (1943) von Douglas Sirk ungenannt.

17   Hanns Eisler an Arnold Schönberg, 28. 5. 1941, Erich-Zeisl-Nachlass, Exilarte Zentrum, Wien.

18   Richard Stöhr an Erich Zeisl, undatiert, zit. n. Karin Wagner (Hg.), *… es grüsst Dich Erichisrael. Briefe von und an Eric Zeisl, Hilde Spiel, Richard Stöhr, Ernst Toch, Hans Kafka u. a.*, Wien 2008, S. 166.

19   Der Komponist Erich Wolfgang Korngold (1897 Brünn – 1957 Los Angeles) war ein Wunderkind, er war der Sohn des konservativen Musikkritikers Julius Korngold (1860 Brünn – 1945 Los Angeles) und ein Schüler von Alexander Zemlinsky. Als Jugendlicher war er eng mit Maria (Mitzi) Kolisch, der älteren Schwester meiner Großmutter, befreundet und widmete ihr ein Liebeslied. In Hollywood war er der erfolgreichste der emigrierten Komponisten. Er prägte den sogenannten Hollywood-Sound und komponierte 16 Filme, für die er zwei Oscars und zwei weitere Nominierungen erhielt. Nach ihrer Ankunft in Los Angeles freundeten sich die Zeisls mit den Korngolds durch ihre gemeinsamen Freunde Fritz und Maria Reitler an. Marias Vater war der Musikkritiker Josef Reitler (1883 Wien – 1948 New York), von 1902 bis 1905 ein früher Musiktheorie-Schüler Schönbergs. Schönberg und Julius Korngold gehörten in Wien unterschiedlichen Lagern an und lernten einander erst in Los Angeles persönlich kennen, wo sie mehrere herzliche Briefe austauschten, die in einem persönlichen Kondolenzbrief nach Korngolds Tod im September 1945 gipfelten. („I had the opportunity – unfortunately only late in our lives – of having contact with your father and I must say that I regret it has not happened earlier. A man like he, whose knowledge and judgement of music was based upon a profound love for this art, such a man should have lived earlier and longer in this country." Arnold Schönberg an Erich Wolfgang und Luzi Korngold, 3. 9. 1945, ASCC 23956. Von der tiefen und sehr engen Freundschaft zwischen Korngold und Zeisl zeugt eine Widmung auf einer Partitur von Korngolds Oper *Die tote Stadt*: „Erich Zeisl – dem alten Freund der ‚toten Stadt' mit allen guten Wünschen: Erich Wolfgang Korngold (der neue Freund in der ganz ‚toten Stadt'!) Hollywood, Weihnachten 1946." Erich-Zeisl-Nachlass, Exilarte Zentrum, Wien.

20   Der Komponist Ernst Toch (1887 Wien – 1964 Santa Monica, Kalif.) scheint mit Schönberg nur wenig Kontakt gehabt zu haben, bevor sie nach 1929 in Berlin lebten. Mit dem Aufstieg der Nationalsozialisten flüchteten beide im Frühjahr 1933 und waren im Mai 1933 gemeinsam in Paris. Zu jener Zeit begann Schönberg ernsthaft über Mittel zur Rettung der europäischen Jüdinnen und Juden durch Gründung eines jüdischen Staates nachzudenken und schrieb an Toch: „Darum will ich eine Bewegung hervorrufen, welche die Juden wieder zu einem Volk macht und sie in einem geschlossenen Land zu einem Staat vereinigt." Arnold Schönberg an Ernst Toch, Mai 1933, ASCC 6587. Ab 1936 lehrte Toch in Los Angeles an der University of Southern California. Er blieb mit Schönberg in gutem Einvernehmen, ihre Töchter wurden Freundinnen. Bei einem Neujahrsempfang 1942 begann die Freundschaft zwischen Zeisl und Toch. Aus der Oral History von Gertrud Zeisl: „Nun, zu diesem Silvesterabend hatte er Eric eingeladen, und da war Ernst Toch, und die beiden haben sich fast sofort angefreundet. Und sie setzten sich ans Klavier, und ohne darüber zu reden, fingen sie an, vierhändig zu spielen, auf eine lustige Art und Weise, und gingen durch die Wiener

Walzer und so weiter und hatten diese Art von Silvesterstimmung. Und es war sehr lustig." Die beiden waren 1948 gemeinsam „composers in residence" im Brandeis Camp in Simi Valley und 1957 in der Huntington Hartford Foundation in Rustic Canyon in Santa Monica.

21 Hugo Strelitzer (1896 Berlin – 1981 Los Angeles) war der Leiter der Opernabteilung am Los Angeles City College. Er war Chorleiter der von Werner Janssen am 18. November 1945 uraufgeführten *Genesis Suite* von Nathaniel Shilkret, die aus Kompositionen von Shilkret selbst und von durch ihn beauftragten Komponisten (Alexandre Tansman, Darius Milhaud, Ernst Toch, Igor Strawinsky, Mario Castelnuovo-Tedesco und Arnold Schönberg) bestand. Für die Aufführung und die Aufnahme 1946 wandelte Shilkret Schönbergs *Prelude to Genesis*, op. 44, in ein Postludium um, da er befürchtete, dass Schönbergs Musik einen negativen Eindruck auf das Publikum machen würde. Es ist nicht bekannt, ob die Zeisls dem Konzert beiwohnten, aber es scheint sehr wahrscheinlich, da Zeisl zu dieser Zeit mit Tansman und Castelnuovo-Tedesco, die er durch seine Arbeit im Filmstudio kennengelernt hatte, sowie mit Milhaud und Strawinsky, die er wieder über Tansman kennengelernt hatte, eng befreundet war. Strelitzer wurde auch ein enger Freund der Zeisls. 1952 wurde in Strelitzers Opera Workshop am Los Angeles City College Zeisls Oper *Leonce und Lena* uraufgeführt. Bei der Hochzeit meiner Eltern am 23. 11. 1965 übernahm Hugo Strelitzer die Rolle des Brautvaters, als er meine Mutter zum Traualtar führte (eigentlich eine Treppe in ihrem Haus am Miler Drive).

22 Nach dieser Begegnung mit Zeisl wurde Wright ein unermüdlicher Fürsprecher seiner Musik. Er leitete den Chor beim Erich-Zeisl-Gedenkkonzert am 23. 11. 1959.

23 Laut Gertrud Zeisls Oral History hatte Strelitzer William Zeisl als Kantor des Fairfax-Tempels empfohlen, über diese Verbindung lernte Rabbi Sonderling Zeisl kennen und schlug ihm vor, Psalm 92 zu vertonen. Siehe Jonathan L. Friedman, John F. Guest, *Songs of Sonderling. Commissioning Jewish Émigré Composers in Los Angeles, 1938–1945* (Modern Jewish History), Lubbock, Tex., 2021.

24 Die Orchesterfassung war am 23. 1. 1948 von der Santa Monica Little Symphony unter Jacques Rachmilovich uraufgeführt worden. Siehe *Los Angeles Times*, 26. 1. 1948, S. 10.

25 Der Dirigent Adolf Heller (1901 Prag – 1954 Santa Barbara, Kalif.) lehrte fünf Jahre lang am Los Angeles City College, wo er zusammen mit Hugo Strelitzer den Opera Workshop leitete. Heller war als Assistenzdirigent an der San Francisco Opera (unter Kurt Herbert Adler) engagiert, als er 1954 bei einem Autounfall starb. Siehe https://www.imdb.com/name/nm0375265/ (abgerufen am 19. 11. 2024). Heller, Strelitzer und Zeisl urlaubten und unterrichteten gemeinsam in Lake Arrowhead, Kalifornien, im Arrowhead Music Camp, das dem Los Angeles Conservatory of Music angeschlossen war. Siehe *Los Angeles Times*, 4. 6. 1950, S. 104. Neben dem *Requiem Ebraico* dirigierte Heller 1952 auch die Premiere von Zeisls Oper *Leonce und Lena* am Los Angeles City College.

26 Arnold Schönberg an Remsen DuBois Bird, Präsident des Occidental College, 22. 5. 1940, ASCC 23646.

27 Erich Zeisl an Arnold Schönberg, 13. 9. 1949, ASCC 19345.

28 *Los Angeles Times*, 7. 12. 1948, S. 42: „Mr. Zeisl is that curiosity among modern composers, one who writes as he feels without regard to formulas or fashions. His brief songs were all quick and definite impressions of childhood [...]. Their main interest lay more in the accompaniments Mr. Zeisl played so expertly and feelingly [...]. [T]hey are varied and attractive songs which should win a place in the repertoire." („Zeisl ist jene Kuriosität unter den modernen Komponisten, einer, der schreibt, wie er empfindet, ohne Rücksicht auf Formeln und Moden. Seine kurzen Lieder sind allesamt rasche und bestimmte Kindheitseindrücke [...]. Das Hauptinteresse dabei lag mehr in der Klavierbegleitung, die Zeisl mit so viel Können und Gefühl darbot [...]. [E]s sind variierte und attraktive Lieder, die einen festen Platz im Repertoire finden sollen.")

29 *Los Angeles Times*, 14. 5. 1950, S. 107.

30 *Los Angeles Times*, 21. 5. 1950, S. 116.

31 Ernst Krenek, ein Schüler von Franz Schreker, der kurzzeitig mit Gustav und Alma Mahlers Tochter Anna verheiratet war, besuchte 1937 Südkalifornien und nahm 1938 eine Stelle am Malkin Conservatory in Boston an (wo auch Schönberg nach seiner Ankunft in den Vereinigten Staaten 1933 zunächst unterrichtet hatte). Krenek kehrte 1947 nach Los Angeles zurück und unterrichtete gemeinsam mit Zeisl an der Southern California School of Music and Arts und am Los Angeles City College. In einer College-Broschüre von 1950/51 wurden fünf Lehrveranstaltungen angeführt: „Contemporary Music" und „Brief History of Opera", unterrichtet von Krenek, „Analysis & Composition" und „Chromatic Harmony", unterrichtet von Zeisl, und der „Opera Workshop", unterrichtet von Heller und Strelitzer. Zeisl übernahm oft Kreneks Unterricht, wenn Krenek auf Reisen war. Siehe z. B. Erich Zeisl an Richard Stöhr, 12. 12. 1951, und Erich Zeisl an Hilde Spiel, undatiert, zit. n. Wagner 2008, wie Anm. 18, S. 264, 271. Bei der Konfirmationsfeier von Ro-

nald Schönberg im Mai 1950 erklärte sich Krenek (auf Bitten Arnold Schönbergs) widerwillig bereit, die Patenschaft für den Jungen zu übernehmen.

32 Eugen(e) Zádor (1894 Bátaszék, Ungarn – 1977 Hollywood) war ein Komponist, der in Wien und in Leipzig bei Max Reger studierte. Ab 1921 lehrte er am Neuen Wiener Konservatorium. Nach seiner Emigration schrieb er viel Musik für MGM (für die er ungenannt blieb), wobei er eng mit Miklós Rózsa zusammenarbeitete.

33 *Los Angeles Times*, 28. 5. 1950, S. 90.

34 Die Uraufführung von *Leonce und Lena* (1937) sollte im Frühjahr 1938 im Hoftheater Schönbrunn unter der Leitung von Kurt Herbert Adler (1905–1988), später Dirigent der San Francisco Opera, stattfinden, doch der „Anschluss" machte eine Aufführung unmöglich. *Leonce und Lena* wurde 2017 in Linz und zuletzt im Eduard-von-Winterstein-Theater in Annaberg-Buchholz im Herbst 2021 aufgeführt.

35 *Los Angeles Evening Citizen News*, 3. 5. 1952, S. 5.

36 Gertrud Schönberg gehörte zum Committee of Friends, das am 22. 5. 1955 das Galakonzert zu Ehren von Zeisls 50. Geburtstag organisierte. Weitere Mitglieder des Komitees waren Kurt Herbert Adler, Erich Wolfgang Korngold, Alma Mahler-Werfel, Darius Milhaud, Edward Muhl, Igor Strawinsky, Hugo Strelitzer, Alexandre Tansman, Ernst Toch, John Vincent, Eugene Zádor und Fritz Zweig. Siehe Malcolm S. Cole, Barbara Barclay, *Armseelchen. The Life and Music of Eric Zeisl*, Westport, Conn., 1984, S. 70.

37 *New York Times*, 22. 3. 1992, Buch 2, S. 32.

38 *Gramophone*, Sept. 1992.

39 Siehe http://www.zeisl.com/books-and-recordings/recordings.htm (abgerufen am 8. 12. 2024).

Die Familie von Barbara Zeisl und Ronald Schoenberg: Frederic Roland Schoenberg, Melanie Raldon Schoenberg, Barbara Zeisl-Schoenberg, Ronald Schoenberg, Marlena Lorand Schoenberg und Eric Randol Schoenberg in Malibu, 2024
Foto: E. Randol Schoenberg

Michael Haas

RABBI SONDERLING AND HIS COMMISSIONS

European Jews arriving in the United States were constantly battling with issues of identity. Jewish communities in the United States were, of course, active and supportive, but for many Austrian, German and Czech refugees, self-identity had not been based on belonging to a particular religious tribe or community. This had been the case for a very long time. With the emancipation of Jews in the second half of the nineteenth century, a natural evolution had taken place with each successive generation taking on more of the characteristics of the surrounding non-Jewish communities in which they were integrating.

Many assimilating Jews celebrated Easter and Christmas not as Christian festivals but as national holidays. By absorbing these ambient festivities into their own traditions, the exotic differences between Christians and Jews began to vanish. With the arrival of the generation born around the turn of the century, Jewish rituals and festivals were celebrated as family occasions at home if indeed they were celebrated at all. To belong to a minority faith while integrating into a larger community, whether Catholic or Protestant, frequently resulted in the total secularisation of younger generations of Jews. If they felt their religious identity placed a barrier between themselves and their friends and colleagues, it was best to get rid of it altogether, while never being quite sure with what, if anything, they might replace it.

With the cataclysm of defeat in 1918 and newer, more modern and efficient systems of governance taking over from emperors and kings, secularisation was not just limited to young Jews. Traditions that had elevated monarchs and the church to be an expression of "God's natural order" were exposed as a useful "opium" to keep the masses under control. Emperors, kings, and the nobility were no longer seen as having a special contract with the Almighty.

Nevertheless, this general secularisation of society was viewed and understood from two very different perspectives. Jews believed it to be a natural evolution that removed barriers between equal citizens. They saw being Jewish as an individual choice of following one religion in preference to another. Many non-Jewish Europeans had, however, existed for centuries with antisemitism so ingrained by church and social traditions that they instinctively sought justification for feelings they could not easily abandon. They held on to the view that being Jewish, far from being a personal denominational decision undertaken by an individual, was in fact a "racial" characteristic that made Jews and non-Jews as different as night and day. The pseudoscientists who called upon Charles Darwin or Herbert Spencer as confirming their racist views, such as Houston Stewart Chamberlain, were often dismissed as silly dilettantes. In reviewing Chamberlain's *The Foundations of the Nineteenth Century*, the critic and philosopher

Ludwig Stein wrote: "In short, this is a very bad book, unclear and illogical in its development of ideas and ungratifying in its style of writing, full of false modesty and real arrogance, of real ignorance and false scholarship."[1]

Ludwig Stein was Jewish, indeed a rabbi, and he would not have anticipated the credibility given to Chamberlain's writings once they were endorsed by Germany's Kaiser Wilhelm II. The views of Stein and the German emperor represented the era's rift of perception: Jews no longer saw themselves as Jews as soon as they signed a notarized document that stated as much, while non-Jews, still searching for scientific justification on which to base their inbred racism, believed that Chamberlain and his followers had miraculously come up with precisely that.

The expulsion, expropriation and internment of Germans and Austrians after 1933 who no longer considered themselves as Jews, or at the very least, thought of themselves as nonobservant, was therefore met with stunned disbelief. This feeling of baffled incomprehension was something that the Los Angeles-based, Polish-born Liberal Rabbi Jacob Sonderling instantly recognized as an opportunity. He did not seek religious renewal among his congregation of Jews who had "forgotten how to be Jews,"[2] to borrow from Joseph Roth's *The Wandering Jews*, but rather, he saw a way of outreach. If Jews had hitherto understood assimilation as necessitating active rejection of their Jewish creed and traditions, Sonderling viewed assimilation as a two-way transaction: Jews needed to reach beyond the liturgy of religious worship to universal self-expressions that could be performed in both temple and secular concert hall, while at the same time remaining fundamentally, defiantly Jewish.

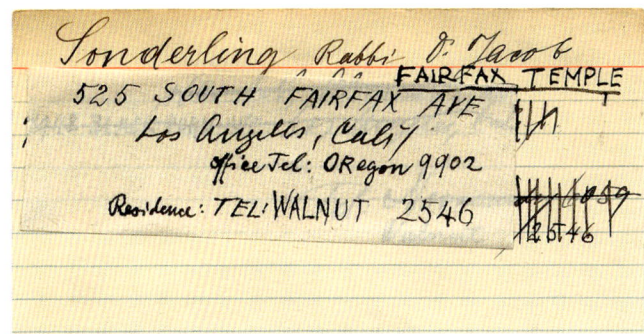

Arnold Schoenberg's address book in Los Angeles opened at the "Sonderling" entry, Fairfax Temple, 525 South Fairfax Ave
Arnold Schönberg Center Privatstiftung, Wien (A-Was)

Sonderling recounted in the *Los Angeles Times* on October 2, 1938, as follows:

[This] relationship between the bible student and the composer of biblical musical texts dawned upon me while studying the composition by the grandfather of Friedrich Schorr, the famous Metropolitan baritone. The composition dealt with a prayer spoken on the Day of Atonement. The penitent sinner begs God to forgive, "Turn from Thy fierce wrath" comes in a heavy bass voice. And, then, suddenly the tempo changes from Andantino to Allegretto. A soprano takes up the melody and repeats these words in a startling Scherzo. The composer, a cantor in Poland and a thorough student of the Bible, sought to interpret in this melody the relationship between the Jew and God. It was to him the kinship of a father and an erring child. It is intensely human. The child, according to Schorr's conception, is horrified because of his sins and so he approaches his father in a repentant mood. But fearing the request for forgiveness will not be granted, he tries with all the winsome tricks of the child to make Him smile. Therefore, the female soprano voice comes trippingly out as though to say, "You cannot punish me. See, I make you smile and since you smile, I know you will forgive."[3]

Sonderling was not alone in trying to renew or redefine Jewish music with a specifically religious dimension. David Putterman of New York's Park Avenue Synagogue was also commissioning works. The difference between him and Sonderling at his Santa Monica Temple was that Putterman specifically commissioned liturgical works, such as Kurt Weill's *Kiddush*, while Sonderling focused on works that were meant to reach out to Jews and non-Jews alike. Putterman's outreach went in quite a different direction, though arguably the intention was the same. He commissioned non-Jews, such as Roy Harris and the African-American composer William Grant Still, to write liturgical works.

A meeting between Sonderling and the composer Ernst Toch, the movie producer Boris Morros, and the actor Leopold Jessner led to the setting of Toch's story of the Haggadah—or the exodus from Egypt. Toch's work was called *Cantata of the Bitter Herbs,* and he went on to explain its concept in an essay found among his personal papers held at UCLA's Performing Arts Library. As the first of Sonderling's commissions, it set the template as "nondenominational" and "universalist." Toch related how it was a sequence of events that led him to meet Sonderling. He had received news of his mother's death in Vienna in December 1937 and knowing how she would never miss the prayers for the dead, he went to the Temple in Santa Monica. He met Rabbi Sonderling after the service who suggested that Toch's daughter might enjoy some

Ernst Toch in conversation with Kurt Weill in Baden-Baden, 1927
Ernst Toch Collection, UCLA Performing Arts Library

Otto Klemperer, Hubertus Friedrich Löwenstein-Wertheim-Freudenberg,
Arnold Schoenberg and Ernst Toch in Los Angeles, 1935
Arnold Schönberg Center Privatstiftung, Wien (A-Was)

Hanukkah events that were currently taking place. This brought Toch closer to the religion and traditions of his childhood, although it did not wholly convince him to embrace the full orthodoxy of belief.[4]

His retelling of the Jewish exodus from Egypt was expressed through the eyes of a child. In 1938, the Shoah was not yet the nightmare it was revealed to be after the war. Yet despite what was still to come, the similarities of Jews fleeing Egypt and Jews fleeing Hitler were all too obvious. The premiere took place in the Temple itself with Toch's daughter taking part.

Following the success of the Toch commission, Sonderling lost no time to approach Arnold Schoenberg, whom he met through the violinist Joseph Achron. In some ways, this is the most unusual work among Sonderling's commissions as, in contrast to the others, it was a liturgical work, at least in name if not in concept. *Kol Nidre* (All vows) is the prayer for Yom Kippur, the Day of Atonement, when unfulfilled vows are nullified. Schoenberg was initially reluctant to commit to the work as he had left the faith, only to return to it in Paris in 1933, which gave the subject matter a personal relevance that he found uncomfortable.

Sonderling convinced Schoenberg that returning to his Jewish religion was indeed atonement for turning his back on the faith and also promised the composer a new text that was less rigid. The revised text was intended to remain compatible with the liturgy of the religious service, but the way Schoenberg carried out the composition ultimately made this impossible. Unusually for Schoenberg, the work is tonal and in G minor, while ending in a blaze of G major. The revised text was indeed too worldly for other synagogues, and the required instrumentation eventually led to the October 1938 premiere taking place in a Los Angeles nightclub with members of the Twentieth Century Fox Orchestra.

Sonderling's next commission would go to Erich Wolfgang Korngold. This was perhaps a more difficult request to fulfil than the others, since Korngold had been raised in a militantly secular family and had little or no knowledge of the Jewish liturgy. Toch and Schoenberg were both children of Vienna's second district, the so-called matzo island, where most of the city's lower-middle-class and working-class Jews lived. Korngold and his wife Luzi (née Sonnenthal) had been raised in upper-class bourgeois families that ceased practicing their religion altogether. Korngold's grandfather-in-law, Adolf von Sonnenthal, however, was one of the first Jews to be raised into the nobility by the Emperor and was a founding father of the city's Jewish Museum.

These families therefore represented the very trajectory of assimilation described in the opening paragraphs. Erich was aware of the ghettoization his parents had experienced as Jews born just before the Constitution of December of 1867, which lifted all restrictions against Jews and placed them as absolute equals with every other citizen in the Habsburg realm. The parents of Korngold and his wife were the first generation to enjoy the privilege of choice, of leaving or staying within their religious community as they pleased. By the time Erich Wolfgang Korngold and Luzi von Sonnenthal were born, the secularisation of assimilated young Jews from bourgeois families was complete. Korngold's love of Catholic pageantry was expressed in his operas *Die tote Stadt* and *Das Wunder der Heliane*. The Korngolds celebrated Christmas and other Christian/national holidays.

Perhaps with Korngold's parents and their religious upbringing in mind, Sonderling convinced him to compose not just a *Passover Psalm*, but also a work called *Prayer*; both works would later be presented to Korngold's parents as a wedding anniversary gift. Correspondence between parents and

Programme

HOLLYWOOD INTER-FAITH FORUM
SUNDAY, APRIL 8, 1945
Held at
HOLLYWOOD FIRST METHODIST CHURCH

Moderators:
REV. JOHN H. ENGLE, Minister, Crescent Heights Methodist Church;
DR. JACOB SONDERLING, Rabbi, Society for Jewish Culture-Fairfax Temple.

Subject:

"The Message of Music in Religion"

Organ Prelude by ERIC ZEISL   NORMAN H. WRIGHT at the organ

DR. GLENN R. PHILLIPS

JESSE J. GOLDBURG, Committee Chairman, Fairfax Temple

REV. JOHN H. ENGLE

Psalm 137: By the rivers of Babylon, there we sat down, yea, we wept, when we remembered Zion. We hanged our harps upon the willows in the midst thereof. For there they that carried us away captive required of us a song; and they that wasted us required of us mirth, saying, Sing us one of the songs of Zion. How shall we sing the Lord's song in a strange land? If I forget thee, O Jerusalem, let my right hand forget her cunning. If I do not remember thee, let my tongue cleave to the roof of my mouth; if I prefer not Jerusalem above my chief joy. Remember, O Lord, the children of Edom in the day of Jerusalem; who said, Rase it, rase it, even to the foundation thereof. O daughter of Babylon, who art to be destroyed; happy shall he be, that rewardeth thee as thou hast served us. Happy shall he be, that taketh and dasheth thy little ones against the stones.

CRESCENT HEIGHTS SIGMATONES.........Director LUVERNE SIGMOND
(a) By the Waters of Babylon.......by CHARLES FRANCOIS GOUNOD
(b) Hymn: I Need Thee Every Hour...............................

RABBI MAX NUSSBAUM

ERNST TOCH..HENRY TEMIANKA
(From Toch's Sonata E Major for Violin and Piano—1912)

DR. EDMUND A. CYKLER

FAIRFAX TEMPLE CHOIR...........Soloists: CANTOR WILLIAM ZEISL,
LILLIAN FAWCETT, RECE SAXON.....DR. HUGO STRELITZER, Conductor.

Psalm 92
Composition by ERIC ZEISL. It is good to give thanks to the Lord, and to sing praises to Thy name, O Most High; to declare Thy lovingkindness in the morning, and Thy faithfulness every night, with an instrument of ten strings and with the psaltery; with a solemn sound upon the harp. For Thou, Lord, hast made me glad through Thy work; I will exult in the works of Thy hands. How great are Thy works, O Lord, Thy thoughts are very deep. A brutish man knoweth not, neither doth a fool understand this. When the wicked spring up as the grass, and when all the workers of iniquity do flourish; it is that they may be destroyed forever. But Thou, O Lord, art on high for evermore. For lo, Thine enemies, O Lord, for lo, Thine enemies shall perish; all the workers of iniquity shall be scattered. But my horn hast Thou exalted like the horn of the wild ox; I am anointed with rich oil. Mine eye also hath gazed on them that lie in wait for me; mine ears have heard my desire of the evil doers that rise up against me. The righteous shall flourish like the palm-tree; he shall grow like a cedar in Lebanon. Planted in the house of the Lord, they shall flourish in the courts of our God. They shall still bring forth fruit in old age; they shall be full of sap and richness; to declare that the Lord is upright, my Rock, in whom there is no unrighteousness.

MARIA JERITZA......................Accompanied by Niclas Kempner.

BENEDICTION

The audience is requested to refrain from applauding, and to remain standing during the recital of "The Lord's Prayer" until the conclusion of the Benediction.

The final session of the current series of The Inter-Faith Forum will be held Sunday, May 13, 1945 at 8 P.M. at the Hollywood-Beverly Christian Church, 1717 N. Gramercy Place, Hollywood. Subject: "PALESTINE and the WORLD'S PEACE." Moderator: Dr. Cleveland Kleihauer.

Concert within the "Hollywood Inter-Faith Forum": Rabbi Sonderling spoke about "The Message of Music in Religion". Zeisl's *Requiem Ebraico* was premiered in the version for organ.
Archiv des Exilarte Zentrum der mdw, Wien (A-Weaz)

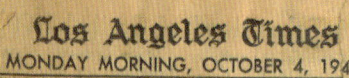

From a review in *The Tidings*, April 13, 1945: "a composer in Hollywood who can still divorce himself from the false glitter of film music and devote his spare time to writing music to a religious text."
Archiv des Exilarte Zentrum der mdw, Wien (A-Weaz)

children nearly always included a "God's blessing" and an indication that some residual religious belief remained at least within the older generation. Once Hitler forced him to acknowledge his Judaism, Korngold was compelled by Sonderling's commission to "take ownership" of it.

Both works radiate the textual and orchestral opulence unique to Korngold with thematic progressions moving ever upwards towards an unknown realm beyond the clouds. The text was a Haggadah text similar to that set by Toch. His setting of *Prayer* was to Franz Werfel's *Adonai Eloheinu* in both English and Hebrew, and the premiere of both works took place on April 12, 1941.

The next works with commissions or input from Sonderling came after the defeat of Nazism and the terrible revelation of Hitler's mass murder. His contribution to Schoenberg's *Survivor from Warsaw* was not that of a commissioning patron but an advisor. His last commission, arguably the most universalist of all the works, went to Eric Zeisl. It was intended to be so nondenominational as to be given the oxymoronic title of *Requiem Ebraico*, a Jewish-Catholic service for the souls of the dead, set to the text of Psalm 92. Adding to the ecumenical character of the work, its premiere was held in Hollywood's First Methodist Church with the Santa Monica Symphony in 1945. It is a rather joyous work and neither typical of a Catholic requiem or a Jewish *Kaddish*, despite being dedicated to Zeisl's parents who were murdered in Treblinka. Zeisl described this paradox as follows:

> At that time war in Europe had just ended and I received the first news of the death of my father and many friends. The sadness of my mood went into my composition which became a Requiem, though I had not intended to write one and scarcely would have chosen the 92nd psalm for it. Yet the completed Requiem thus received a deeper meaning than I could have achieved by planning it that way.[5]

It is in summation a work in which Zeisl attempts a reconciliation with God despite profound tragedy. One critic was reported as writing that it was "one of the most gripping pieces of elegiac composition in the history of music."[6]

The Sonderling commissions represent a trajectory of exile starting with the common theme of exodus and exile as described in the Haggadah, interpreted by Toch and Korngold, along with a reaffirmation of faith set by Korngold *(Adonai Eloheinu)* and Schoenberg, ending with the despair and hope of Zeisl's *Requiem Ebraico*. Hitler stood for an exclusionary view of Judaism. Sonderling's commissions, as demonstrated by these displaced Jews who had "forgotten how to be Jews," were inclusive and led to rationalisation, healing, and ultimately, acceptance.

---

1   Ludwig Stein is quoting one "H. C(onrad?)." Ludwig Stein, "Der Rassenimperialismus Chamberlains", *Neue Freie Presse*, Jan. 29, 1905, pp. 33–36 at 34.

2   Joseph Roth, *The Wandering Jews*, trans. Michael Hoffmann (New York, 2001), p. 124.

3   "The Jews Are Changing Their Music," *Los Angeles Times*, Oct. 2, 1938, p. H7.

4   Personal papers of Ernst Toch, UCLA Performing Arts Library, Box 91.

5   Quoted in Karin Wagner, "Eric Zeisl (1905–1959) – Life and Works," in: *Endstation Schein-Heiligenstadt: Eric Zeisls Flucht nach Hollywood*, exh. cat. Jewish Museum Vienna (Vienna, 2005), p. 49.

6   Malcolm S. Cole and Barbara Barclay, *Armseelchen: The Life and Music of Eric Zeisl* (Westport, CT, 1984), p. 50.

Michael Haas

RABBI SONDERLING UND SEINE AUFTRÄGE

Permanent sahen sich die aus Europa in die Vereinigten Staaten immigrierten Jüdinnen und Juden mit Identitätsfragen konfrontiert. Zwar waren jüdische Gemeinden in den USA aktiv und leisteten Unterstützung, doch viele österreichische, deutsche und tschechische Flüchtlinge definierten ihre Identität nicht über die Zugehörigkeit zu einer bestimmten religiösen Gemeinschaft. Das war damals schon sehr lange so. Die Emanzipation der Jüdinnen und Juden in der zweiten Hälfte des 19. Jahrhunderts brachte mit sich, dass die Nachfolgegenerationen die Merkmale der nichtjüdischen Gemeinschaften übernahmen, in die sie sich integriert hatten.

Viele sich assimilierende Jüdinnen und Juden feierten Ostern und Weihnachten nicht als christliche Feste, sondern als nationale Feiertage. Indem diese Feste in die eigenen Traditionen aufgenommen wurden, verschwanden die eigentümlichen Unterschiede zwischen Christ:innen und Jüdinnen/Juden allmählich. Sofern sie überhaupt gefeiert wurden, verlagerten sich jüdische Rituale und Feste mit der um die Jahrhundertwende geborenen Generation in den familiären Raum. Die Zugehörigkeit zu einer Minderheitenreligion bei gleichzeitiger Integration in eine größere Gemeinschaft, ob katholisch oder protestantisch, führte häufig zur vollständigen Säkularisierung der jüngeren Generationen. Wenn jüdische Menschen ihre religiöse Identität als Barriere zwischen sich und ihren Freund:innen und Kolleg:innen empfanden, so schien es ihnen oft am besten, sie ganz abzulegen, auch wenn nicht klar war, was sie ersetzen könnte.

Mit der Katastrophe der Niederlage von 1918, dem Niedergang der Adelshäuser und der Entwicklung hin zu moderneren und effizienteren Regierungssystemen beschränkte sich die Säkularisierung nicht mehr auf die junge jüdische Bevölkerung. Traditionen, welche die Monarchie und die Kirche als Ausdruck einer „göttlichen Ordnung" gesehen hatten, wurden als „Opium" entlarvt, mit dem man die Masse unter Kontrolle halten konnte. Die vormals als besonders dargestellte Verbindung von Königen, Kaisern und Adel mit Gott wurde nicht mehr anerkannt.

Diese allgemeine Säkularisierung der Gesellschaft hatte zwei sehr unterschiedliche Perspektiven zur Folge. Für die Jüdinnen und Juden zeigte sie sich als eine natürliche Entwicklung, welche die Barrieren innerhalb der gleichberechtigten Bevölkerung beseitigte. Jüdisch zu sein galt als individuelle Entscheidung dafür, eine Religion einer anderen vorzuziehen. Viele nichtjüdische Europäer:innen lebten jedoch seit Generationen in einem tief verwurzelten, durch kirchliche und gesellschaftliche Traditionen geprägten Antisemitismus, sodass sie nach einer Rechtfertigung für ihre latenten Gefühle suchten. Ihrer Ansicht nach war Jüdischsein keine persönliche Entscheidung, sondern vielmehr eine „rassische" Eigenschaft, die Juden und Nichtjuden so unterschiedlich mache wie Tag und Nacht. Sich auf Charles Darwin oder Herbert Spencer berufende Pseudowissenschaftler wie Houston Stewart Chamberlain, die durch diesen Rückbezug ihre rassistischen Ansichten untermauerten, wurden zuerst oft noch als lächerliche Dilettanten abgetan. In seiner Rezension von Chamberlains *Die Grundlagen des neunzehnten Jahrhunderts* (1899) gab der Kritiker und Philosoph Ludwig Stein einen Überblick über die Aufnahme des Werks und zitierte einen Kollegen: „[...] kurz, es ist ein schlechtes Buch, unklar und unlogisch im Gedankengang und unerfreulich im Stil, voll falscher Bescheidenheit und echtem Hochmut, voll echter Unwissenheit und falscher Gelehrsamkeit."[1]

Ludwig Stein war Jude, sogar ein Rabbiner. Er hätte es nicht für möglich gehalten, dass man Chamberlains Schriften nach der Unterstützung durch Kaiser Wilhelm II. Glaubwürdigkeit schenken würde. Die Ansichten Steins und des deutschen Kaisers spiegelten die damalige Diskrepanz in der Wahrnehmung wider. Juden sahen sich nicht länger als Juden, sobald sie ein notariell beglaubigtes Dokument, das dies bestätigte, unterzeichneten, während Nichtjuden, die weiterhin nach einer wissenschaftlichen Rechtfertigung für ihren immanenten Rassismus suchten, in den Ausführungen Chamberlains und seiner Anhänger:innen die auf wundersame Weise gefundene Antwort auf diese Fragen sahen.

Nach 1933 stand man daher der Vertreibung, Enteignung und Internierung von Deutschen und Österreicher:innen, die sich nicht mehr als Jüdinnen und Juden betrachteten (oder zumindest als nicht praktizierend), fassungslos und ungläubig gegenüber. Der in Los Angeles ansässige, in Schlesien geborene liberale Rabbiner Jacob Sonderling begriff dieses Gefühl des Nichtverstehens solcher Mechanismen sofort als Chance. Er suchte nicht nach religiöser Erneuerung in seiner Gemeinde von Juden, die „verlernt [hatten], Juden zu sein"[2], um Joseph Roth zu zitieren, sondern erkannte vielmehr ein Mittel der Kommunikation. Während Jüdinnen und Juden die Assimilation bisher als aktive Ablehnung ihres jüdischen Glaubens und ihrer Traditionen verstanden hatten, sah Sonderling Assimilation als Transaktion: Bei einem grundlegenden Beharren auf ihrem Judentum müssten Jüdinnen und Juden über die Liturgie des Gottesdienstes hinaus universelle Ausdrucksformen finden, die sowohl im Tempel als auch im weltlichen Konzertsaal aufgeführt werden könnten.

Sonderling berichtete in der *Los Angeles Times* vom 2. Oktober 1938 Folgendes:

> [Diese] Beziehung zwischen dem Bibelschüler und dem Komponisten biblischer Musiktexte wurde mir bewusst, als ich das Werk des Großvaters von Friedrich Schorr, dem berühmten Bariton der Metropolitan Opera, studierte. Die Komposition handelte von einem Gebet, das am Versöhnungstag gesprochen wird. Der reuige Sünder bittet Gott um Vergebung, „Wende Dich von Deinem grimmigen Zorn ab", kommt in einer schweren Bassstimme. Und dann ändert sich plötzlich das Tempo von Andantino zu Allegretto. Eine Sopranistin übernimmt die Melodie und wiederholt diese Worte in einem überraschenden Scherzo. Der Komponist, ein Kantor in Polen und ein gründlicher Bibelgelehrter, wollte in dieser Melodie die Beziehung zwischen dem Juden und Gott interpretieren. Für ihn war es das Verhältnis zwischen einem Vater und einem fehlbaren Kind. Es ist zutiefst menschlich. Das Kind, nach Schorrs Vorstellung, ist entsetzt über seine Sünden und nähert sich seinem Vater in reuiger Stimmung. Doch aus Angst, dass die Bitte um Vergebung nicht gewährt wird, versucht es mit allen liebenswerten Tricks eines Kindes, Gott zum Lächeln

Los Angeles Times, 2. Oktober 1938: Jacob Sonderlings Text „The Jews Are Changing Their Music" zeigt sein Portrait sowie Schönberg und Toch.
Ernst Toch Collection, UCLA Performing Arts Library

zu bringen. Daher kommt die weibliche Sopranstimme beschwingt heraus, als wollte sie sagen: „Du kannst mich nicht bestrafen. Sieh, ich bringe Dich zum Lächeln, und da Du lächelst, weiß ich, dass Du mir verzeihst."[3]

Sonderling war nicht allein in seinem Versuch, die jüdische Musik mit einer spezifisch religiösen Dimension zu erneuern oder neu zu definieren. Auch David Putterman von der Park-Avenue-Synagoge in New York gab Kompositionen in Auftrag. Der Unterschied zwischen Putterman und Sonderling in seinem Tempel in Santa Monica war, dass Putterman spezifisch liturgische Werke wie Kurt Weills *Kiddush* bestellte, während Sonderling Werke anregte, die sowohl jüdische als auch nichtjüdische Menschen ansprechen sollten. Putterman verfolgte eine ganz andere Richtung, auch wenn die Absicht möglicherweise dieselbe war. Er beauftragte Nichtjuden wie Roy Harris und den afroamerikanischen Komponisten William Grant Still, liturgische Werke zu schreiben.

Ein Treffen zwischen Sonderling, dem Komponisten Ernst Toch, dem Filmproduzenten Boris Morros und dem Schauspieler Leopold Jessner führte zur Vertonung von Tochs Version der in der Haggada erzählten Geschichte der Flucht aus Ägypten. Tochs Werk trug den Titel *Cantata of the Bitter Herbs*; in einem Essay, der in seinen persönlichen Unterlagen an der Performing Arts Library der UCLA gefunden wurde, erläuterte er das Konzept dazu. Als erster Auftrag von Sonderling überhaupt legte das Werk das Format fest, mit den Kennzeichen „überkonfessionell" und „universell". Toch berichtete über die Ereignisse, die ihn zu Sonderling geführt hatten. Er hatte im Dezember 1937 die Nachricht vom Tod seiner Mutter in Wien erhalten, und da er wusste, dass sie die Gebete für die Toten nie ausgelassen hätte, ging er in den Tempel in Santa Monica. Nach dem Gottesdienst traf er Rabbi Sonderling, der darauf hinwies, dass seine Tochter eventuell Gefallen an den Chanukka-Veranstaltungen haben könnte, die gerade stattfanden. Dies führte zu einer Annäherung Tochs an die Religion und die Traditionen seiner Kindheit, ohne dass er die orthodoxen Überzeugungen vollständig angenommen hätte.[4]

Tochs Erzählung von der Flucht der Juden aus Ägypten wurde daher aus dem Blickwinkel eines Kindes dargestellt. 1938 war die Schoah noch nicht der Horror, als der sie sich nach dem Krieg offenbaren sollte. Doch trotz der bevorstehenden Ereignisse waren die Parallelen zwischen der Flucht der Juden aus Ägypten und der Flucht vor Hitler allzu offensichtlich. Die Uraufführung, bei der auch Tochs Tochter mitwirkte, fand im Tempel selbst statt.

Nach dem Erfolg von Tochs Auftragswerk zögerte Sonderling nicht, Arnold Schönberg zu kontaktieren. Er hatte ihn durch den Geiger Joseph Achron kennengelernt. In gewisser Weise resultierte daraus das ungewöhnlichste Werk unter Sonderlings Aufträgen, da es zumindest dem Namen nach als liturgisch anzusehen ist, wenngleich das Konzept anderes reflektiert. *Kol Nidre* (Alle Gelübde) ist das Gebet für Jom Kippur – den Versöhnungstag, an dem nicht eingehaltene Gelübde gesühnt werden. Schönberg zögerte zunächst, sich auf das Werk einzulassen, weil er ursprünglich den Glauben verloren hatte und 1933 in Paris doch wieder in die jüdische Glaubensgemeinschaft eingetreten war. Dies verlieh dem Thema eine persönliche Bedeutung für ihn, die ihm unangenehm war.

Sonderling überzeugte Schönberg, dass er durch seine Rückkehr zum jüdischen Glauben tatsächlich sein gebrochenes Gelübde, also seine Abkehr, sühne, und versprach ihm einen neuen, weniger starren Text. Der überarbeitete Text sollte mit der Liturgie des Gottesdienstes vereinbar bleiben, doch

Ernst Toch, ca. 1922
Ernst Toch Collection, UCLA Performing Arts Library

Erich Wolfgang Korngold in seinem Haus in der Toluca Lake Avenue, ca. 1940
The Brendan G Carroll Collection

Schönbergs Art der Ausführung machte das letztlich unmöglich. Ungewöhnlich für Schönberg ist, dass das Werk tonal und in g-Moll gehalten ist, aber in einem strahlenden G-Dur endet. Der überarbeitete Text war tatsächlich zu weltlich für andere Synagogen und erforderte ein derart überwältigendes Instrumentarium, dass die Uraufführung im Oktober 1938 in einem Nachtklub in Los Angeles mit Mitgliedern des Orchesters von Twentieth Century Fox stattfand.

Sonderlings nächster Auftrag ging an Erich Wolfgang Korngold. Vermutlich gestaltete sich das als ein schwierigeres Unterfangen, denn Korngold war in einer streng säkularen Familie aufgewachsen und wusste nur wenig oder nichts über die jüdische Liturgie. Toch und Schönberg waren Kinder des zweiten Wiener Gemeindebezirks, der sogenannten Mazzesinsel, wo die meisten Angehörigen der jüdischen Arbeiterschaft und des jüdischen Kleinbürgertums lebten. Korngold und seine Frau Luzi (geborene Sonnenthal) dagegen waren in großbürgerlichen Familien aufgewachsen, die ihre Religion vollständig aufgegeben hatten. Korngolds Schwiegervater, Adolf von Sonnenthal, war jedoch einer der ersten Juden, die vom Kaiser in den Adelsstand erhoben wurden, weiters war er Mitbegründer des Jüdischen Museums in Wien.

Diese Familien repräsentierten somit genau die in den einleitenden Absätzen beschriebene Geschichte der Assimilation. Korngold war sich der Ghettoisierung seiner Eltern als Juden, die kurz vor der Verfassung von Dezember 1867 geboren worden waren, bewusst. Diese Verfassung hob alle Beschränkungen für Jüdinnen und Juden auf und stellte sie auf eine Stufe mit allen anderen Bürger:innen des Habsburgerreichs. Die Eltern von Korngold und seiner Frau konnten als Erste das Privileg genießen, ihre religiöse Gemeinschaft zu verlassen oder in ihr zu bleiben. Als Erich Wolfgang Korngold und Luzi von Sonnenthal geboren wurden, war die Säkularisierung junger, integrierter Jüdinnen und Juden aus bürgerlichen Familien vollständig abgeschlossen. Korngolds Liebe zur katholischen Prachtentfaltung zeigte sich in seinen Opern *Die tote Stadt* und *Das Wunder der Heliane*. Die Korngolds feierten Weihnachten und andere christliche/nationale Feiertage.

Vielleicht mit Blick auf Korngolds Eltern und ihre religiöse Kindheit überzeugte Sonderling ihn, nicht nur einen Pessach-Psalm zu komponieren, sondern auch ein Werk mit dem Titel *Gebet*. Beide Werke wurden später Korngolds Eltern zu ihrem Hochzeitsjubiläum überreicht. Der Briefwechsel in der Familie Korngold zwischen Eltern und Kindern enthielt fast immer die Phrase „Gottes Segen" – ein Hinweis darauf, dass zumindest in der älteren Generation noch ein Rest religiösen Glaubens vorhanden war. Nachdem Hitler ihn gezwungen hatte, sich zu seinem Judentum zu bekennen, wurde Korngold durch Sonderlings Auftrag dazu angeregt, es sich tatsächlich anzueignen.

Beide Werke strahlen die für Korngold typische textliche und orchestrale Opulenz aus, mit thematischen Fortschreitungen, die sich immer weiter nach oben in unbekannte Sphären bewegen. Der Text zu dem einen Werk ging ähnlich wie bei Toch auf die Haggada zurück. Dem *Gebet* wiederum lag Franz Werfels *Adonai Eloheinu* zugrunde, sowohl auf Englisch als auch auf Hebräisch. Die Uraufführung beider Werke fand am 12. April 1941 statt.

Die nächsten Werke, die auf einen Auftrag oder eine Anregung Sonderlings zurückgingen, entstanden nach der Niederlage des Nationalsozialismus und der schrecklichen Enthüllung von Hitlers Massenmord. Bei Schönbergs *Ein Überlebender aus Warschau* fungierte Sonderling nicht als

Auftraggeber, sondern als Berater. Sein letzter Auftrag ging an Erich Zeisl, der wohl das universellste aller Werke präsentierte. Allein schon im widersprüchlichen Titel *Requiem Ebraico* zeigt sich die Überkonfessionalität – ein jüdisch-katholisches Requiem, eine Vertonung von Psalm 92. Dass die Uraufführung 1945 in der First Methodist Church in Hollywood mit dem Santa Monica Symphony Orchestra stattfand, trug zum ökumenischen Charakter des Werks bei. Obwohl das *Requiem Ebraico* Zeisls in Treblinka ermordeten Eltern gewidmet ist, ist es ein eher freudiges Werk und weder typisch für ein katholisches Requiem noch für ein jüdisches Kaddisch. Zeisl beschrieb dieses Paradoxon wie folgt:

> At that time war in Europe had just ended and I received the first news of the death of my father and many friends. The sadness of my mood went into my composition which became a Requiem, though I had not intended to write one and scarcely would have chosen the 92nd psalm for it. Yet the completed Requiem thus received a deeper meaning than I could have achieved by planning it that way.[5]

Zusammengefasst ist es ein Stück, in dem Zeisl versucht, sich trotz tiefer Tragödie mit Gott zu versöhnen. Ein Kritiker soll es als „eines der ergreifendsten elegischen Werke in der Geschichte der Musik"[6] beschrieben haben.

Die Sonderling-Aufträge stehen für eine Exilgeschichte, die mit dem gemeinsamen Thema von Flucht und Exil beginnt, wie es in der Haggada beschrieben und von Toch und Korngold interpretiert wird, zusammen mit einer erneuten Bekräftigung des Glaubens durch Korngold *(Adonai Eloheinu)* und Schönberg, und die mit der Verzweiflung und Hoffnung in Zeisls *Requiem Ebraico* endet. Hitler stand für eine Sichtweise, die das Judentum ausgrenzte. Sonderlings Aufträge – wie diese vertriebenen Juden zeigten, die „verlernt [hatten], Juden zu sein" – waren inklusiv und führten zu einer Konfrontation mit der Realität, zu Heilung und letztlich zu Akzeptanz.

Rabbi Sonderling assistiert beim Pflanzen eines Baumes, 3. Mai 1946
American Jewish University, Special Collections, Ostrow Library

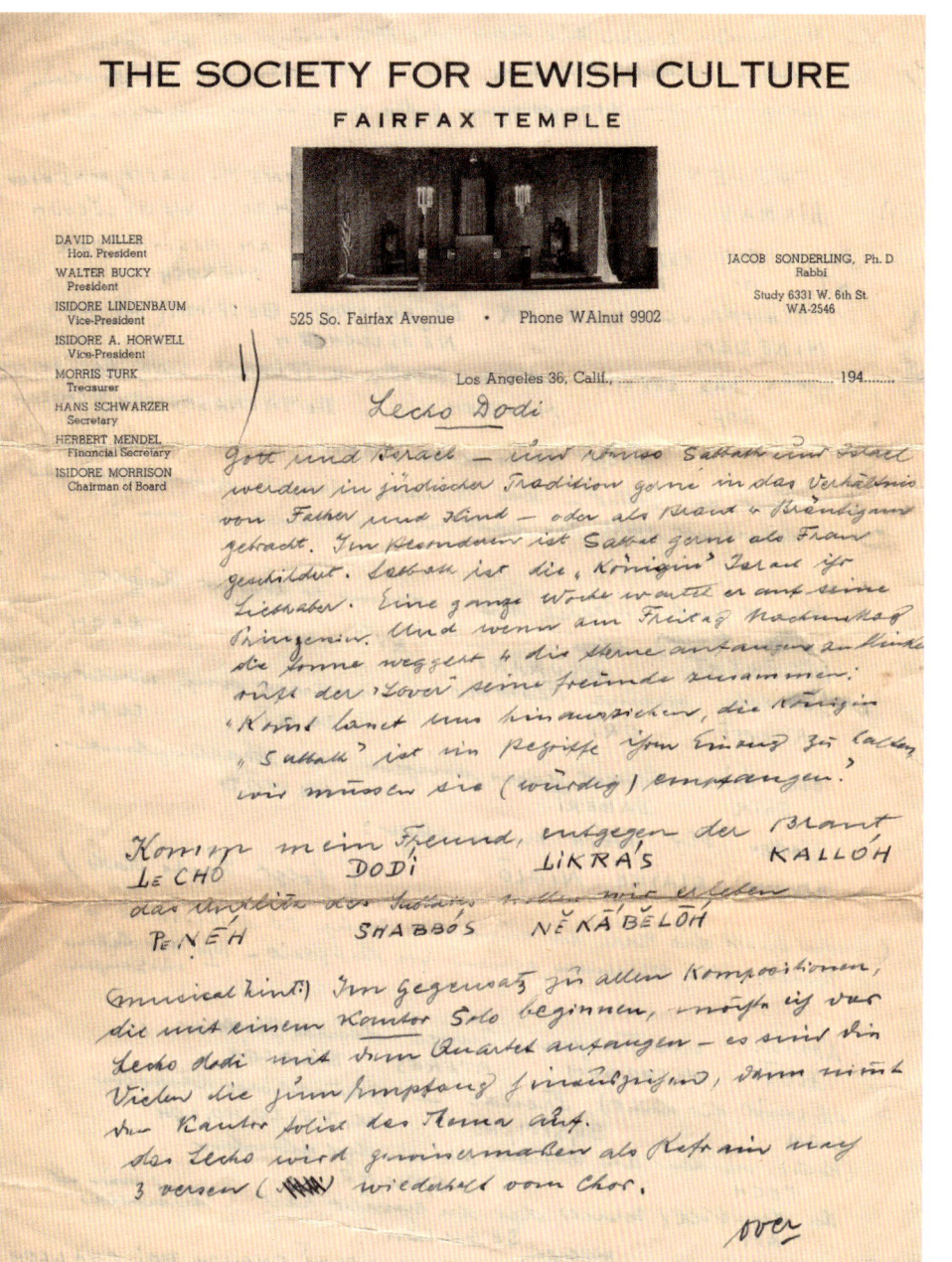

Brief von Rabbi Jacob Sonderling an Erich Zeisl: Sonderling erklärt die Bedeutung der mystisch-liturgischen Hymne *Lecha Dodi*, mit welcher der Schabbat willkommen geheißen wird.
Archiv des Exilarte Zentrum der mdw, Wien (A-Weaz)

Erich Zeisls Adressbuch in Los Angeles: Eintrag rechts unten: „Sonderling"
Archiv des Exilarte Zentrum der mdw, Wien (A-Weaz)

1   Stein zitiert hier einen „H. C(onrad?)". Ludwig Stein, „Der Rassenimperialismus Chamberlains", in: *Neue Freie Presse*, 29. 1. 1905, S. 33–36, hier S. 34.
2   Joseph Roth, „Vorrede zur neuen Auflage", in: ders., *Juden auf Wanderschaft*, Köln 1985, S. 75–85, hier S. 77.
3   „The Jews Are Changing Their Music", in: *Los Angeles Times*, 2. 10. 1938.
4   Persönliche Unterlagen von Ernst Toch, UCLA Performing Arts Library, Box 91.
5   Zit. n. Karin Wagner, „Eric Zeisl (1905–1959) – Leben und Werk", in: *Endstation Schein-Heiligenstadt. Eric Zeisls Flucht nach Hollywood*, Ausst.-Kat. Jüdisches Museum Wien, Wien 2005, S. 22–54, hier S. 48.
6   Malcolm S. Cole, Barbara Barclay, *Armseelchen. The Life and Music of Eric Zeisl*, Westport, Conn./London 1984, S. 50.

Karin Wagner

„A SORT OF HEBREW TANGLEWOOD"
Erich Zeisl im Brandeis Music Camp

Tanglewood ist in der Musikwelt ein klingender Name: Es handelt sich um eine Aufführungsstätte in Berkshire County im Westen von Massachusetts, bekannt vor allem durch ein Sommerfestival mit Konzerten in großer stilistischer Vielfalt. Besonders die Jugend fühlt sich in Tanglewood angesprochen: Das Boston University Tanglewood Institute und das Tanglewood Music Center bieten dort musikalische Fortbildung an. Seit den späten 1930er-Jahren verbringt das Boston Symphony Orchestra die Sommermonate in Tanglewood, 1938 und 1939 spielte es unter Sergej Koussevitzky (1874–1951) dort jeweils sechs Konzerte und 1940 gründete Koussevitzky schließlich das Berkshire Music Center (heute Tanglewood Music Center). In seiner Eröffnungsrede betonte er die einende Kraft der Musik gerade in Kriegszeiten. Das Angebot in Tanglewood wurde um Instrumentalkurse erweitert, Aaron Copland (1900–1990) war als „composer in residence" zugegen und Mitglieder des Boston Symphony Orchestra betreuten das Studierendenorchester. Eine Pädagogik, die sich an den Studierenden orientierte, die Perfektionierung instrumentaler Fertigkeiten und eine gemeinschaftliche Musizierpraxis sollten einander auf höchstem Niveau ergänzen.

Denkt man an die ungezwungene Atmosphäre in Tanglewood und an den Kontakt zur Jugend, kommt einem sogleich der Name Leonard Bernstein (1918–1990) in den Sinn: Als junger Dirigent nahm Bernstein an den Kursen Koussevitzkys teil, er wurde sein Assistent und bald auch Mitglied des Berkshire Music Center. Bernsteins Vorlesungen und Dirigate, immer in unverbraucht frischer Nähe zu den Studierenden, bedeuteten Wissensvermittlung, Inspiration und ein Musizieren nach höchsten Ansprüchen. Die amerikanische Musikergeneration der Nachkriegsjahre erlebte in Tanglewood eine offene, von musikalischem Selbstbewusstsein und Eigendefinierung getragene Haltung.

Sollte nicht auch dezidiert für jüdische Studierende und die jüdische Kunstäußerung solch ein Ort der Zusammenkunft, des Austauschs und der Zukunftsvisionen geschaffen werden? Wo, wenn nicht in den Vereinigten Staaten, wo vor dem Hintergrund der Katastrophe in Europa die Herausbildung eines neuen jüdischen Kulturbewusstseins sowohl der amerikanisch-jüdischen Künstlerschaft als auch den aus Europa Vertriebenen ein vordringliches Anliegen war?

Der in Polen geborene Max Helfman (1901–1963) war der Richtige für den Aufbau jüdischer künstlerisch-pädagogischer Projekte. Im Alter von acht Jahren kam der spätere Komponist, Organist, Dirigent und Musikkritiker in die Neue Welt, seine erste musikalische Ausbildung erhielt er am Mannes College of Music in New York, danach studierte er am Curtis Institute of Music in Philadelphia bei Ralph Leopold (Klavier), Rosario Scalero (Komposition) und Fritz Reiner (Dirigieren). Musizierpraxis erwarb Helfman am Temple Israel in Manhattan, in der Komposition wollte er die jüdische Liturgie in eine zeitgemäße Sprache übersetzen. Eine besondere Herzensangelegenheit war ihm die Arbeit mit der Jugend: Helfman, seit 1938 im Vorstand der Jewish Music Alliance, wurde 1944 an die School of Sacred Music des Hebrew Union College in New York berufen und gründete 1961 die School of Fine Arts an der University of Judaism in Los Angeles. Mit der Organisation der Musikkurse im Brandeis Camp fiel ihm 1947 eine exquisite Aufgabe zu, die er 17 Jahre lang erfüllte.

1942 hatte Shlomo Bardin (1898–1976) in Winterdale, Pennsylvania, ein Sommertrainingsprogramm für junge Erwachsene gegründet, das sich innerhalb einiger Jahre gut etablieren hatte können. Das Leitbild dafür war das Leben im Kibbuz – einschließlich Studieren, Gartenarbeit und Hochhalten des Schabbats. 1943 nannte Bardin das Projekt nach Louis Dembitz Brandeis (1856–1941) Brandeis Camp Institute (heute Brandeis-Bardin Institute):[1] Der zwei Jahre zuvor verstorbene Brandeis war der erste jüdische Richter am Supreme Court gewesen; von seinem Ansatz, amerikanische Ideale mit dem Bekenntnis zum Zionismus in Einklang zu bringen, war Bardin angetan. 1947 richtete Bardin in Simi Valley nahe Santa Susana, nordwestlich von Los Angeles, ein weiteres Brandeis Camp Institute ein.

Shlomo Bardin stammte aus der Ukraine, 1918 gelangte er nach Palästina, zum Studium ging er nach Berlin und London. Zurück in Haifa unterrichtete er an der Hebrew Boarding School, bevor er seine Ausbildung am Teachers' College der Columbia University abschloss. 1939 wurde er Leiter des Youth Department von Hadassah, einer zionistischen Frauenorganisation, und der kurz zuvor eingerichteten American Zionist Youth Commission, unter deren Schirmherrschaft er das Sommertrainingsprogramm etablierte. Die Zielgruppe des Brandeis Camp war weit gefasst, willkommen waren Studierende aus reformwilligen, konservativen, zionistischen und orthodoxen Kreisen. Mit der Expertise der Lehrenden setzte das Brandeis Camp Maßstäbe für jüdische künstlerisch-pädagogische Formate.

In seiner Funktion als Artistic Director der Brandeis Youth Foundation schrieb Max Helfman am 27. Mai 1948 an Erich Zeisl:

> Dear Mr. Zeisl:
>
> Both as a serious artist and conscious Jew, you will, I am sure, be deeply interested in the Hebrew Arts Project sponsored by the Brandeis Youth Foundation. Believing as we do, that the most precious asset of a people is its creative youth, and that we, in America, have a vast artistic potential in our Jewish youth, the Foundation is establishing an Arts Institute on its estate Santa Susana, California, where a selected group of qualified students between the ages of 18 – 27 will be enabled to live and work together with distinguished leaders in their respective arts in a creative Jewish atmosphere. In other words, – a sort of Hebrew Tanglewood.[2]

Über die begabte Jugend, die künftigen Komponist:innen, Dirigent:innen, Sänger:innen, Autor:innen, Schauspieler:innen und Tänzer:innen, sprach Helfman als „the treasures of our artistic heritage and resources"[3]. Ihnen wollte er die Fähigkeiten vermitteln, das Erbe jüdischer Kunst zeitgemäß anzutreten, sodass sie das kulturelle Leben in den Vereinigten Staaten und auch über die Landesgrenzen hinaus bereichern konnten. „To my knowledge" – so Helfman weiter – „it is the first attempt to systematize the special problems of the Hebrew Arts."[4] Helfman lud Zeisl ein, Ehrengast im Brandeis Camp zu sein, zu unterrichten und Vorträge zu halten. Zeisl folgte diesem Vorschlag: Von 1948 bis 1950 lehrte er in den Sommermonaten als „composer in residence" am Brandeis Camp Institute in Santa Susana.

Studierende und Lehrende im Brandeis Camp Institute (heute: Brandeis-Bardin Institute): Letzte Reihe, dritte Person von links: Erich Zeisl, dritte Person von rechts: Julius Chajes, links davon: Max Helfman. Erste Reihe in der Mitte: Barbara Zeisl
Archiv des Exilarte Zentrum der mdw, Wien (A-Weaz)

Im Haupthaus, genannt „Patio", sitzt Shlomo Bardin auf der Stiege und spricht zu den Teilnehmenden im Brandeis Camp Institute, 1949. Zweite Person links hinten: Barbara Zeisl, rechts daneben hinter der Säule: Gertrud Zeisl
American Jewish University, Special Collections, Ostrow Library

Shlomo Bardins und Max Helfmans Programmidee war einer jüdischen Ethik verpflichtet. Diese Haltung wurde sowohl durch die Kursinhalte als auch durch die Art der Vermittlung erkennbar. Moderne und tradierte jüdische Musik (Kunstmusik, Musik mit religiösem Kontext, Folklore) wurde mit entsprechender Tanzkunst verbunden. Man ging auf die musikalische Individualität der Jugend ein und förderte zugleich Persönlichkeiten mit dem Potenzial für Führungspositionen im jüdisch-amerikanischen Kulturleben. In Hinblick auf die Breitenwirkung und vor allem den lebendigen Kontakt zur Jugend waren die durch Leonard Bernstein populären Kurse in Tanglewood Vorbild.

Bardins Gedanken zu den Kursteilnehmer:innen finden sich in einer Broschüre aus den späten 1940er-Jahren zusammengefasst:

> They come to acquaint themselves more fully with Jewish values, draw inspiration from the reborn state of Israel, study the methods of democratic leadership and thus be trained as youth leaders for the American Jewish community. The Brandeis Camp of the West with its 2,000 acres of picturesque southern California country immediately suggests the hills of Judea to the imaginative young person. Exposed to skillful direction and programming, the Brandeis camper acquires a new understanding and pride in his Jewish heritage and a new dignity as a human being. Upon leaving, the Brandeis camper carries with him a sense of personal responsibility for his Jewish community and for the future of the Jewish people.[5]

Neben Zeisl unterrichteten um 1948 im Brandeis Camp in Simi Valley auch die Komponisten Mario Castelnuovo-Tedesco (1895–1968), Ernst Toch (1887–1964) und Heinrich Schalit (1886–1976), die Pianisten-Komponisten Julius Chajes (1910–1985) und Louis Gruenberg (1884–1964), der Dirigent Izler Solomon (1910–1987), der Kantor und Komponist Solomon Rosowsky (1878–1962), der Dirigent, Organist und Chorleiter Erwin Jospe (1907–1983), die Musikwissenschaftlerin Anneliese Landau (1903–1991), der Autor Irving Fineman (1893–1976) oder der Tänzer und Choreograf Benjamin Zemach (1901–1997). Im Juni 1950 zog Helfman in Erwägung, Arnold Schönberg (1874–1951) für ein oder zwei Wochen nach Santa Susana zu holen, und erkundigte sich bei Zeisl nach den eventuellen Konditionen dafür.[6] Der Plan dürfte nicht weiterverfolgt worden sein, Schönbergs Gesundheitszustand hätte einen Aufenthalt dort ohnedies nicht erlaubt.

Julius Chajes, ehemals Zeisls Mitstreiter im Wiener Zirkel „Junge Kunst", propagierte in seiner Funktion als Leiter des Jewish Community Center in Detroit Zeisls Werk in den Vereinigten Staaten. Mit Mario Castelnuovo-Tedesco und Ernst Toch war Zeisl über den Filmbetrieb in Hollywood befreundet. Anneliese Landau, die aus Deutschland geflüchtet war, war als musikalische Leiterin des Westside Jewish Community Center in Los Angeles und als Executive Secretary des Jewish Music Council of Los Angeles tätig. Das Jewish Music Council wurde 1944 vom National Jewish Welfare Board und der National Association of Jewish Center Workers gegründet; die Organisationen des Council bemühten sich in den Vereinigten Staaten landesweit um die Etablierung jüdischer Kunstschaffender. In ihren Funktionen stand Anneliese Landau in stetigem Austausch mit Zeisl, den sie in einer 1946 verfassten Studie zur zeitgenössischen jüdischen Komponistenschaft neben Ernest Bloch, Paul Dessau, Stefan Wolpe, Karol Rathaus, Jaromír Weinberger, Erich Wolfgang Korngold, Marc Blitzstein, Kurt Weill, Leo Ornstein, Ernst Toch oder Rubin Goldmark stellte und als „the youngest of the conscious Jewish composers"[7] beschrieb.

Studierende im Brandeis Camp Institute arbeiten unter der Anleitung der Bildhauerin Ruth Bardin an ihren Kunstwerken, ca. 1940
American Jewish University, Special Collections, Ostrow Library

Max Helfman leitet vom Klavier aus den Chor im Brandeis Camp, ca. 1950
American Jewish University, Special Collections, Ostrow Library

Bedeutend für Zeisl im Kreis der Brandeis-Lehrenden war Benjamin Zemach: Der Tänzer und Choreograf war mit der Habimah-Theatergruppe von Moskau nach New York gekommen und setzte in Los Angeles Impulse für den zeitgenössischen Tanz. In Zusammenarbeit mit ihm schuf Zeisl die biblischen Ballette *Naboth's Vineyard* (1953) und *Jacob and Rachel* (1954). Die *University News* der University of Judaism in Los Angeles kündigte im Februar 1955 für Mai eine Aufführung von *Jacob and Rachel* im Wilshire Ebell Theatre in Los Angeles durch Studierende von Zemachs Tanzklasse an.[8]

„A serious artist and conscious Jew"

Erich Zeisl war in der amerikanisch-jüdischen Musikwelt über Jahre hinweg präsent. Durch Veranstaltungen unterschiedlichen Zuschnitts profilierte er sich als der „serious artist and conscious Jew", als den ihn Max Helfman bezeichnete und den man ins Brandeis Camp holen wollte. So führte bereits im Oktober 1943 das Studio Symphony Orchestra unter Walter Scharf (1910–2003) im Rahmen eines *All Jewish-Palestinian Program*, „presented by Los Angeles Chapters League for Labor Palestine", die *Overture* und den *Folk Dance* aus der Oper *Job* (*Hiob*) auf.[9] Ebenfalls programmiert waren Walter Scharfs *Palestine Suite* und *Hatikvah Requiem*, Julius Chajes' *Adarim* oder Marc Lavrys (1903–1967) symphonische Dichtung *Emek*.

Von großem Nachklang für Zeisl war die Uraufführung des *Requiem Ebraico* in der Orgelfassung: Der Fairfax-Temple-Chor unter der Leitung von Hugo Strelitzer (1896–1981) interpretierte am 8. April 1945 in einem Konzert beim „Hollywood Inter-Faith Forum" in der Hollywood First Methodist Church den althebräischen Psalm 92. Erich Zeisls Bruder William (Wilhelm) Zeisl (1907–1972) sang den Kantor, Norman Söreng Wright (1905–1982) eröffnete das Programm mit dem *Organ Prelude* (entstanden 1939 als Ouvertüre zur Bühnenversion von Joseph Roths *Hiob* in Paris), der Rabbiner Jacob Sonderling (1878–1964) referierte zum Thema „The Message of Music in Religion".[10]

Ein zu diesem tiefgründigen Konzert ganz konträres Populärevent war die als „Palestine Spectacle" angekündigte und vom Palestine Emergency Fund organisierte Zusammenstellung *That we may live* unter der Leitung von Paul Gordon. Gordon war der Initiator der *Hiob*-Bühnenaufführung in Paris gewesen, nun sorgte er in Hollywood-Manier für ein kräftiges Lebenszeichen der jüdischen Exilwelt. Im Stilmix ging das Spektakel im Dezember 1946 in Los Angeles über die Bühne, publikumswirksam inszeniert mit einem Großaufgebot an Stars: Howard Da Silva, Marta Eggerth, Bela Lugosi, Hugo Haas und Jan Kiepura, ebenso Erich Wolfgang Korngold, Jakob Gimpel, Hugo Strelitzer und Erich Zeisl. Korngold war als Komponist und Dirigent der Oper *Die tote Stadt* eingebunden, von Zeisl standen die *Overture* und der *Cossack Dance* aus *Job* (*Hiob*) auf dem Programm. Die zusammenhanglose Collage zum Naziterror und zur Vertreibung jüdischer Menschen aus Europa zeigte Berlin, Genua, London, Zuchnow (den fiktiven polnischen Heimatort der *Hiob*-Romanfigur), Buchenwald und Wien als Stationen des Geschehens. Mit dem Sujet *Before the Gates of Palestine* endete das

Ankündigung für ein außergewöhnliches Event im Dezember 1946: *That we may live* wurde vom Palestine Emergency Fund organisiert und war ein kräftiges Lebenszeichen der jüdischen Exilwelt.
Archiv des Exilarte Zentrum der mdw, Wien (A-Weaz)

Spektakel in einer zionistischen Botschaft, Kerngedanke der Schau war die Kritik an der britischen Mandatspolitik in Palästina. Die *Los Angeles Evening Citizen News* skizzierte die Dimension der bevorstehenden Aufführung:

> For two nights only, Dec. 17 and 18, the Shrine Auditorium will be turned into a gigantic tribunal when the Palestine Emergency Fund, Inc., presents "That we may live," with a cast of 500. Starring roles will be played by Jan Kiepura, Marta Eggerth and Hugo Haas. "That we may live" is a dramatic portrayal and indictment against the British Palestine policy.[11]

Die Show *That we may live* wurde vermutlich nach New York übertragen: Auf den Leuchtreklamen wurde auch der Veranstaltungsort Madison Square Garden genannt und ein Plakat wies auf eine dortige Ausstrahlung hin.

Ebenfalls in New York wurde die Proklamation des Staates Israel durch den jüdischen Nationalrat am 14. Mai 1948 gefeiert. So fand am 18. Mai 1948 ein *Carnegie "POP" Concert* unter dem Titel *Palestine Night* statt.[12] Eröffnet wurde das Fest mit den Staatshymnen *The Star-Spangled Banner* und *Hatikvah*. Siegfried Landau (1921–2007) dirigierte an diesem der zionistischen Idee verschriebenen Abend mit Julius Chajes' *Hebrew Suite* und Erich Zeisls hier erstmals präsentierter Suite *To the Promised Land* zwei Werke vormals in Wien tätiger Komponisten. Zeisls Stück mit seinem verheißungsvollen Titel stützt sich in den Teilen *Folk Dance* und *Menuhim's Song* auf *Cossack Song and Dance* und *Menuhim's Song* aus *Job* (*Hiob*), der dritte Teil, *Lullaby*, ist eine leicht veränderte Version des *Wiegenlieds* aus dem Jahr 1928. Als vierten Teil arrangierte Zeisl das jüdische Volkslied *Kuma Echa Hora* aus Palästina. Louis Biancolli zog ein positives Resümee: „Maybe the names were new to most concert fans, names like David

Brief von Erwin Jospe an Erich Zeisl, 15. September 1950: „I was sad that our schedule at Brandeis did not permit me to spend much more time with you. I should have liked to."
Archiv des Exilarte Zentrum der mdw, Wien (A-Weaz)

Die Musikwissenschafterin Anneliese Landau stand als musikalische Leiterin des Westside Jewish Community Center in Los Angeles mit Zeisl in Kontakt.
Archiv des Exilarte Zentrum der mdw, Wien (A-Weaz)

Scheinfeld, Salomo Rosowsky, Nardi, Julius Chayes [sic], and Eric Zeisl. Yet taken together, they spelt out the promise of a great future for Jewish music."[13]

Ein neuer Name in der Szene und ein Garant für ihre vielversprechende Zukunft – so wurde Erich Zeisl von der Fachwelt wahrgenommen. Zeisl verfolgte nie aktiv zionistische Ideen, doch mit der Teilnahme an den genannten Konzerten gab auch er ein Statement zur Festigung eines neuen jüdischen Selbstbildes ab und zeigte Sympathie für den jungen israelischen Staat. To the Promised Land ist ein pointiert öffentlichkeitswirksamer Beitrag, bedingt durch die Zeitumstände. Dass Zeisl zu seiner eigenen „jüdisch" intonierten Musik fand, ist allerdings einem inneren Prozess zuzuschreiben, in dem er sehr wohl auf die äußeren Umstände reagierte; auf stringent realpolitische oder zionistische Botschaften verzichtete er aber.

„Wahrhaft jüdische Musik"

Angeregt durch das Ambiente im Brandeis Camp komponierte Zeisl 1949/50 die Alexandre Tansman (1897–1986) gewidmete Sonata for Violin and Piano (Brandeis Sonata). Eine „Voraufführung"[14] der Sonate fand am 13. August 1950 mit dem Geiger Israel Baker (1919–2011) und der Pianistin Yaltah Menuhin (1921–2001) im Brandeis Camp statt, am 24. September 1950 führte das Duo die Brandeis Sonata in Santa Monica[15] erstmals öffentlich auf.

Yehudi Menuhins Schwester Yaltah lebte während der 1950er-Jahre in Los Angeles, als Interpretin zeitgenössischer Werke kam ihr eine wichtige Rolle zu. Sie übernahm etwa auch Uraufführungen von George Antheil, Ernst Krenek, Louis Gruenberg, Mario Castelnuovo-Tedesco oder Walter Piston.

Das Duo Israel Baker und Yaltah Menuhin spielte am 24. September 1950 die Uraufführung von Zeisls Brandeis Sonata für Violine und Klavier.
Archiv des Exilarte Zentrum der mdw, Wien (A-Weaz)

Mit Israel Baker feierte sie 1951 in New York das Duo-Debüt. Baker unterrichtete am Scripps College im kalifornischen Claremont; als Violinist der Heifetz-Piatigorsky-Kammerkonzerte und Interpret der Werke Igor Strawinskys, Arnold Schönbergs und Alban Bergs prägte er das Konzertleben an der amerikanischen Westküste.

Die *Brandeis Sonata* mit den Sätzen *Grave*, *Andante religioso (hebraique)* und *Rondo* verdeutlicht die Synthese von Wiener Tradition und Anklängen an „jüdische Sphären". Mächtig ist die *Grave*-Einleitung im insistierenden lombardischen Rhythmus, aus dem heraus die Violine frei aufsteigt und die Szenerie eröffnet. Über ostinat pulsierender Begleitung bringt das *Allegretto* ein tänzerisches Thema in der von Zeisl gern verwendeten folkloristischen Moll-Tonleiter (auf E) mit der erhöhten vierten Stufe. Das dazu kontrastierende zweite Thema grenzt sich durch expressive Kantilenen in b-Moll ab. Zur zentralen Aussage des Stücks wird das *Andante religioso*, dessen Zusatzbezeichnung „hebraique" den Gestus expressiven jüdischen Gebets bekräftigt. Ausdrucksstark, doch nach innen gewandt. Ein vitales *Rondo*, das den Einleitungsrhythmus der Sonate abermals aufnimmt, vermittelt Spielfreude im Sinne osteuropäischer Folklore.

Die Exilzeitschrift *Aufbau* berichtete im Oktober 1950 unter der Rubrik „Neue Musik in Los Angeles":

> Dem Duo Yaltah Menuhin (Klavier) und Israel Baker (Violine) verdanken wir mehrere Abende mit interessanter neuer Musik. Beide setzten sich unlängst für die Sonate in e-moll (Brandeis) von Eric Zeisl ein, zu der der Komponist bei seiner Lehrtätigkeit in dem nahe bei Los Angeles gelegenen Brandeis Camp durch die betont jüdische Atmosphäre angeregt wurde. Unter den vielen Neuerscheinungen der letzten Jahre hörte ich selten ein Kammermusikwerk von solcher Geschlossenheit: jeder der drei Sätze ist gleich stark und fesselnd. Ohne ein bereits bestehendes jüdisches Motiv zu zitieren, schrieb Zeisl hier, im besten Sinne inspiriert, wahrhaft jüdische Musik, die unserem heutigen Empfinden entspricht.[16]

1 Siehe Jenna Leventhal, *The Brandeis-Bardin Institute. A Living History*, Los Angeles 2012.

2 Max Helfman an Erich Zeisl, 27. 5. 1948, zit. n. Karin Wagner (Hg.), *… es grüsst Dich Erichisrael. Briefe von und an Eric Zeisl, Hilde Spiel, Richard Stöhr, Ernst Toch, Hans Kafka u. a.*, Wien 2008, S. 245.

3 Ebd., S. 246.

4 Ebd.

5 Informationsheft *A Program for American Jewish Youth. Brandeis Camp Institute*, Erich-Zeisl-Nachlass, Exilarte Zentrum, Wien.

6 Max Helfman an Erich Zeisl, 9. 6. 1950, Erich-Zeisl-Nachlass, Exilarte Zentrum, Wien.

7 Anneliese Landau, *The Contribution of Jewish Composers to the Music of the Modern World*, [Cincinnati, Ohio, 1946], S. 64.

8 *University News* der University of Judaism, Febr. 1955, American Jewish University, Los Angeles, Special Collections.

9 Programmzettel *All Jewish-Palestinian Program*, 2. 10. 1943, Erich-Zeisl-Nachlass, Exilarte Zentrum, Wien.

10 Programmzettel *The Message of Music in Religion*, Hollywood First Methodist Church, 8. 4. 1945, Erich-Zeisl-Nachlass, Exilarte Zentrum, Wien.

11 *Los Angeles Evening Citizen News*, 28. 11. 1946.

12 Programmzettel *Palestine Night*, Carnegie Hall, 18. 5. 1948, Erich-Zeisl-Nachlass, Exilarte Zentrum, Wien.

13 Zeitungsausschnitt ohne Angaben, Erich-Zeisl-Nachlass, Exilarte Zentrum, Wien.

14 Programmzettel *Brandeis Camp Institute Concert*, Brandeis Camp, 13. 8. 1950, Erich-Zeisl-Nachlass, Exilarte Zentrum, Wien.

15 Programmzettel *Israel Baker, Yaltah Menuhin Sonata Recital*, Barnum Hall, Santa Monica, 24. 9. 1950, Erich-Zeisl-Nachlass, Exilarte Zentrum, Wien.

16 Martin Hausdorff, „Neue Musik in Los Angeles", in: *Aufbau*, 20. 10. 1950, Erich-Zeisl-Nachlass, Exilarte Zentrum, Wien.

Announcement of a scholarship to take part in the music and dance courses at the Brandeis Camp Institute (today: Brandeis-Bardin Institute)
Archiv des Exilarte Zentrum der mdw, Wien (A-Weaz)

Karin Wagner

"A SORT OF HEBREW TANGLEWOOD"
Eric Zeisl at the Brandeis Music Camp

Tanglewood is a name that resonates deeply within the music world. Located in Berkshire County in western Massachusetts, it is renowned as a performance venue, particularly for its summer festival featuring concerts in a wide range of styles. Young musicians find Tanglewood especially appealing, thanks to educational opportunities provided by the Boston University Tanglewood Institute and the Tanglewood Music Center. Since the late 1930s, the Boston Symphony Orchestra (BSO) has spent its summers at Tanglewood. In 1938 and 1939, under the direction of Serge Koussevitzky (1874–1951), the orchestra performed six concerts each season. In 1940, Koussevitzky founded the Berkshire Music Center, now known as the Tanglewood Music Center. In his inaugural address, Koussevitzky emphasized the importance of music as a unifying force, particularly in times of war. The offerings at Tanglewood expanded to include instrumental courses, with Aaron Copland (1900–1990) serving as a composer in residence and members of the Boston Symphony Orchestra tutoring the student orchestra. The program focused on students' needs, striving to blend the perfectioning of instrumental skills with ensemble music-making at the highest level.

When thinking of the relaxed atmosphere at Tanglewood and its connection to youth, the name Leonard Bernstein (1918–1990) inevitably comes to mind. As a young conductor, Bernstein participated in Serge Koussevitzky's courses, became his assistant, and soon joined the faculty at the Berkshire Music Center. Bernstein's lectures and conducting, always marked by a fresh, vibrant engagement with the students, combined inspirational knowledge-sharing and music-making of the highest standards. For American musicians of the postwar generation, Tanglewood represented an open-minded environment, characterized by musical self-confidence and individual self-definition.

Should such a place of encounter, exchange, and visionary thinking not also be created specifically for Jewish students and Jewish artistic expression? And if so, where, if not in the United States, where the cultivation of a new Jewish cultural consciousness against the backdrop of the catastrophe in Europe was an urgent concern both for American-Jewish artists and for those exiled from Europe?

Max Helfman (1901–1963), born in Poland, was the ideal person to help establish Jewish artistic and educational projects. At the age of eight, the future composer, organist, conductor, and music critic immigrated to the New World. He received his initial musical training at the Mannes College of Music in New York and continued his studies at the Curtis Institute of Music in Philadelphia, where he trained under Ralph Leopold (piano), Rosario Scalero (composition), and Fritz Reiner (conducting). Helfman honed his practical musicianship at Temple Israel; as a composer, he sought to trans-

BRANDEIS YOUTH FOUNDATION

National Headquarters for: BRANDEIS CAMP INSTITUTES *at*

WINTERDALE, PA. • SANTA SUSANA, CALIF. • HENDERSONVILLE, N.C.

Office of Executive Director:
DR. SHLOMO BARDIN

May 27, 1948

381 FOURTH AVENUE
NEW YORK 16, N. Y.

MUrray Hill 7-7763

Mr. Eric Zeisl
8578 West Knoll Drive
Hollywood 46, Calif.

Dear Mr. Zeisl:

Both as a serious artist and a conscious Jew, you will, I am sure, be deeply interested in the Hebrew Arts Project sponsored by the Brandeis Youth Foundation.

Believing as we do, that the most precious asset of a people is its creative youth, and that we, in America, have a vast artistic potential in our Jewish youth, the Foundation is establishing an Arts Institute on its estate Santa Susana, California, where a selected group of qualified students between the ages of 18 - 27 will be enabled to live and work together with distinguished leaders in their respective arts in a creative Jewish atmosphere.

In other words, - a sort of Hebrew Tanglewood.

We feel that by opening up for these gifted young men and women - the future composers, conductors, singers, dancers, - the treasures of our artistic heritage and resources, and by making them aware of the possibilities for the continued contemporary development of this heritage and these resources, we shall notably, profoundly enrich them, make it possible for them, in turn, to enrich our cultural life here in America and indeed everywhere.

I am enclosing the Prospectus which will give you a more detailed idea of what we are trying to do. To my knowledge, it is the first attempt to systematize the special problems of the Hebrew Arts.

I hope you will read it and, if at all possible, let me have your reactions. And because - if this Project is to be developed properly - we must have the sympathetic interest, advice and collaboration of those significant artists who are truly concerned with the continuance of Jewish creativity in this country, I take the liberty of asking you:

Invitation from Max Helfman to Eric Zeisl to teach at the Brandeis Camp Institute, May 27, 1948
Archiv des Exilarte Zentrum der mdw, Wien (A-Weaz)

Eric Zeisl with Max Helfman, Artistic Director of the Brandeis Youth Foundation
Archiv des Exilarte Zentrum der mdw, Wien (A-Weaz)

Ernst Toch shares a glance with the violinist Henri Temianka in an Ernest Bloch score in preparation of a performance at Brandeis, 1960
American Jewish University, Special Collections, Ostrow Library

late liturgical music into a contemporary musical language. He had a particular passion for working with young people: a board member of the Jewish Music Alliance since 1938, in 1944, he was appointed to the School of Sacred Music at the Hebrew Union College in New York. In 1961, he founded the School of Fine Arts at the University of Judaism in Los Angeles. The notable task of organizing the music courses at the Brandeis Camp was a responsibility he took on in 1947 and continued for seventeen years to come.

In 1942, Shlomo Bardin (1898–1976) started a summer training program for young adults in Winterdale, Pennsylvania; modeled on life in a kibbutz, it combined study, horticulture, and strict observance of Shabbat and established itself well within a few years. In 1943, Bardin renamed the project Brandeis Camp Institute (now the Brandeis-Bardin Institute)[1] after Louis Dembitz Brandeis (1856–1941), the first Jewish justice on the U.S. Supreme Court, who had died two years earlier. Bardin was inspired by Brandeis's approach of trying to harmonize American ideals with a commitment to Zionism. In 1947, Bardin initiated another Brandeis Camp Institute in Simi Valley near Santa Susana, northwest of Los Angeles.

Bardin was born in Ukraine and immigrated to Palestine in 1918. He later pursued studies in Berlin and London. Upon returning to Haifa, he taught at the Hebrew Boarding School before completing his studies at Columbia University's Teachers College. In 1939, Bardin was appointed director of the Youth Department of Hadassah, the Women's Zionist organization of America, and the newly established American Zionist Youth Commission, under whose auspices he then established the summer training camp program. The Brandeis Camp welcomed a diverse audience, including students from reform, conservative, Zionist, and orthodox backgrounds. With its exceptional faculty, the camp set new standards for future Jewish artistic and educational formats.

In his capacity as artistic director of the Brandeis Youth Foundation, Max Helfman wrote to Eric Zeisl on May 27, 1948:

Dear Mr. Zeisl:

Both as a serious artist and conscious Jew, you will, I am sure, be deeply interested in the Hebrew Arts Project sponsored by the Brandeis Youth Foundation. Believing as we do, that the most precious asset of a people is its creative youth, and that we, in America, have a vast artistic potential in our Jewish youth, the Foundation is establishing an Arts Institute on its estate Santa Susana, California, where a selected group of qualified students between the ages of 18 – 27 will be enabled to live and work together with distinguished leaders in their respective arts in a creative Jewish atmosphere. In other words,—a sort of Hebrew Tanglewood.[2]

Speaking of the talented young generation—the future composers, conductors, singers, authors, actors, and dancers—Helfman referred to them as "the treasures of our artistic heritage and resources."[3] He aimed to equip them with the skills to embrace the legacy of Jewish art in a contemporary manner so that they would be able to enrich cultural life both in the United States and beyond its borders. "To my knowledge," Helfman continued, "it is the first attempt to systematize the special problems of the Hebrew Arts."[4] Helfman invited Zeisl to be a guest of honor at the Brandeis Camp, to teach and give lectures. Zeisl accepted the invitation: from 1948 to 1950, he taught during the summer months as composer in residence at the Brandeis Camp Institute in Santa Susana.

Shlomo Bardin and Max Helfman's program concept was rooted in Jewish ethics, a commitment that reflected on both the course content and in the methods of instruction. Contemporary and traditional Jewish music, including art music, religious music, and folklore, were combined with dance and movement. The program embraced the musical individuality of young participants while also fostering those with the potential to take on future leadership roles in Jewish-American cultural life. Its broad outreach and, above all, its vibrant engagement with youth were inspired by the courses popularized by Leonard Bernstein at Tanglewood.

Bardin's thoughts on the participants are summarized in a brochure from the late 1940s:

They come to acquaint themselves more fully with Jewish values, draw inspiration from the reborn state of Israel, study the methods of democratic leadership and thus be trained as youth leaders for the American Jewish community. The Brandeis Camp of the West, with its 2,000 acres of picturesque southern California countryside, immediately suggests the hills of Judea to the imaginative young person. Exposed to skillful direction and programming, the Brandeis camper acquires a new understanding and pride in their Jewish heritage and a new dignity as a human being. Upon leaving, the Brandeis camper carries with them a sense of personal responsibility for their Jewish community and for the future of the Jewish people.[5]

Teaching alongside Eric Zeisl at the Brandeis Camp in Simi Valley around 1948 were composers Mario Castelnuovo-Tedesco (1895–1968), Ernst Toch (1887–1964), and Heinrich Schalit (1886–1976); pianist-composers Julius Chajes (1910–1985) and Louis Gruenberg (1884–1964); conductor Izler Solomon (1910–1987); cantor and composer Solomon Rosowsky (1878–1962); conductor, organist, and choir director Erwin Jospe (1907–1983); musicologist Anneliese Landau (1903–1991); author Irving Fineman (1893–1976); and dancer and choreographer Benjamin Zemach (1901–1997). In June 1950, Helfman considered inviting Arnold Schoenberg (1874–1951) to Santa Susana for one or two weeks. He consulted Zeisl regarding possible conditions for such a visit.[6] However, the plan does not appear to have been pursued further, as Schoenberg's health would not have allowed to come there anyway.

Julius Chajes, formerly a confrere of Zeisl in the "Young Art" circle in Vienna, championed Zeisl's work in the United States in his role as director of the Jewish Community Center in Detroit. Through his work in the Hollywood film industry, Zeisl maintained friendships with the composers Mario Castelnuovo-Tedesco and Ernst Toch. The German émigré musicologist Anneliese Landau served as music director of the Westside Jewish Community Center in Los Angeles and as executive secretary of the Jewish Music Council of Los Angeles. The Jewish Music Council, founded in 1944 by the National Jewish Welfare Board and the National Association of Jewish Center Workers, worked nationwide in the United States to promote Jewish artists. In these capacities, Landau maintained regular contact with Zeisl, whom she, in a study on contemporary Jewish composers she authored in 1946, listed on par with Ernest Bloch, Paul Dessau, Stefan Wolpe, Karol Rathaus, Jaromír Weinberger, Erich Wolfgang Korngold, Marc Blitzstein, Kurt Weill, Leo Ornstein, Ernst Toch, and Rubin Goldmark, describing him as "the youngest of the conscious Jewish composers."[7]

A significant figure for Eric Zeisl among the Brandeis faculty was Benjamin Zemach. The dancer and choreographer had come to New York with the Habima Theatre group from Moscow and became a key influence on contemporary dance in Los Angeles. In collaboration with Zemach, Zeisl composed the biblical ballets *Naboth's Vineyard* (1953) and *Jacob and Rachel* (1954). The *University News* of the University of Judaism in Los Angeles announced in February 1955 a performance of *Jacob and Rachel* scheduled in May 1955 at the Wilshire Ebell Theatre in Los Angeles and featuring students from Zemach's dance class.[8]

"A Serious Artist and Conscious Jew"

Over years, Eric Zeisl maintained a prominent presence in the American-Jewish musical world. Through a variety of events, he established himself as the "serious artist and conscious Jew" that Max Helfman had envisioned for the Brandeis Camp. As early as October 1943, the Studio Symphony Orchestra, conducted by Walter Scharf (1910–2003), performed the *Overture* and *Folk Dance* from Zeisl's opera *Job* (*Hiob*) as part of an *All Jewish-Palestinian Program* "presented by the Los Angeles Chapters League for Labor Palestine."[9] The program also featured Scharf's *Palestine Suite* and *Hatikvah Requiem*, Julius Chajes' *Adarim*, and Marc Lavry's (1903–1967) symphonic poem *Emek*.

A significant milestone for Eric Zeisl was the premiere of his *Requiem Ebraico* in the organ version. Conducted by Hugo Strelitzer (1896–1981), the Fairfax Temple Choir performed the ancient Hebrew Psalm 92 as part of a concert at the "Hollywood Inter-Faith Forum" at the Hollywood First Methodist Church on April 8, 1945. Zeisl's brother William (Wilhelm) Zeisl (1907–1972) sang the cantor role, while Norman Söreng Wright (1905–1982) opened the program with the *Organ Prelude*, originally composed in 1939 as the overture to the stage adaptation of Joseph Roth's *Hiob* in Paris. Rabbi Jacob Sonderling (1878–1964) delivered a lecture on the theme "The Message of Music in Religion."[10]

A striking contrast to the heartfelt performance of Zeisl's *Requiem Ebraico* was the popular revue event *That we may live*, announced as the "Palestine Spectacle" and organized by the Palestine Emergency Fund under the direction of Paul Gordon. Gordon, who had previously initiated the stage adaptation of *Hiob* in Paris, now orchestrated a Hollywood-style display of vitality of the Jewish exile community. A wild mix of styles, the spectacle was staged in December 1946 in Los Angeles, drawing in audiences with a star-studded lineup: Howard Da Silva, Marta Eggerth, Bela Lugosi, Hugo Haas, and Jan Kiepura, alongside Erich Wolfgang Korngold, Jakob Gimpel, Hugo Strelitzer, and Eric Zeisl. Korngold participated as composer and conductor of his opera *Die tote Stadt*, while Zeisl's contributions included the *Overture* and *Cossack Dance* from his opera *Job* (*Hiob*). Without a consistent storyline, this collage about the Nazi terror and the expulsion of Jews from Europe was set in Berlin, Genoa, London, the Polish town of Zuchnow (the fictional hometown of the novel *Hiob*'s protagonist), Buchenwald, and Vienna. The spectacle concluded with the segment *Before the Gates of Palestine*, delivering a Zionist message. At its core, the production criticized British mandate policies in Palestine. The *Los Angeles Evening Citizen News* highlighted the scale and ambition of the upcoming performance:

A group of students at the Brandeis Camp Institute are given tips about working on the land from Jacob Aronowicz, 1947
American Jewish University, Special Collections, Ostrow Library

Dancing to Jewish folklore at Brandeis Camp, 1948
American Jewish University, Special Collections, Ostrow Library

For two nights only, Dec. 17 and 18, the Shrine Auditorium will be turned into a gigantic tribunal when the Palestine Emergency Fund, Inc., presents "That we may live," with a cast of 500. Starring roles will be played by Jan Kiepura, Marta Eggerth and Hugo Haas. "That we may live" is a dramatic portrayal and indictment against the British Palestine policy.[11]

The show *That we may live* likely reached New York audiences through a broadcast, with Madison Square Garden prominently advertised as venue in neon signs and on posters.

New York was also where the proclamation of the State of Israel by the Jewish National Council was celebrated on May 14, 1948. Just days later, on May 18, 1948, a *Carnegie "POP" Concert* took place under the title of *Palestine Night*.[12] The event opened with the national anthems *The Star-Spangled Banner* and *Hatikvah*. On an evening dedicated to the Zionist idea, Siegfried Landau (1921–2007) conducted works by two composers from Vienna, Julius Chajes' *Hebrew Suite* and Eric Zeisl's suite *To the Promised Land*, which had its premiere on the occasion. Zeisl's piece with its evocative title in part drew on other works of his, with *Folk Dance* and *Menuhim's Song* being adaptations of the *Cossack Song and Dance* and *Menuhim's Song* from his opera *Job* (*Hiob*), and *Lullaby* a slightly altered version of his 1928 *Wiegenlied*. As a fourth segment, Zeisl arranged a Jewish folk song from Palestine, *Kuma Echa Hora*. Louis Biancolli summed up the evening with praise: "Maybe the names were new to most concert fans, names like David Scheinfeld, Salomo Rosowsky, Nardi, Julius Chayes [sic], and Eric Zeisl. Yet taken together, they spelt out the promise of a great future for Jewish music."[13]

A new name on the scene and a guarantor of its promising future—that was how Eric Zeisl was perceived by music expert circles. Zeisl never actively pursued Zionist ideas, yet his participation in the mentioned concerts was a statement in support of a new Jewish identity and expressed his sympathy with the young state of Israel. His composition *To the Promised Land* stands out as a poignantly effective contribution reflecting circumstances of the era. However, Zeisl's development of his own "Jewishly" inflected music stemmed from an inner process, which, while responding to external circumstances, consistently avoided outspokenly political or Zionist messages.

"Truly Jewish Music"

Inspired by the atmosphere of the Brandeis Camp, Eric Zeisl composed the *Sonata for Violin and Piano (Brandeis Sonata)* in 1949/50, dedicating it to Alexandre Tansman (1897–1986). A "pre-premiere"[14] of the work took place on August 13, 1950, at the Brandeis Camp, performed by violinist Israel Baker (1919–2011) and pianist Yaltah Menuhin (1921–2001). The duo also gave the public premiere of the *Brandeis Sonata* on September 24, 1950, in Santa Monica.[15]

Yaltah Menuhin, the sister of Yehudi Menuhin, lived in Los Angeles during the 1950s and played a significant role as a performer of contemporary works. She premiered compositions by George Antheil, Ernst Krenek, Louis Gruenberg,

Carnegie "POP" Concerts — SEASON OF 1948

Tuesday Evening, May 18th, at 8:30 o'clock
PALESTINE NIGHT
CARNEGIE "POP" ORCHESTRA

Conductor: SIEGFRIED LANDAU
Soloists: SIDOR BELARSKY, Bass
CHORAL SOCIETY of TEMPLE EMANUEL,
Paterson, N. J.

PART I

Pastorale and Hora .... David Scheinfeld
ORCHESTRA

Ode for Mourning .... Salomo Rosowsky
(In memory of those who have fallen for Palestine)
Vocal obbligato: Mildred Meditz, Soprano
ORCHESTRA

Sadod Shebaemek .... Ben Haim*
Shir Hachamishah .... Zaira*
Yo Adir .... Jacob Weinberg
Zemer Chaluzim .... Nardi*
SIDOR BELARSKY

Hebrew Suite .... Julius Chajes
  a) Prayer
  b) Melody and Dance
  c) Hora†
ORCHESTRA

INTERMISSION

PART II

"To the Promised Land" .... Eric Zeisl
  a) Con moto (Folk-dance)
  b) Moderato (Lullaby)
  c) Allegretto con fuoco (Hora)†
    (First Performance)
ORCHESTRA

Shir Ha-emek .... Lavri-Binder*
Yaaleh .... Joel Engel*
Liberation Hymn .... Salomo Rosowsky
CHORAL SOCIETY of TEMPLE EMANUEL,
Paterson, N. J.

Palestinian Song Suite .... Nardi
  a) Uru Achim
  b) Ssissi Admat Hasharon
  c) Yeleth Li Natan (Lullaby)
  d) Hymnon La-Avoda
    (First Performance in America)
SIDOR BELARSKY, CHORAL SOCIETY
and ORCHESTRA

*Orchestrated by Siegfried Landau
†Through the courtesy of the Transcontinental Music Co.

SMOKING PERMITTED IN LOGES ONLY

Announcement of a concert on the founding of the State of Israel: On May 18, 1948, *Palestine Night* with music by Eric Zeisl took place at Carnegie Hall.
Archiv des Exilarte Zentrum der mdw, Wien (A-Weaz)

The duo Israel Baker and Yaltah Menuhin often performed Zeisl's *Brandeis Sonata* in performances of Jewish-American music.
Archiv des Exilarte Zentrum der mdw, Wien (A-Weaz)

Mario Castelnuovo-Tedesco, and Walter Piston, among others. In 1951, she made her New York debut as part of a duo with Israel Baker. Israel Baker taught at Scripps College in Claremont, California, and was a prominent figure in West Coast concert life as a violinist in the Heifetz-Piatigorsky chamber concerts and a noted interpreter of works by Igor Stravinsky, Arnold Schoenberg, and Alban Berg.

The *Brandeis Sonata*, with its movements *Grave*, *Andante religioso (hebraique)*, and *Rondo*, exemplifies the synthesis of Zeisl's Viennese tradition with "Jewish sphere" echoes. The *Grave* introduction is powerful, with an insistent Lombard rhythm from which the violin rises freely, setting the stage. Over an ostinato-like pulsating accompaniment, the *Allegretto* introduces a dance-like theme in Zeisl's favored folkloristic minor scale (in E) with the raised fourth degree. A contrasting second theme stands out with expressive cantilenas in B minor. The *Andante religioso* becomes the emotional centerpiece of the work, with its subtitle "hebraique" underscoring the mode of expressive Jewish prayer. It is emphatic yet introspective. The concluding vibrant *Rondo* revisits the sonata's opening rhythmic motif, radiating a sense of joy and playfulness in the spirit of Eastern European folk music.

Aufbau, the German-language newspaper for refugees, reported in October 1950, under the section "New Music in Los Angeles":

We owe several evenings of interesting new music to the duo of Yaltah Menuhin (piano) and Israel Baker (violin). Recently, they championed the Sonata in E Minor (Brandeis) by Eric Zeisl, a work inspired by the distinctly Jewish atmosphere at the Brandeis Camp near Los Angeles, where the composer has been teaching. Among the many new works of recent years, I have rarely heard a piece of chamber music of such consistency: each of the three movements is equally strong and captivating. Without quoting any preexisting Jewish motif, Zeisl, inspired in the best sense of the word, has created truly Jewish music here, deeply resonant with our contemporary sensibilities.[16]

1   See Jenna Leventhal, *The Brandeis-Bardin Institute: A Living History* (Los Angeles, 2012).
2   Max Helfman to Eric Zeisl, May 27, 1948, quoted in Karin Wagner (ed.), *… es grüsst Dich Erichisrael: Briefe von und an Eric Zeisl, Hilde Spiel, Richard Stöhr, Ernst Toch, Hans Kafka u. a.* (Vienna, 2008), p. 245.
3   Ibid., p. 246.
4   Ibid.
5   Information brochure *A Program for American Jewish Youth: Brandeis Camp Institute*, Santa Susana, California, Eric Zeisl Estate, Exilarte Center, Vienna.
6   Max Helfman to Eric Zeisl, June 9, 1950, Eric Zeisl Estate, Exilarte Center, Vienna.
7   Anneliese Landau, *The Contribution of Jewish Composers to the Music of the Modern World*, [Cincinnati, OH, 1946], p. 64.
8   *University News of University of Judaism*, Feb. 1955, American Jewish University, Special Collections, Los Angeles.
9   Program flyer *All Jewish-Palestinian Program*, Oct. 2, 1943, Eric Zeisl Estate, Exilarte Center, Vienna.
10 Program flyer *The Message of Music in Religion*, Hollywood First Methodist Church, Apr. 8, 1945, Eric Zeisl Estate, Exilarte Center, Vienna.
11 *Los Angeles Evening Citizen News*, Nov. 28, 1946.
12 Program flyer *Palestine Night*, Carnegie Hall, May 18, 1948, Eric Zeisl Estate, Exilarte Center, Vienna.
13 Newspaper clipping without any details, Eric Zeisl Estate, Exilarte Center, Vienna.
14 Program flyer *Brandeis Camp Institute Concert*, Brandeis Camp, Aug. 13, 1950, Eric Zeisl Estate, Exilarte Center, Vienna.
15 Program flyer *Israel Baker, Yaltah Menuhin Sonata Recital*, Barnum Hall, Santa Monica, Sept. 24, 1950, Eric Zeisl Estate, Exilarte Center, Vienna.
16 Martin Hausdorff, "Neue Musik in Los Angeles," *Aufbau*, Oct. 20, 1950, Eric Zeisl Estate, Exilarte Center, Vienna.

BILDNACHWEISE

Archiv des Exilarte Zentrum der mdw – Universität für Musik und darstellende Kunst Wien (A-Weaz)

Arnold Schönberg Center Privatstiftung, Wien (A-Was)

    S. 25: ASCI PH9397, S. 104: ASCI PH3285,
    S. 106: ASCI PH3296, S. 120: ASCI PH1002
    S. 127: ASCI PH8677, S. 131: ASCI PH1811
    S. 139: ASCI A2632, S. 141: ASCI PH2003

American Jewish University, Special Collections, Ostrow Library

    S. 159, 160, 171, 175

Ernst Toch Collection, UCLA Performing Arts Library

    S. 140, 148, 150

Bricht Family Collection

    S. 77, 81, 82, 92

E. Randol Schoenberg

    S. 98, 137

The Brendan G Carroll Collection

    S. 151

Cover photos:

    Eric Zeisl: exiled in Los Angeles, c. 1955 (A-Weaz)
    Eric Zeisl with his daughter Barbara on the beach in Santa Monica, December 1947 (A-Weaz)

Wikipedia:

S. 60: Ferdinand Küss oder Michael Frankenstein, Galerie Bassenge, PD, https://commons.wikimedia.org/wiki/File:Wien_Nordbahnhof_19c.jpg?uselang=de

S. 65: H. Wolfgang, 2022, CC BY-SA 4.0, https://commons.wikimedia.org/wiki/File:1020_Heinestra%C3%9Fe_2.jpg?uselang=de

S. 61: Österreichische Nationalbibliothek, USIS – United States Information Services, PD, https://commons.wikimedia.org/wiki/File:Lise_Meitner_(1878%E2%80%931968)_1953_OeNB_USIS_2955727.jpg?uselang=de, https://onb.digital/result/BAG_2955727 US 11.031 C POR MAG

S. 61: Max Fenichel, vor März 1938, Österreichische National-bibliothek, PD, https://commons.wikimedia.org/wiki/File:Max_Grunwald.jpg, https://onb.digital/result/BAG_18245351 Pf 29548 : C (1) POR MAG

S. 63: Fotograf unbekannt, Dokumentationsarchiv des österreichi-schen Widerstandes, PD, https://commons.wikimedia.org/wiki/File:Jura_Soyfer_und_Marika_(Maria)_Sz%C3%A9csi.jpg, https://www.doew.at/erinnern/biographien/spurensuche/jura-soyfer-1912-1939

S. 65: Nella Katz, Library of Israel, Schwadron Collection, CC BY 3.0, https://commons.wikimedia.org/wiki/File:Tzvi-Peretz_Hayot.jpg, https://www.nli.org.il/en

S. 69: H. Wolfgang, 2022, CC BY-SA 4.0, https://commons.wikimedia.org/wiki/File:1020_Heinestra%C3%9Fe_4.jpg?uselang=de

S. 70: Bryn Mawr College, CC BY-SA 2.0, https://commons.wikimedia.org/wiki/File:Chemist_Lise_Meitner_with_students.jpg?uselang=de, https://www.flickr.com/photos/nrcgov/15422785493

S. 70: Hebrew Free Burial Society, 2011, CC BY-SA 3.0, https://commons.wikimedia.org/wiki/File:Jura_Soyfer%27s_gravesite_at_Hebrew_Free_Burial_Association%27s_Mount_Richmond_Cemetery.jpg

S. 72: Los Angeles Times, CC BY 4.0, https://commons.wikimedia.org/wiki/File:Richard_J._Neutra_holding_photograph_of_Beard_House.jpg, https://digital.library.ucla.edu/catalog/ark:/21198/zz002cwx90

S. 74: Pierre Genée, Wiener Synagogen 1825–1938, PD, https://commons.wikimedia.org/wiki/File:Pazmanitentempel.PNG